Taste *of* Home.

Pizza, Pasta,
and more

TASTE OF HOME BOOKS • RDA ENTHUSIAST BRANDS, LLC • MILWAUKEE, WI

© 2024 RDA Enthusiast Brands, LLC.
1610 N. 2nd St., Suite 102, Milwaukee WI
53212-3906

Visit us at **tasteofhome.com** for other
Taste of Home books and products.

International Standard Book Number:
979-8-88977-027-5

Chief Content Officer: Jason Buhrmester
Content Director: Mark Hagen
Creative Director: Raeann Thompson
Senior Editor: Christine Rukavena
Editor: Hazel Wheaton
Senior Art Director: Courtney Lovetere
Assistant Art Director: Jazmin Delgado
Senior Print Publication Designer: Jogesh Antony
Deputy Editor, Copy Desk: Ann Walter
Copy Editor: Suchismita Ukil
Contributing Copy Editor: Pam Grandy

Cover Photography:
Photographer: Mark Derse
Set Stylist: Stacey Genaw
Food Stylist: Josh Rink

Pictured on front cover:
The Best Sausage Pizzas, p. 108
Pictured on back cover:
Lasagna with Bechamel, p. 206; Rich & Creamy
Tiramisu, p. 300; Fried Cheese Ravioli, p. 31;
Great Garlic Bread , p. 74; Deep-Dish Sausage
Pizza, p. 116

Printed in China
3 5 7 9 10 8 6 4 2

Table of Contents

P.192

P.122

P.279

MORE WAYS TO CONNECT WITH US:

Bring Italian flair to your table any night of the week.

Italian cooking is one of the world's most widely loved cuisines. Odds are, if you're looking for a crowd-pleasing dish for a party, pizza is on the menu. If you want a quick weeknight meal, a stovetop pasta dish is a perfect choice. For savory, heartwarming comfort, lasagna or another baked pasta recipe is pure perfection. The timeless appeal of classic Italian dishes is in fresh, delicious ingredients prepared without frills, just a clear focus on flavors the family will love.

In *Pizza, Pasta & More*, you'll find not only beloved Italian dishes, but also fresh, innovative spins. The basics of Italian cooking are endlessly adaptable, leading to pizzas and pastas with flavor profiles from places far from Rome—like Cajun Chicken & Pasta (p. 174), Grilled Elote Flatbread (p. 97) and Chinese Cashew Chicken Pizza (p. 124). Two special chapters, "Pizza with a Twist," (pp. 130-155) and "Dessert Pizzas" (pp. 306-317) explore how pizza has sparked entirely new culinary inventions. You're encouraged to do your own inventing too! Throughout the book, tips from the experts in our Test Kitchen guide you when you want to follow the recipe and suggest alternatives when you want to use the recipe as a starting point to create something new.

Of course, Italian cooking isn't just pizza and pasta! There are antipasti, soups, breads, salads and side dishes here to make your meal complete. And of course, you can try your hand at one of Italy's world-famous sweets—including Almond Biscotti (p. 296), Chocolate Cannoli (p. 304), Dark Chocolate Panna Cotta (p. 305) and Rich & Creamy Tiramisu (p. 300).

So get ready to dive into the diverse and delicious world of Italian cooking, where simple ingredients come together to create meals that are as satisfying to make as they are to eat. This is your invitation to bring the taste of Italy home—with no passport required!

Make it your own— or make it yourself!

There are countless ways to transform convenient store-bought items into something wholly new and uniquely yours. If you start with refrigerated pizza dough or prebaked crusts, you have plenty to choose from. Modern shoppers are almost spoiled for choice, with even vegan and gluten-free options available on store shelves. If you're using a store-bought dough, you can make it your own by adding herbs or other ingredients. You can even roll a bit of mozzarella cheese into the edge of the crust to imitate those gooey, tempting crusts from your regular takeout place.

P.267

Store-bought sauces are a huge timesaver, and they still give you the opportunity to improvise. Just because a sauce came from a jar doesn't mean it has to taste like everyone else's! Begin with your favorite pasta sauce—everyone has their own!—then start adding. Red pepper flakes for heat, seasoned salt for layers of flavor, ricotta or cream cheese for richness, and mushrooms, olives, capers and vegetables of all kinds.

P.259

But when time permits, why not make your own sauces and crusts from scratch? Making pizza crust at home lets you turn out a classic crust (p. 270) or a gluten-free option (p. 266) whenever needed. And homemade gnocchi (p. 161) and pasta dough (p. 195) may seem intimidating, but once you've tried it, you'll be hooked. Best of all, you can use your own dough to create any shape you like!

And sauces? Classic Marinara (p. 257), hearty Bolognese (p. 265), creamy Alfredo (p. 263), pizza sauce in both red (p. 254) and white (p. 271), and many more are a perfect way to make a homemade meal truly your own.

P.254

MARINATED CHEESE
(PAGE 22)

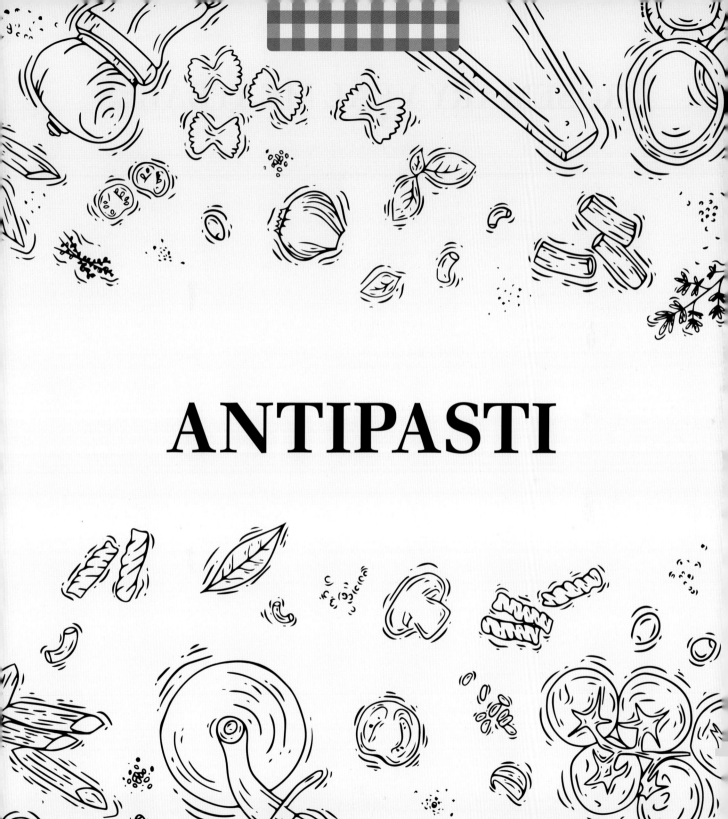

ANTIPASTI

ROSEMARY VEAL MEATBALLS

These savory appetizer meatballs, seasoned with rosemary and garlic, get a touch of sweetness from chopped golden raisins. They will be a hit at your next gathering.

—Rhonda Maiani, Chapel Hill, NC

PREP: 25 min. • **COOK:** 20 min. • **MAKES:** 3½ dozen (1½ cups sauce)

1   cup plain yogurt
1   jar (7½ oz.) marinated artichoke hearts, drained and chopped
2   Tbsp. prepared Italian salad dressing
1   garlic clove, minced

MEATBALLS
2   large eggs, lightly beaten
¾   cup soft bread crumbs
½   cup golden raisins, finely chopped
3   garlic cloves, minced
4   tsp. dried rosemary, crushed
1½ tsp. salt
1   tsp. pepper
1   lb. ground veal
¼   cup canola oil

1. In a small bowl, combine yogurt, artichokes, salad dressing and garlic; cover and refrigerate until serving.

2. For meatballs, in a large bowl, combine eggs, bread crumbs, raisins, garlic, rosemary, salt and pepper. Crumble veal over mixture and mix well. Shape into 1-in. balls.

3. In a large skillet, brown meatballs in oil in small batches until no longer pink. Remove with a slotted spoon and keep warm. Serve with yogurt sauce.

3 MEATBALLS 188 cal., 13g fat (3g sat. fat), 73mg chol., 513mg sod., 10g carb. (6g sugars, 1g fiber), 9g pro.

OVEN-BAKED MEATBALLS

If you like, you can bake your meatballs in the oven instead of cooking them in a skillet. Place meatballs in a single layer in a shallow rimmed baking pan, with space between them. You can line the pan with foil to help catch the grease. Bake at 375°F for 18-20 minutes.

GREEN CHILE PROSCIUTTO ROLLS

I created these for my husband, who adores green chiles.
He loves these rolls so much he could eat a whole pan.
—Paula Mchargue, Richmond, KY

TAKES: 25 min. • **MAKES:** 14

1 tube (8 oz.) refrigerated crescent rolls
3 oz. cream cheese, softened
1 can (4 oz.) chopped green chiles, drained
1 Tbsp. sweet hot mustard
½ cup thinly sliced prosciutto, cooked and crumbled
1 large egg, beaten
3 Tbsp. grated Parmesan cheese

1. Preheat oven to 375°. Unroll crescent dough into 1 long rectangle; press perforations to seal. In a small bowl, beat cream cheese, green chiles and mustard. Spread over dough to within ½ in. of edges. Sprinkle with prosciutto. Roll up the left and right sides toward center, jelly-roll style, until roll meets in middle. Cut into 1-in. slices.

2. Place slices on a parchment-lined baking sheet. Brush with egg; sprinkle with Parmesan cheese. Bake until golden brown, 12-15 minutes. If desired, top with additional Parmesan cheese.

1 ROLL 98 cal., 6g fat (2g sat. fat), 23mg chol., 258mg sod., 8g carb. (2g sugars, 0 fiber), 3g pro.

ANTIPASTO PLATTER

We entertain often, and antipasto is one of our favorite crowd-pleasers. Guests love having their choice of so many delicious nibbles, including pepperoni and cubes of provolone.

—*Teri Lindquist, Gurnee, IL*

PREP: 10 min. + chilling • **MAKES:** 16 servings (3 qt.)

1 jar (24 oz.) pepperoncini, drained
1 can (15 oz.) garbanzo beans or chickpeas, rinsed and drained
2 cups halved fresh mushrooms
2 cups halved cherry tomatoes
½ lb. provolone cheese, cubed
1 can (6 oz.) pitted ripe olives, drained
1 pkg. (3½ oz.) sliced pepperoni
1 bottle (8 oz.) Italian vinaigrette dressing
  Lettuce leaves

1. In a large bowl, combine the first 7 ingredients. Pour vinaigrette over mixture; toss to coat.

2. Refrigerate at least 30 minutes or overnight. Arrange on a lettuce-lined platter. Serve with toothpicks.

1 CUP 178 cal., 13g fat (4g sat. fat), 15mg chol., 852mg sod., 8g carb. (2g sugars, 2g fiber), 6g pro.

SUGGESTED ADDITIONS

When it comes to antipasto platters or charcuterie boards, the sky is the limit. Whatever dried fruits you have on hand would be good to have on the side. Almost any type of nut is a welcome add—toast the nuts first so they'll have the most flavor possible. Fresh fruits, like apples, pears, grapes, apricots and berries, also work well on an antipasto platter. For fruits that turn brown quickly, like apples and pears, toss them in a little lemon juice mixed with water after you slice them.

SLOW-COOKER CAPONATA

This Italian eggplant dip preps quickly and actually gets better as it stands. Serve it warm or at room temperature. Try adding a little leftover caponata to scrambled eggs for a savory breakfast.

—*Nancy Beckman, Helena, MT*

PREP: 20 min. • **COOK:** 5 hours • **MAKES:** 6 cups

2 medium eggplants, cut into ½-in. pieces
1 medium onion, chopped
1 can (14½ oz.) diced tomatoes, undrained
12 garlic cloves, sliced
½ cup dry red wine
3 Tbsp. olive oil
2 Tbsp. red wine vinegar
4 tsp. capers, undrained
5 bay leaves
1½ tsp. salt
¼ tsp. coarsely ground pepper
French bread baguette slices, toasted
Optional: Fresh basil leaves, toasted pine nuts and additional olive oil

1. Place first 11 ingredients in a 6-qt. slow cooker (do not stir). Cook, covered, on high for 3 hours.

2. Stir gently; replace cover. Cook on high 2 hours longer or until vegetables are tender.

3. Cool slightly; discard bay leaves. Serve with toasted baguette slices, adding toppings as desired.

¼ CUP 34 cal., 2g fat (0 sat. fat), 0 chol., 189mg sod., 4g carb. (2g sugars, 2g fiber), 1g pro.

"My sister always bought caponata from Arthur Avenue in the Bronx for Christmas Eve dinner. Since we moved to Florida we haven't been able to find it. I stumbled on this recipe and tried it. LOVED it! It's just as good as Little Italy's! Very happy to have found this recipe. I will use it often."
—CHRIS7810, TASTEOFHOME.COM

EGGPLANT PARMESAN SLIDERS

I wanted something that was easy for guests to grab, and vegetarian friendly.
The lemon ricotta spread really adds a level of flavor to these delicious bites. Be sure
not to rush the eggplant; it's important to cook it until it's buttery and tender.

—*Debbie Glasscock, Conway, AR*

PREP: 45 min. • **BAKE:** 15 min. • **MAKES:** 2 dozen

4 large eggs, beaten
1½ cups seasoned bread crumbs
2 medium eggplant, peeled and cut into ¼-in. slices
½ cup olive oil
2 pkg. (18 oz. each) Hawaiian sweet rolls
1 container (15 oz.) whole-milk ricotta cheese
⅓ cup plus ¼ cup grated Parmesan cheese, divided
2 Tbsp. lemon juice
2 tsp. dried parsley flakes, divided
1 tsp. grated lemon zest
½ tsp. kosher salt
1½ cups marinara sauce
24 slices fresh mozzarella cheese
½ cup butter, melted

1. Preheat oven to 350°. Place eggs and bread crumbs in separate shallow bowls. Dip eggplant slices into eggs, then coat with crumbs. In a large skillet, cook eggplant in oil in batches until golden brown on both sides; drain on paper towels.

2. Without separating rolls, cut rolls in half horizontally; arrange bottom halves in two greased 13x9-in. baking dishes. In a small bowl, mix ricotta, ⅓ cup Parmesan, lemon juice, 1 tsp. parsley flakes, lemon zest and kosher salt. Spread over roll bottoms. Top with eggplant, marinara and mozzarella. Replace top halves of rolls. Brush with melted butter; sprinkle with remaining ¼ cup Parmesan cheese and 1 tsp. parsley.

3. Bake, uncovered, until golden brown and cheese is melted, 15-20 minutes. Serve with additional warmed marinara.

1 SLIDER 347 cal., 19g fat (9g sat. fat), 68mg chol., 420mg sod., 33g carb. (13g sugars, 3g fiber), 13g pro.

⏱ MIXED OLIVE CROSTINI

These little toasts are pretty and irresistible—they're always a big hit. Even though they look as if you fussed, the ingredients are probably already in your pantry.
—*Laurie LaClair, North Richland Hills, TX*

TAKES: 25 min. • **MAKES:** 2 dozen

1   can (4¼ oz.) chopped ripe olives
½   cup pimiento-stuffed olives, finely chopped
½   cup grated Parmesan cheese
¼   cup butter, softened
1   Tbsp. olive oil
2   garlic cloves, minced
¾   cup shredded part-skim mozzarella cheese
¼   cup minced fresh parsley
1   French bread baguette (10½ oz.)

1. In a small bowl, combine the first 6 ingredients; stir in mozzarella cheese and parsley. Cut baguette into 24 slices; place on an ungreased baking sheet. Spread with olive mixture.

2. Broil 3-4 in. from heat until edges are lightly browned and cheese is melted, 2-3 minutes.

1 PIECE 102 cal., 6g fat (2g sat. fat), 9mg chol., 221mg sod., 10g carb. (0 sugars, 1g fiber), 3g pro.

⏱ ARTICHOKE CAPRESE PLATTER

I dressed up the classic Italian trio of mozzarella, tomatoes and basil with marinated artichokes.
It looks so yummy on a pretty platter set out on a buffet. Using fresh mozzarella is the key to its great taste.
—*Margaret Wilson, San Bernardino, CA*

TAKES: 15 min. • **MAKES:** 12 servings

2 jars (7½ oz. each) marinated artichoke hearts
2 Tbsp. red wine vinegar
2 Tbsp. olive oil
6 plum tomatoes, sliced
1 lb. fresh mozzarella cheese, sliced
2 cups loosely packed fresh basil leaves
  Coarsely ground pepper, optional

1. Drain artichokes, reserving ½ cup marinade. In a small bowl, whisk vinegar, oil and the reserved marinade.

2. On a large serving platter, arrange artichokes, tomatoes, mozzarella and basil. Drizzle with vinaigrette. If desired, sprinkle with coarsely ground pepper.

½ CUP 192 cal., 16g fat (7g sat. fat), 30mg chol., 179mg sod., 5g carb. (2g sugars, 1g fiber), 7g pro.

"We liked this variation of a caprese salad from our usual version with balsamic dressing. I took this to a football party potluck. We accompanied the salad with baguette slices and we didn't have anything left."
—GUEST13196636, TASTEOFHOME.COM

AIR-FRYER PROSCIUTTO TORTELLINI

This recipe is my take on Italian street food, and these tortellini are crunchy and gooey. Use the best-quality tomatoes you can find for the sauce—it's so good that you'll want to double it and serve it over pasta. If you don't have an air fryer, you can make these in a deep fryer, an electric skillet or on the stovetop.
—*Angela Lemoine, Howell, NJ*

PREP: 25 min. • **COOK:** 10 min./batch • **MAKES:** about 3½ dozen

1   Tbsp. olive oil
3   Tbsp. finely chopped onion
4   garlic cloves, coarsely chopped
1   can (15 oz.) tomato puree
1   Tbsp. minced fresh basil
¼   tsp. salt
¼   tsp. pepper

TORTELLINI
2   large eggs
2   Tbsp. 2% milk
⅔   cup seasoned bread crumbs
1   tsp. garlic powder
2   Tbsp. grated pecorino
    Romano cheese
1   Tbsp. minced fresh parsley
½   tsp. salt
1   pkg. (12 oz.) refrigerated
    prosciutto ricotta tortellini
    Cooking spray

1. In a small saucepan, heat oil over medium-high heat. Add onion and garlic; cook and stir until tender, 3-4 minutes. Stir in tomato puree, basil, salt and pepper. Bring to a boil; reduce heat. Simmer, uncovered, 10 minutes. Keep warm.

2. Meanwhile, preheat air fryer to 350°. In a small bowl, whisk eggs and milk. In another bowl, combine bread crumbs, garlic powder, cheese, parsley and salt.

3. Dip tortellini in egg mixture, then in bread crumb mixture to coat. In batches, arrange tortellini in a single layer on greased tray in air-fryer basket; spritz with cooking spray. Cook until golden brown, 4-5 minutes. Turn; spritz with cooking spray. Cook until golden brown, 4-5 minutes longer. Serve with sauce; sprinkle with additional minced fresh basil.

1 APPETIZER 38 cal., 1g fat (0 sat. fat), 9mg chol., 96mg sod., 5g carb. (0 sugars, 0 fiber), 1g pro.

FRIED BURRATA

It's hard to beat the combination of flavors and textures of rich, creamy fried burrata.
Enjoy it with crisp crostini and smoky, sweet romesco sauce. To make crostini,
brush baguette slices with olive oil and toast until crisp and golden brown.
—Taste of Home *Test Kitchen*

PREP: 20 min. + freezing • **COOK:** 5 min. • **MAKES:** 10 servings

½ cup slivered almonds, toasted
½ cup soft whole wheat or
  white bread crumbs
½ cup fire-roasted crushed tomatoes
1 jar (8 oz.) roasted sweet red
  peppers, drained
2 Tbsp. minced fresh parsley
2 garlic cloves
1 tsp. sweet paprika
½ tsp. salt
¼ tsp. freshly ground pepper
¼ cup sherry
½ cup olive oil
½ cup all-purpose flour
1 large egg, lightly beaten
½ cup panko bread crumbs
1 ball (8 oz.) burrata cheese
  Oil for deep-fat frying
  Crostini

1. Pulse almonds, bread crumbs, tomatoes, red peppers, parsley, garlic, paprika, salt and pepper in a food processor until finely chopped. Add sherry; process until blended. Continue processing while gradually adding oil in a steady stream.

2. In three separate shallow bowls, place flour, egg and bread crumbs. Dip burrata in flour, then in egg; coat with bread crumbs. Place on a parchment-lined plate; freeze for 20 minutes.

3. In an electric skillet or deep-fat fryer, heat oil to 375°. Fry cheese until golden brown, 2-3 minutes on each side. Drain on paper towels. Serve with sauce and crostini.

1 SERVING 262 cal., 21g fat (5g sat. fat), 25mg chol., 312mg sod., 9g carb. (3g sugars, 1g fiber), 7g pro.

FREEZING THE CHEESE

It's important to freeze the burrata before deep-frying—it ensures that the cheese doesn't immediately melt when it hits the hot oil, so don't skip that step. However, don't freeze it too long, or else the outside will get crisp but the inside will still be cold.

GARLIC TOMATO BRUSCHETTA

I drew inspiration from my grandma's recipe for this garden-fresh bruschetta. The crisp bread and tomato goodness make a great party appetizer, but the dish also works alongside your favorite Italian entree.
—*Jean Franzoni, Rutland, VT*

PREP: 30 min. + chilling • **MAKES:** 2 dozen

¼ cup olive oil
3 Tbsp. chopped fresh basil
3 to 4 garlic cloves, minced
½ tsp. salt
¼ tsp. pepper
4 medium tomatoes, diced
2 Tbsp. grated Parmesan cheese
1 loaf (1 lb.) unsliced French bread

1. In a large bowl, combine oil, basil, garlic, salt and pepper. Add tomatoes and toss gently. Sprinkle with cheese. Refrigerate at least 1 hour.

2. Bring to room temperature before serving. Slice bread into 24 pieces; toast under broiler until lightly browned. Top with tomato mixture. Serve immediately.

1 PIECE 77 cal., 3g fat (0 sat. fat), 0 chol., 172mg sod., 11g carb. (1g sugars, 1g fiber), 2g pro. **DIABETIC EXCHANGES** ½ starch, ½ fat.

SUGGESTED ADDITIONS

If you want your bruschetta to have a little bite, add 2 Tbsp. of minced seeded jalapeno peppers and 2 tsp. of balsamic vinegar to the mixture. If you want some creaminess, spread ricotta on the toast before putting the tomatoes on top.

MARINATED CHEESE

This special appetizer always makes it to our neighborhood parties and is the first to disappear from the buffet table. It's attractive, delicious—and so easy!

—Laurie Casper, Coraopolis, PA

PREP: 30 min. + marinating • **MAKES:** about 2 lbs.

2   blocks (8 oz. each) white cheddar cheese
2   pkg. (8 oz. each) cream cheese
¾   cup chopped roasted sweet red peppers
½   cup olive oil
¼   cup white wine vinegar
¼   cup balsamic vinegar
3   Tbsp. chopped green onions
3   Tbsp. minced fresh parsley
2   Tbsp. minced fresh basil
1   Tbsp. sugar
3   garlic cloves, minced
½   tsp. salt
½   tsp. pepper
    Assorted crackers or toasted sliced French bread

1. Slice each block of cheddar cheese into twenty ¼-in. slices. Cut each block of cream cheese into 18 slices. Create four 6-in.-long blocks of stacked cheeses, sandwiching 9 cream cheese slices between 10 cheddar slices for each stack. Place in a 13x9-in. dish.

2. In a small bowl, combine peppers, oil, vinegars, onions, herbs, sugar, garlic, salt and pepper; pour over cheese stacks.

3. Cover; refrigerate overnight, turning cheese blocks once. Drain excess marinade. Serve cheese slices with crackers or toasted bread.

1 OZ. CHEESE 121 cal., 11g fat (6g sat. fat), 30mg chol., 153mg sod., 1g carb. (0 sugars, 0 fiber), 5g pro.

⏱ ASPARAGUS WITH FRESH BASIL SAUCE

Add zip to your party with this easy appetizer. The dip can also double as a flavorful sandwich spread.
—*Janie Colle, Hutchinson, KS*

TAKES: 15 min. • **MAKES:** 12 servings

¾ cup reduced-fat mayonnaise
2 Tbsp. prepared pesto
1 Tbsp. grated Parmesan cheese
1 Tbsp. minced fresh basil
1 tsp. lemon juice
1 garlic clove, minced
1½ lbs. fresh asparagus, trimmed

1. In a small bowl, mix mayonnaise, pesto, Parmesan, basil, lemon juice and garlic until blended; refrigerate until serving.

2. In a Dutch oven, bring 12 cups water to a boil. Add asparagus in batches; cook, uncovered, until crisp-tender, 2-3 minutes. Remove and immediately drop into ice water. Drain and pat dry. Serve with sauce.

1 SERVING 72 cal., 6g fat (1g sat. fat), 6mg chol., 149mg sod., 3g carb. (1g sugars, 1g fiber), 1g pro. **DIABETIC EXCHANGES** 1½ fat.

CRUMB-TOPPED CLAMS

In my family, it wouldn't be Christmas Eve without baked clams. However, they make a special bite for any occasion and are easy to make and always a hit.
—*Annmarie Lucente, Monroe, NY*

PREP: 35 min. • **BROIL:** 10 min. • **MAKES:** 2 dozen

2 lbs. kosher salt
2 dozen fresh littleneck clams
½ cup dry bread crumbs
¼ cup chicken broth
1 Tbsp. minced fresh parsley
2 Tbsp. olive oil
2 garlic cloves, minced
¼ tsp. dried oregano
   Dash pepper
1 Tbsp. panko bread crumbs
   Lemon wedges

1. Spread salt onto a cast-iron 15x10x1-in. baking pan or other ovenproof metal serving plater. Shuck clams, leaving clams and juices in bottom shells. Arrange in prepared platter; divide juices among shells.

2. In a small bowl, mix dry bread crumbs, chicken broth, parsley, oil, garlic, oregano and pepper; spoon over clams. Sprinkle with panko bread crumbs.

3. Broil 4-6 in. from heat until clams are firm and crumb mixture is crisp and golden brown, 6-8 minutes. Serve immediately with lemon wedges.

1 CLAM 31 cal., 1g fat (0 sat. fat), 5mg chol., 35mg sod., 2g carb. (0 sugars, 0 fiber), 2g pro.

⏱ BRUSCHETTA WITH PROSCIUTTO

A crowd-pleaser any time of year, this savory appetizer is perfect for get-togethers.
—*Debbie Manno, Fort Mill, SC*

TAKES: 25 min. • **MAKES:** about 6½ dozen

8 plum tomatoes, seeded and chopped
1 cup chopped sweet onion
¼ cup grated Romano cheese
¼ cup minced fresh basil
2 oz. thinly sliced prosciutto, finely chopped
1 shallot, finely chopped
3 garlic cloves, minced
⅓ cup olive oil
⅓ cup balsamic vinegar
1 tsp. minced fresh rosemary
¼ tsp. pepper
⅛ tsp. hot pepper sauce, optional
2 French bread baguettes (10½ oz. each), cut into ¼-in. slices

1. In a large bowl, combine the first 7 ingredients. In another bowl, whisk oil, vinegar, rosemary, pepper and, if desired, pepper sauce. Pour over tomato mixture; toss to coat.

2. Place bread slices on ungreased baking sheets. Broil 3-4 in. from heat or until golden brown, 1-2 minutes. With a slotted spoon, top each slice with tomato mixture.

1 APPETIZER 33 cal., 1g fat (0 sat. fat), 1mg chol., 67mg sod., 5g carb. (1g sugars, 0 fiber), 1g pro.

CHICKEN PICCATA MEATBALLS

The classic chicken piccata entree is my favorite dish, but I wanted another way to have all the same flavors. These chicken piccata meatballs are the perfect solution, whether served alone or with a sauce like marinara or Buffalo! Serve over buttered noodles if you'd like, or stick toothpicks in them for appetizers.

—*Dawn Collins, Rowley, MA*

PREP: 20 min. • **COOK:** 25 min. • **MAKES:** 2 dozen

½ cup dry bread crumbs
⅓ cup grated Parmesan cheese
1 large egg, lightly beaten
1 tsp. garlic powder
¼ tsp. salt
⅛ tsp. pepper
1 lb. ground chicken
2 Tbsp. canola oil, divided
2 garlic cloves, minced
⅓ cup chicken broth
¼ cup white wine
1 jar (3½ oz.) capers, drained
1 Tbsp. lemon juice
2 Tbsp. butter
Shredded Parmesan cheese and lemon wedges

1. In a large bowl, combine the first 6 ingredients. Add chicken; mix lightly but thoroughly. With wet hands, shape into 1-in. balls.

2. In a large skillet, heat 1 Tbsp. oil over medium heat. Brown meatballs in batches; drain. Remove and keep warm. In same skillet, heat remaining 1 Tbsp. oil over medium heat. Add garlic; cook 1 minute.

3. Add broth and wine to pan; increase heat to medium-high. Cook 1 minute, stirring to loosen browned bits from pan. Add capers and lemon juice; bring to a boil. Add meatballs. Reduce heat; simmer, uncovered, until meatballs are cooked through, 5-7 minutes, stirring occasionally. Remove from heat; stir in butter until melted. Sprinkle with Parmesan cheese and serve with lemon wedges.

1 MEATBALL 63 cal., 4g fat (1g sat. fat), 24mg chol., 193mg sod., 2g carb. (0 sugars, 0 fiber), 4g pro.

⏱ QUINOA ARANCINI

I wanted to make a healthier version of arancini, which is a popular appetizer, by substituting quinoa for rice. I prefer baking them than frying, too, and this way we can enjoy them guilt-free.

—*Sabrina Ovadia, New York, NY*

TAKES: 30 min. • **MAKES:** 3 servings

1 pkg. (9 oz.) ready-to-serve quinoa or 1¾ cups cooked quinoa
2 large eggs, lightly beaten, divided use
1 cup seasoned bread crumbs, divided
¼ cup shredded Parmesan cheese
1 Tbsp. olive oil
2 Tbsp. minced fresh basil or 2 tsp. dried basil
½ tsp. garlic powder
½ tsp. salt
⅛ tsp. pepper
6 cubes part-skim mozzarella cheese (¾ in. each)
Cooking spray
Warmed pasta sauce, optional

1. Preheat oven to 425°. Prepare quinoa according to package directions. Stir in 1 egg, ½ cup bread crumbs, Parmesan cheese, oil, basil and seasonings.

2. Divide mixture into 6 portions. Shape each portion around a cheese cube to cover cheese completely, forming a ball.

3. Place remaining egg and ½ cup bread crumbs in separate shallow bowls. Dip quinoa balls in egg, then roll in bread crumbs. Place on a greased 15x10x1-in. baking pan; spritz with cooking spray. Bake until golden brown, 15-20 minutes. If desired, serve with pasta sauce.

2 ARANCINI 423 cal., 19g fat (6g sat. fat), 142mg chol., 1283mg sod., 40g carb. (4g sugars, 5g fiber), 21g pro.

TO USE AN AIR FRYER

You can also make this recipe in an air fryer if you prefer. Prepare the arancini as directed, then place on greased tray in the air-fryer basket; spritz with cooking spray. Cook at 375° for 6-8 minutes.

FRIED CHEESE RAVIOLI

Be sure to make enough of these crispy, coated ravioli. They're bound to be the hit
of your party. The golden brown pillows are easy to pick up and dip in tomato sauce.

—*Kate Dampier, Quail Valley, CA*

PREP: 15 min. • **COOK:** 20 min. • **MAKES:** about 2½ dozen

1 pkg. (9 oz.) refrigerated cheese ravioli
1 large egg
1 cup seasoned bread crumbs
¼ cup shredded Parmesan cheese
1½ tsp. dried basil
½ cup canola oil
    Additional shredded Parmesan cheese, optional
1 cup marinara sauce or meatless spaghetti sauce, warmed

1. Cook ravioli according to package directions; drain and pat dry. In a shallow bowl, lightly beat egg. In another shallow bowl, combine bread crumbs, Parmesan cheese and basil. Dip ravioli in egg, then in bread crumb mixture.

2. In a large skillet or deep-fat fryer, heat ¼ cup oil over medium heat. Fry ravioli in batches for 30-60 seconds on each side or until golden brown and crispy; drain on paper towels. Halfway through frying, replace oil; wipe skillet with paper towels if necessary.

3. Sprinkle with additional cheese as desired. Serve with marinara sauce.

1 RAVIOLI 58 cal., 2g fat (1g sat. fat), 11mg chol., 158mg sod., 7g carb. (1g sugars, 1g fiber), 2g pro.

VARIATION SUGGESTIONS

Consider trying beef or sausage ravioli, or specialty ravioli, such as those stuffed with butternut squash, mushroom or lobster. Whether they are fresh, refrigerated or frozen, first cook the ravioli in boiling water, drain, then pat them dry before dredging.

⏱ PROSCIUTTO-WRAPPED ASPARAGUS WITH RASPBERRY SAUCE

Grilling the prosciutto with the asparagus gives this appetizer a salty crunch that's perfect for dipping into a sweet glaze. When a delicious appetizer is this easy to prepare, you owe it to yourself to try it!
—*Noelle Myers, Grand Forks, ND*

TAKES: 30 min. • **MAKES:** 16 appetizers

⅓ lb. thinly sliced prosciutto
   or deli ham
16 fresh asparagus spears, trimmed
½ cup seedless raspberry jam
2 Tbsp. balsamic vinegar

1. Cut prosciutto slices in half. Wrap a prosciutto piece around each asparagus spear; secure ends with toothpicks.

2. Grill asparagus, covered, on a greased rack over medium heat until prosciutto is crisp, 6-8 minutes, turning once. Discard toothpicks.

3. In a small microwave-safe bowl, microwave jam and vinegar on high until jam is melted, 15-20 seconds. Serve with asparagus.

1 ASPARAGUS SPEAR WITH 1½ TSP. SAUCE 50 cal., 1g fat (0 sat. fat), 8mg chol., 184mg sod., 7g carb. (7g sugars, 0 fiber), 3g pro. **DIABETIC EXCHANGES** ½ starch.

TURKEY BOLOGNESE POLENTA NESTS

This delicious appetizer combines two of my favorite foods, polenta and bolognese meat sauce, uniting them into one incredibly tasty bite!

—Lidia Haddadian, Pasadena, CA

PREP: 40 min. • **BAKE:** 25 min. + cooling • **MAKES:** 2 dozen

3½ cups chicken stock, divided
1 cup yellow cornmeal
¾ cup grated Parmigiano-Reggiano cheese, divided
½ cup heavy whipping cream
¼ tsp. salt
¼ tsp. pepper
1 Tbsp. olive oil
1 cup chopped onion
3 garlic cloves, minced
½ lb. ground turkey
⅓ cup tomato paste
1½ tsp. Italian seasoning

1. Preheat oven to 350°. Coat 24 mini muffin cups with cooking spray. Set aside.

2. In a large heavy saucepan, bring 3 cups chicken stock to a boil. Reduce heat to a gentle boil; slowly whisk in cornmeal. Cook and stir with a wooden spoon until polenta is thickened and pulls away cleanly from side of pan, 15-20 minutes (mixture will be very thick). Stir in ½ cup cheese, cream, salt and pepper.

3. Spoon 2 Tbsp. polenta mixture into each mini muffin cup. As polenta cools, press an indentation in center of each with end of wooden spoon handle to create a nest shape. Set aside. Wipe out pan.

4. In same saucepan, heat oil over medium-high heat. Add onion; saute until translucent, 2-3 minutes. Add garlic; cook 1 minute longer. Add turkey; saute until no longer pink. Stir in tomato paste, Italian seasoning and remaining ½ cup chicken stock. Cook, stirring occasionally, until thickened, about 5 minutes.

5. Fill each polenta indention with about 2 tsp. turkey mixture. Sprinkle with remaining ¼ cup cheese; bake until edges are golden, 25-30 minutes. Remove from oven; cool at least 10 minutes before removing from muffin cups. Refrigerate or freeze for later use.

1 APPETIZER 80 cal., 4g fat (2g sat. fat), 14mg chol., 154mg sod., 7g carb. (1g sugars, 0 fiber), 4g pro.

SAVORY STUFFED CHERRY PEPPERS

Our family's holiday dinners always include a giant antipasto, and the showpiece when we were growing up was Mom's stuffed hot peppers on top of the display. Regardless of how spicy the peppers were, every year we would sneak into the refrigerator and steal one of those thrilling little flavor bombs! There isn't a holiday that we don't make them in her honor. These stuffed peppers are remarkable hot or cold. Serve with a nice loaf of Italian bread and a glass of wine.

—Donna Scarano, East Hanover, NJ

PREP: 20 min. • **BAKE:** 40 min. • **MAKES:** about 3 dozen

- 3 jars (16 oz. each) pickled hot cherry peppers, drained
- 1 can (2 oz.) anchovy fillets
- 1 large tomato, seeded and finely chopped
- 1 cup pimiento-stuffed olives, finely chopped
- 1 cup ripe olives, finely chopped
- 3 Tbsp. olive oil, divided
- ¼ cup grated Parmesan cheese
- 2 Tbsp. seasoned bread crumbs
- 1 tsp. capers, drained
- 1 Tbsp. minced fresh parsley or 1 tsp. dried parsley flakes
- 1 tsp. garlic powder
- ½ tsp. pepper
- ½ tsp. dried basil

1. Preheat oven to 350°. Cut tops off peppers and remove seeds; set aside. Drain and chop anchovies, reserving oil.

2. In a large bowl, combine tomato, olives, 1 Tbsp. olive oil, Parmesan cheese, anchovies, anchovy oil, bread crumbs, capers, parsley and seasonings. Spoon into peppers.

3. Place in a greased 13x9-in. baking dish. Drizzle with remaining 2 Tbsp. olive oil. Bake until tops are light golden brown, about 40 minutes.

FREEZE OPTION Cover and freeze cooled peppers in a greased 13x9-in. baking dish. To use, partially thaw in refrigerator overnight. Remove from refrigerator 30 minutes before baking. Preheat oven to 350°. Reheat peppers, covered, until heated through, 20-30 minutes.

1 APPETIZER 49 cal., 3g fat (0 sat. fat), 2mg chol., 612mg sod., 4g carb. (1g sugars, 1g fiber), 2g pro.

"These were a fabulous appetizer! I had never eaten anchovies before and it was my first time cooking with them as well. They are quite salty, yet with all the other ingredients it was like antipasto heaven! I had leftover filling and added it to a salad. That was very good also."
—SUSAN8783, TASTEOFHOME.COM

ITALIAN BREAD
SALAD WITH OLIVES
(PAGE 52)

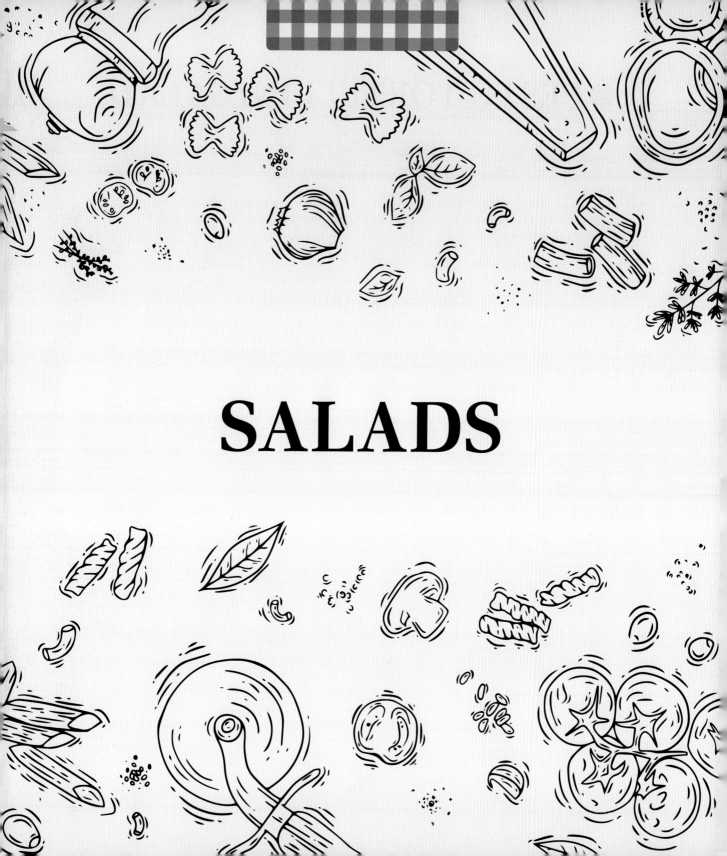

SALADS

⏱ PESTO TORTELLINI SALAD

I came up with this recipe when I tried re-creating a pasta salad I had at a wedding rehearsal.
It's easy to make and I'm always asked to bring it to potlucks and parties.
—*Danielle Weets, Grandview, WA*

TAKES: 20 min. • **MAKES:** 6 servings

1 pkg. (19 oz.) frozen cheese tortellini
¾ cup shredded Parmesan cheese
1 can (2¼ oz.) sliced ripe olives,
   drained
5 bacon strips, cooked and crumbled
¼ cup prepared pesto

Cook tortellini according to package directions; drain and rinse in cold water. Place in a large bowl. Add remaining ingredients; toss to coat.

¾ CUP 320 cal., 14g fat (6g sat. fat), 44mg chol., 724mg sod., 32g carb. (2g sugars, 2g fiber), 15g pro.

SUGGESTED ADDITIONS

As with most cold pasta salad recipes, it's easy to mix and match ingredients for this salad. Try stirring in grape tomatoes, miniature fresh mozzarella cheese balls, lightly steamed asparagus or sun-dried tomatoes.

ITALIAN PASTA SALAD

This zesty Italian pasta salad recipe combines vegetables and pasta in a creamy dressing.
Refreshing and filling, this change-of-pace salad is perfect as a side dish. It's always popular at a potluck.

—Tina Dierking, Skowhegan, ME

PREP: 15 min. + chilling • **COOK:** 10 min. • **MAKES:** 6 servings

1   cup uncooked spiral pasta
1½ cups halved cherry tomatoes
1   cup sliced fresh mushrooms
¼   cup chopped sweet red pepper
¼   cup chopped green pepper
3   Tbsp. thinly sliced green onions
1   cup zesty Italian salad dressing
¾   cup mayonnaise
½   cup grated Parmesan cheese
⅓   cup cubed provolone cheese
1   can (2¼ oz.) sliced ripe olives,
    drained

1. Cook pasta according to package directions; rinse with cold water and drain. Place pasta in a large bowl; add the tomatoes, mushrooms, peppers, onions and salad dressing. Refrigerate, covered, at least 4 hours or overnight; drain.

2. In a small bowl, combine mayonnaise and Parmesan cheese; stir in provolone cheese and olives. Gently fold into the pasta mixture.

1 CUP 371 cal., 30g fat (6g sat. fat), 13mg chol., 707mg sod., 17g carb. (4g sugars, 2g fiber), 7g pro.

"This is an excellent pasta salad. I didn't have any provolone cheese on hand so I used mozzarella. I don't know how using provolone could have made it any better!"
—ALLENFIVE, TASTEOFHOME.COM

MUSHROOM PANZANELLA

My fresh take on classic Italian bread salad pairs well with grilled or roasted meats.
—*Jennifer Beckman, Falls Church, VA*

PREP: 35 min. • **MAKES:** 8 servings

4 cups cubed sourdough bread
6 Tbsp. olive oil, divided
1 tsp. salt, divided
1 lb. sliced fresh assorted mushrooms (such as shiitake, oyster and cremini)
1 garlic clove, minced
2 Tbsp. balsamic vinegar
1 Tbsp. stone-ground mustard
1 tsp. honey
4 cups fresh arugula
1 cup grape tomatoes, halved
2 Tbsp. pine nuts, toasted
2 Tbsp. golden raisins
2 oz. fresh goat cheese, crumbled

1. Preheat oven to 450°. In a large bowl, combine bread, 2 Tbsp. oil and ¼ tsp. salt; toss to coat. Transfer bread cubes to an ungreased baking sheet. Bake until golden brown, 8-10 minutes. Cool to room temperature.

2. Combine mushrooms, 2 Tbsp. oil, garlic and ¼ tsp. salt; transfer to a greased baking sheet. Bake until tender, 10-12 minutes.

3. In another large bowl, whisk vinegar, mustard, honey, and the remaining 2 Tbsp. oil and ½ tsp. salt. Add arugula, tomatoes, pine nuts, raisins, toasted bread and mushrooms; toss to coat. Sprinkle with goat cheese. Serve immediately.

NOTE Arugula is a small and tender leafy green with a peppery taste; it's also known as rocket. It's often used in salads, alone or as part of a mix of greens, or in pizzas, sandwiches and pesto sauces. Arugula pairs well with prosciutto, goat cheese, figs, sun-dried tomatoes and Parmesan cheese.

1 CUP 210 cal., 13g fat (2g sat. fat), 5mg chol., 506mg sod., 20g carb. (5g sugars, 2g fiber), 6g pro. **DIABETIC EXCHANGES** 2 fat, 1 starch, 1 vegetable.

🕐 SIMPLE ITALIAN SALAD

Homemade croutons star in this easy Italian salad filled with grape tomatoes,
olives and pepperoncinis. It's the perfect side dish to practically any meal.
—*Nancy Granaman, Burlington, IA*

TAKES: 30 min. • **MAKES:** 6 servings

3 slices Italian bread, cubed
   Butter-flavored cooking spray
1 tsp. Italian seasoning
½ tsp. garlic powder
2 bunches romaine, torn
2 cups grape tomatoes, halved
1 can (2¼ oz.) sliced ripe olives,
   drained
¼ cup grated Parmesan cheese
1 small red onion, thinly sliced and
   separated into rings
8 pepperoncini
½ cup fat-free Italian salad dressing

1. Preheat oven to 450°. For croutons, spritz bread cubes with butter-flavored spray; place in a bowl. Sprinkle with Italian seasoning and garlic powder; toss to coat evenly.

2. Transfer to a greased 15x10x1-in. baking pan. Bake until golden brown, 8-10 minutes, stirring once or twice. Cool.

3. Meanwhile, in a large bowl, combine romaine, tomatoes, olives, Parmesan cheese, onion and pepperoncini. Drizzle with salad dressing; toss to coat. Top with croutons.

NOTE Look for pepperoncini (pickled peppers) in the pickle and olive section of your grocery store.

1½ CUPS 120 cal., 3g fat (1g sat. fat), 3mg chol., 943mg sod., 18g carb. (5g sugars, 4g fiber), 6g pro.

ACINI DI PEPE SALAD

Looking for a quick lunch idea or fun new side dish? Try this blend of veggies, tiny pasta and juicy pineapple bits for a change-of-pace salad jam-packed with flavor.

—June Herke, Watertown, SD

PREP: 20 min. + chilling • **MAKES:** 2 servings

¼ cup uncooked acini di pepe pasta
¼ cup mayonnaise
¼ cup whipped topping
1 Tbsp. finely chopped onion
Dash celery seed
¾ cup chopped fresh cauliflower
1 snack-size cup (4 oz.) pineapple tidbits, drained
⅓ cup frozen peas, partially thawed
1 Tbsp. raisins
Optional: Lettuce leaves and minced fresh parsley

1. Cook the pasta according to the package directions; drain and rinse in cold water.

2. In a small bowl, combine the mayonnaise, whipped topping, onion and celery seed. Add cauliflower, pineapple, peas, raisins and pasta; toss to coat. Cover and refrigerate 1 hour.

3. If desired, serve on a lettuce-lined plate and sprinkle with parsley.

¾ CUP 295 cal., 11g fat (3g sat. fat), 11mg chol., 284mg sod., 42g carb. (14g sugars, 4g fiber), 7g pro.

PASTA OPTIONS

If you don't have acini di pepe on hand, or if your market doesn't carry it, you could use orzo or ditalini for this recipe.

⏱ ANTIPASTO SALAD PLATTER

I used to work in a pizza shop where this salad was the most popular item on the menu. The dish is perfect for nights when it's just too hot to cook.
—*Webbie Carvajal, Alpine, TX*

TAKES: 25 min. • **MAKES:** 8 servings

1½ cups cubed fully cooked ham
1 jar (10 oz.) pimiento-stuffed olives, drained and sliced
1 can (3.8 oz.) sliced ripe olives, drained
1 pkg. (3½ oz.) sliced pepperoni, quartered
8 cups shredded lettuce
10 to 12 cherry tomatoes, quartered
1 cup Italian salad dressing
1½ cups shredded part-skim mozzarella cheese

In a large bowl, combine the ham, olives and pepperoni. On a platter or individual salad plates, arrange the lettuce, olive mixture and tomatoes. Drizzle with dressing; sprinkle with shredded cheese.

1 SERVING 342 cal., 29g fat (7g sat. fat), 41mg chol., 1830mg sod., 9g carb. (3g sugars, 2g fiber), 13g pro.

CAPRESE PASTA SALAD

This easy pasta salad is always a favorite, especially when summer tomatoes
are at their peak. It comes together quickly, but if you can make it ahead
of time, the flavors seem to get better after it's chilled for a few hours.

—Debby Harden, Lansing, MI

PREP: 35 min. • **MAKES:** 17 servings

1   pkg. (16 oz.) penne pasta
3   large heirloom tomatoes (about
    2 lbs.), seeded and chopped
¾   lb. fresh mozzarella cheese,
    cut into ½-in. pieces
½   cup loosely packed basil leaves,
    chopped
⅓   cup olive oil
¼   cup lemon juice
1   shallot, finely chopped
1   garlic clove, minced
1   tsp. sugar
¾   tsp. salt
½   tsp. grated lemon zest
¼   tsp. pepper

1. Cook pasta according to package directions. Drain and rinse in cold water.
Transfer to a large bowl. Gently stir in the tomatoes, cheese and basil.

2. In a small bowl, whisk the remaining ingredients. Drizzle over salad and toss
to coat. Refrigerate until serving.

¾ CUP 204 cal., 9g fat (4g sat. fat), 16mg chol., 137mg sod., 23g carb. (3g sugars,
2g fiber), 8g pro.

MAKING IT AHEAD

Caprese pasta salad can be made ahead of time and stored
covered in the fridge. For best results, use it within 3 to 4 days, and
wait to add the basil until you're ready to serve so it doesn't wilt.

🕐 GRILLED PEACH COUSCOUS SALAD

You'll feel inspired at the farmers market with the recipe for this couscous salad in your pocket. Grilled peaches and limes plus a subtly sweet dressing bring pizazz.
—*Emily King, Fayetteville, AR*

TAKES: 30 min. • **MAKES:** 8 servings

½ cup uncooked couscous
1 medium lime
2 medium firm ripe peaches, halved and pitted
1 tsp. plus ¼ cup canola oil, divided
1 English cucumber, halved and sliced
1 cup cherry tomatoes, halved
¼ medium red onion, thinly sliced
1 Tbsp. agave nectar
2 tsp. white wine vinegar
½ tsp. salt
¼ tsp. pepper

1. Prepare couscous according to package directions; fluff. Transfer to a large bowl; let cool.

2. Meanwhile, finely grate enough zest from lime to measure 1½ tsp.; set aside for dressing. Slice lime in half. Brush peach and lime halves with 1 tsp. oil. Grill peaches, covered, over medium heat until tender, 3-4 minutes on each side. Remove to a cutting board. Grill lime halves just until tender, about 1 minute.

3. When cool enough to handle, chop peaches and add to couscous. Stir in cucumber, tomatoes and red onion. Squeeze juice from lime into a small bowl. Add agave, vinegar, salt, pepper, reserved lime zest and remaining ¼ cup oil. Whisk until blended. Pour over salad; toss to coat.

¾ **CUP** 144 cal., 8g fat (1g sat. fat), 0 chol., 150mg sod., 18g carb. (7g sugars, 2g fiber), 2g pro. **DIABETIC EXCHANGES** 1½ fat, 1 starch.

⏱ ORZO WITH FETA & ARUGULA

In my family, we love salads because they're an interesting way to blend many different flavors.
This orzo salad is one of our favorites—it tastes delicious served either warm or cool.

—*Laura Adamsky, Decatur, AL*

TAKES: 30 min. • **MAKES:** 6 servings

1   cup uncooked orzo pasta
6   cups fresh arugula
½   cup crumbled feta cheese
½   cup sliced almonds, toasted
½   cup dried cherries or dried
    cranberries
2   Tbsp. extra virgin olive oil
¼   tsp. salt
⅛   tsp. pepper
    Lemon wedges, optional

1. Cook pasta according to package directions for al dente. Drain orzo; rinse with cold water and drain well.

2. In a large bowl, combine arugula, feta, almonds, cherries, oil, salt and pepper. Add orzo; toss to coat. If desired, serve with lemon wedges.

1 CUP 279 cal., 11g fat (2g sat. fat), 5mg chol., 198mg sod., 38g carb. (11g sugars, 3g fiber), 8g pro.

FOR THE NEXT DAY

Turn leftovers into lunch by adding sliced grilled chicken.

SICILIAN POTATO SALAD

Fresh basil is the star of this mayo-free, Italian-inspired take on potato salad.

—*Susan Falk, Sterling Heights, MI*

PREP: 20 min. • **COOK:** 20 min. • **MAKES:** 26 servings

10 small russet potatoes, unpeeled
1½ tsp. salt, divided
½ lb. fresh green beans, cut into 1½-in. pieces
¼ tsp. pepper
2 medium cucumbers, halved lengthwise and cut into ¼-in. slices
½ lb. cherry tomatoes, halved
1 large red onion, halved and thinly sliced
1 cup thinly sliced fresh basil leaves, divided
½ cup olive oil
4 Tbsp. cider vinegar
3 garlic cloves, minced

1. Place potatoes and ½ tsp. salt in a Dutch oven; add water to cover. Bring to a boil. Reduce heat; cook, uncovered, until tender, 12-15 minutes. Drain; rinse with cold water. Pat dry.

2. Meanwhile, in a small saucepan, bring 1 cup water to a boil. Add beans; cook, uncovered, just until crisp-tender, 3-4 minutes. Drain; immediately drop into ice water. Drain and pat dry.

3. Peel and cube potatoes; sprinkle with remaining 1 tsp. salt and the pepper. Transfer to a serving bowl. Add beans, cucumbers, tomatoes, onion and ¾ cup basil leaves. Whisk together oil, vinegar and garlic. Drizzle over vegetables; toss to coat. Sprinkle with remaining ¼ cup basil.

¾ CUP 96 cal., 4g fat (1g sat. fat), 0 chol., 143mg sod., 13g carb. (2g sugars, 2g fiber), 2g pro. **DIABETIC EXCHANGES** 1 starch, 1 fat.

COOKING GREEN BEANS

Instead of blanching the green beans in a large amount of water, you can steam them for a few minutes. Be sure to put the beans in ice water immediately after they're cooked, otherwise they'll lose their crunch and fade in color.

⏱ ITALIAN BREAD SALAD WITH OLIVES

This quick and flavorful bread salad always gets rave reviews from my friends and family. The panzanella-style dish is a timesaver during the holidays, as it can be made ahead of time. Just keep the bread cubes separate and add them right before serving.

—*Angela Spengler, Niceville, FL*

TAKES: 30 min. • **MAKES:** 9 servings

1   loaf (14 oz.) ciabatta bread, cut into ½-in. cubes (about 10 cups)
¾   cup olive oil
3   garlic cloves, minced
¼   tsp. pepper
¼   cup balsamic vinegar
¼   tsp. salt
2   large tomatoes, chopped
¼   cup sliced olives
⅓   cup coarsely chopped fresh basil
2   Tbsp. chopped fresh Italian parsley
¼   cup shredded Parmesan cheese

1. Preheat oven to 350°. Place bread cubes in a large bowl. In another bowl, mix oil, garlic and pepper; drizzle 3 Tbsp. over bread and toss to coat. Reserve the remaining oil mixture. Spread bread cubes in a single layer on two 15x10x1-in. baking pans.

2. Bake until crisp and light brown, 12-18 minutes, stirring occasionally.

3. Meanwhile, whisk vinegar and salt into the reserved oil mixture. Add tomatoes, olives and herbs; toss to coat.

4. Cool bread cubes slightly. Add to the tomato mixture; toss to combine. Sprinkle with shredded cheese; serve immediately.

1 CUP 316 cal., 21g fat (3g sat. fat), 2mg chol., 345mg sod., 31g carb. (5g sugars, 2g fiber), 5g pro.

54 EASY ITALIAN POTATO SALAD

You'll want to take this simple-to-assemble potato salad to all your picnics and outings. It's always on the menu when my tomato plants yield a bumper crop. Feel free to improvise by adding other fresh vegetables.

—Jeannette Macera, Utica, NY

TAKES: 20 min. • **MAKES:** 10 servings

6   medium red potatoes, cooked and cut into 1-in. pieces
2   garlic cloves, minced
½   cup chopped red onion
3   to 4 plum tomatoes, quartered
⅓   cup olive oil
3   to 4 fresh basil leaves, chopped
1   jar (5¾ oz.) pimiento-stuffed olives, drained and halved
1   tsp. dried oregano
1½   tsp. salt
¼   tsp. pepper

In a large bowl, combine all the ingredients; toss to coat. Refrigerate, covered, until ready to serve.

¾ CUP 170 cal., 10g fat (1g sat. fat), 0 chol., 638mg sod., 19g carb. (2g sugars, 2g fiber), 2g pro. **DIABETIC EXCHANGES** 2 fat, 1 starch.

COOKING POTATOES

When cooking potatoes for potato salad, don't overcook them; you want them to hold their shape and to absorb a minimal amount of water. Cook them whole in boiling water until just tender. When cool enough to handle, cut as directed.

🔒 HONEYDEW & PROSCIUTTO SALAD

For parties, I turn melon and prosciutto into an easy salad with a honey mustard dressing. To add zip, stir in fresh basil and mint.
—*Julie Merriman, Seattle, WA*

TAKES: 30 min. • **MAKES:** 12 servings

1. Place the first 8 ingredients in a blender; cover and process until smooth. Place arugula and herbs in a large bowl. Drizzle with ⅓ cup vinaigrette and toss lightly to coat.

2. In large serving bowl, layer a quarter of the arugula mixture, honeydew, mozzarella cheese and prosciutto layers. Repeat layers 3 times. Serve with the remaining vinaigrette.

1 SERVING 186 cal., 12g fat (4g sat. fat), 23mg chol., 294mg sod., 15g carb. (13g sugars, 1g fiber), 7g pro. **DIABETIC EXCHANGES** 1 fruit, 1 vegetable, 1 medium-fat meat, 1 fat.

"Great recipe! I used bocconcini pearls instead of traditional mozzarella to save a few bucks and it worked quite well. Followed everything else to a T and it was a big hit. Would definitely make again."
—MATT866, TASTEOFHOME.COM

SALAD

- ⅓ cup olive oil
- ½ tsp. grated lime zest
- 2 Tbsp. lime juice
- 2 Tbsp. white wine vinegar
- 2 Tbsp. honey
- 1 tsp. Dijon mustard
- ¼ tsp. salt
- ¾ cup fresh cilantro leaves
- 8 cups fresh arugula or baby spinach (about 5 oz.)
- ½ medium red onion, thinly sliced
- ¼ cup thinly sliced fresh mint leaves
- ¼ cup thinly sliced fresh basil leaves
- 8 cups diced honeydew melon
- 1 pkg. (8 oz.) fresh mozzarella cheese pearls
- ¼ lb. thinly sliced prosciutto, cut into wide strips

FENNEL SALAD WITH ORANGE-BALSAMIC VINAIGRETTE

A sweet balsamic vinaigrette always pulls everything together in a delicious harmony of flavors. Raspberries are one of my very favorite fruits, so I'm always eager to find a new use for them.
—*Susan Gauthier, Falmouth, ME*

TAKES: 25 min. • **MAKES:** 8 servings

¼ cup balsamic vinegar
¼ cup maple syrup
2 Tbsp. orange marmalade
2 Tbsp. seedless raspberry preserves
½ tsp. ground mustard
¼ tsp. salt
⅛ tsp. pepper
½ cup olive oil

SALAD
1 pkg. (5 oz.) spring mix salad greens
2 fennel bulbs, thinly sliced
1 can (15 oz.) mandarin oranges, drained
¼ cup coarsely chopped pistachios, toasted

1. In a small bowl, whisk the first 7 ingredients. Gradually whisk in oil until blended.

2. In a large bowl, combine salad greens, fennel and oranges. Divide salad mixture among 8 plates. Sprinkle with pistachios; drizzle with dressing.

1½ CUPS 240 cal., 16g fat (2g sat. fat), 0 chol., 133mg sod., 25g carb. (18g sugars, 3g fiber), 2g pro.

SUMMER ORZO

I'm always looking for fun ways to use the fresh veggies that come in my Community Supported Agriculture box, and this salad is one of my favorite creations. I like to improvise, so feel free to do the same here! The recipe makes enough for a crowd, so it's perfect for summer parties, but it can easily be cut back for a smaller group.
—*Shayna Marmar, Philadelphia, PA*

PREP: 30 min. + chilling • **MAKES:** 16 servings

1   pkg. (16 oz.) orzo pasta
¼   cup water
1½ cups fresh or frozen corn
24 cherry tomatoes, halved
2   cups crumbled feta cheese
1   medium cucumber, seeded and chopped
1   small red onion, finely chopped
¼   cup minced fresh mint
2   Tbsp. capers, drained and chopped, optional
½   cup olive oil
¼   cup lemon juice
1   Tbsp. grated lemon zest
1½ tsp. salt
1   tsp. pepper
1   cup sliced almonds, toasted

1. Cook orzo according to package directions for al dente. Drain orzo; rinse with cold water and drain well. Transfer to a large bowl.

2. In a large nonstick skillet, heat ¼ cup water over medium heat. Add corn; cook and stir until crisp-tender, 3-4 minutes. Add to orzo; stir in tomatoes, feta cheese, cucumber, onion, mint and, if desired, capers.

3. In a small bowl, whisk oil, lemon juice, lemon zest, salt and pepper until blended. Pour over orzo mixture; toss to coat. Refrigerate 30 minutes.

4. Just before serving, stir in almonds.

¾ CUP 291 cal., 15g fat (4g sat. fat), 15mg chol., 501mg sod., 28g carb. (3g sugars, 3g fiber), 11g pro.

SUGGESTED ADDITIONS

This salad can be customized with almost any vegetable you like. Try adding grilled zucchini, roasted asparagus or sauteed bell peppers, or include a handful of fresh herbs such as basil or parsley. To make the salad into a main course, add a protein like chicken, shrimp, tofu or chickpeas. Diced avocado is never a bad idea, either; it would add some creaminess to the salad.

ITALIAN SPAGHETTI SALAD

This attractive, fresh-tasting salad is a terrific option for parties—it's easy to make in advance, and it makes enough for a crowd! Thin spaghetti or angel hair pasta works best; dice your vegetables small to balance the pasta size.

—Lucia Johnson, Massena, NY

PREP: 20 min. + chilling • **MAKES:** 16 servings

1   pkg. (16 oz.) thin spaghetti, halved
3   medium tomatoes, diced
3   small zucchini, diced
1   large cucumber, halved, seeded and diced
1   medium green pepper, diced
1   medium sweet red pepper, diced
1   bottle (8 oz.) Italian salad dressing
2   Tbsp. grated Parmesan cheese
1½ tsp. sesame seeds
1½ tsp. poppy seeds
½   tsp. paprika
¼   tsp. celery seed
⅛   tsp. garlic powder
    Chopped fresh parsley, optional

1. Cook spaghetti according to package directions; drain and rinse in cold water. Place in a large bowl; add tomatoes, zucchini, cucumber and peppers.

2. Combine the next 7 ingredients; pour over salad and toss to coat. Cover and refrigerate for at least 2 hours. If desired, sprinkle with parsley.

1 CUP 158 cal., 3g fat (1g sat. fat), 1mg chol., 168mg sod., 26g carb. (4g sugars, 2g fiber), 5g pro. **DIABETIC EXCHANGES** 1½ starch, 1 vegetable, ½ fat.

MAKING AHEAD

This recipe calls for refrigerating for at least 2 hours, but allowing the salad to sit overnight will allow more flavors to develop and blend. This salad will last 3 to 5 days in the refrigerator.

⏱ PEACH MANGO CAPRESE SALAD

Summer in the Midwest offers a bounty of fresh produce. I wanted to come up with a new recipe for the harvested goods, and this bright, flavorful salad is the refreshing end result. If you don't like cilantro, you can substitute parsley or mint.
—*Richard Robinson, Park Forest, IL*

TAKES: 25 min. • **MAKES:** about 6 servings

2 medium peaches, cut into
   ½-in. pieces
2 cups grape tomatoes, halved
1 carton (8 oz.) fresh mozzarella
   cheese pearls, drained
1 cup chopped peeled mango
2 Tbsp. minced fresh cilantro
2 Tbsp. minced fresh basil

DRESSING
3 Tbsp. balsamic vinegar
3 fresh basil leaves
2 tsp. honey
¼ tsp. salt
⅛ tsp. pepper
¼ cup olive oil

Place the first 6 ingredients in a large bowl. For the dressing, place vinegar, basil, honey, salt and pepper in a blender. While processing, gradually add oil in a steady stream. Pour over peach mixture; gently toss to coat. Refrigerate until serving. Garnish with additional basil.

¾ CUP 248 cal., 17g fat (7g sat. fat), 30mg chol., 156mg sod., 16g carb. (14g sugars, 2g fiber), 8g pro.

"What an amazing salad! Rather than getting out my blender, I minced the basil and placed the remaining dressing ingredients in a small jar with a lid ... shaking worked great."
—SGRONHOLZ, TASTEOFHOME.COM

EASY CAESAR SALAD

Fans of Caesar salad will find the dressing used in this tasty version one of the best. My sister, Jan, developed this recipe and was nice enough to share her secret with me.

—Dianne Nash, Kaslo, British Columbia

TAKES: 15 min. • **MAKES:** 8 servings

- ¼ cup grated Parmesan cheese
- ¼ cup mayonnaise
- 2 tablespoons milk
- 1 tablespoon lemon juice
- 1 tablespoon Dijon-mayonnaise blend
- 1 garlic clove, minced
  Dash cayenne pepper
- 1 bunch romaine, torn
  Optional: Salad croutons and additional grated Parmesan cheese

In a small bowl, whisk the first 7 ingredients. Place romaine in a large bowl. Drizzle with dressing and toss to coat. Serve with salad croutons and additional cheese if desired.

1 CUP 73 cal., 6g fat (1g sat. fat), 5mg chol., 126mg sod., 2g carb. (0 sugars, 1g fiber), 2g pro. **DIABETIC EXCHANGES** 1 vegetable, 1 fat.

WHITE BEAN SOUP
WITH ESCAROLE
(PAGE 75)

SOUPS & BREADS

FOCACCIA BARESE

This focaccia has been in my mom's family for several generations. It is one of my most-requested recipes whenever I am invited to a party—I am not allowed to attend unless I bring it!

—*Dora Travaglio, Mount Prospect, IL*

PREP: 30 min. + rising • **BAKE:** 30 min. • **MAKES:** 8 servings

1⅛ tsp. active dry yeast
¾ cup warm water (110° to 115°), divided
½ tsp. sugar
⅓ cup mashed potato flakes
1½ tsp. plus 2 Tbsp. olive oil, divided
¼ tsp. salt
1¾ cups bread flour

TOPPING
2 medium tomatoes, thinly sliced
¼ cup pitted Greek olives, halved
1½ tsp. minced fresh or dried oregano
½ tsp. coarse salt

1. In a large bowl, dissolve yeast in ½ cup warm water. Add sugar; let stand for 5 minutes. Add potato flakes, 1½ tsp. oil, salt, 1 cup flour and remaining ¼ cup water. Beat until smooth. Stir in enough remaining flour to form a soft dough.

2. Turn onto a floured surface; knead until smooth and elastic, 6-8 minutes. Place in a greased bowl, turning once to grease top. Cover and let rise in a warm place until doubled, about 1 hour. Punch dough down. Cover and let rest for 10 minutes.

3. Place 1 Tbsp. olive oil in a 10-in. cast-iron or other ovenproof skillet; tilt pan to evenly coat. Add dough; shape to fit pan. Cover and let rise until doubled, about 30 minutes.

4. With fingertips, make several dimples over top of dough. Brush with remaining 1 Tbsp. oil. Blot tomato slices with paper towels. Arrange tomato slices and olives over dough; sprinkle with oregano and salt.

5. Bake at 375° for 30-35 minutes or until golden brown.

NOTE Also known as kalamata olives, Greek olives are almond-shaped and range in size from ½-1 in. long. Dark eggplant in color, the kalamata olive is rich and fruity in flavor and can be found packed in either a vinegar brine or olive oil.

1 PIECE 142 cal., 4g fat (1g sat. fat), 0 chol., 269mg sod., 24g carb. (1g sugars, 1g fiber), 4g pro.

CHIPOTLE FOCACCIA WITH GARLIC-ONION TOPPING

Chipotle peppers make some people grab their water glasses, while others can't get enough of the smoky heat. I came up with this recipe to fit right in the middle. Add more chipotle if you crave spiciness.

—*Frances Kay Bouma, Trail, BC*

PREP: 1¼ hours + rising • **BAKE:** 20 min. • **MAKES:** 1 loaf (16 pieces)

1 cup water (70° to 80°)
2 Tbsp. olive oil
2½ cups all-purpose flour
1 tsp. salt
1 Tbsp. chopped chipotle pepper in adobo sauce
1½ tsp. active dry yeast

TOPPING
6 garlic cloves, peeled
¼ tsp. plus 7 Tbsp. olive oil, divided
2 large onions, cut into ¼-in. slices
2 Tbsp. chopped chipotle peppers in adobo sauce
¼ tsp. salt
Chopped chives, optional

1. In bread machine pan, place first 6 ingredients in order suggested by manufacturer. Select dough setting (check after 5 minutes of mixing; add 1-2 Tbsp. water or flour if needed). When cycle is completed, turn onto a lightly floured surface. Punch down dough; cover and let rest 15 minutes.

2. Place garlic in a small microwave-safe bowl. Drizzle with ¼ tsp. oil. Microwave on high for 20-60 seconds or until softened. Mash garlic.

3. Roll dough into a 12x10-in. rectangle. Transfer to a well-greased baking sheet. Set, covered, in a warm place until slightly risen, about 20 minutes.

4. With fingertips, make several dimples over top of dough. Brush dough with 1 Tbsp. oil. Bake at 400° for 10 minutes or until lightly browned.

5. Meanwhile, in a large skillet, saute onions in remaining oil until tender. Add chipotle peppers, salt and mashed garlic; saute 2-3 minutes longer. Sprinkle over dough.

6. Bake until golden brown, 10-15 minutes longer. If desired, top with chives. Cut into serving portions; serve warm.

1 PIECE 159 cal., 8g fat (1g sat. fat), 0 chol., 206mg sod., 19g carb. (2g sugars, 1g fiber), 3g pro.

ITALIAN MEATBALL & BEAN SOUP

Tender meatballs in a savory, chili-like soup deliver a taste sensation the whole family will love.
You can use sweet, medium or hot Italian sausage, depending on your heat preferences!
—*Amanda Bowyer, Caldwell, ID*

PREP: 30 min. • **COOK:** 5 hours • **MAKES:** 6 servings

1 large egg
3 Tbsp. 2% milk
⅓ cup seasoned bread crumbs
1 lb. bulk Italian sausage
½ lb. ground turkey
2 cans (14½ oz. each) diced tomatoes
1 can (15 oz.) cannellini beans,
   rinsed and drained
1 can (15 oz.) black beans, rinsed
   and drained
1 can (8 oz.) tomato sauce
1 cup water
2 green onions, thinly sliced
1 tsp. Italian seasoning
1 tsp. dried minced garlic
½ tsp. crushed red pepper flakes
   Additional thinly sliced
   green onions, optional

1. In a large bowl, combine egg, milk and bread crumbs. Crumble sausage and turkey over mixture and mix well. Shape into 1-in. balls. In a large skillet, brown meatballs in batches; drain.

2. Transfer meatballs to a 3-qt. slow cooker. Stir in remaining ingredients. Cover and cook on low for 5-6 hours or until a thermometer inserted in a meatball reaches 160°. If desired, top with additional sliced green onion.

1½ CUPS 529 cal., 31g fat (11g sat. fat), 119mg chol., 1273mg sod., 35g carb. (6g sugars, 8g fiber), 27g pro.

"I used frozen meatballs to save time, but followed the other instructions as written. Still used the slow cooker, but only cooked for 3 hours on high. In the end it was good and my wife liked it too. It was easy, and I'll make it again."
—GUEST9175, TASTEOFHOME.COM

UPSTATE MINESTRONE SOUP

If you love vegetables, you'll find this minestrone especially satisfying.
Keep the recipe in mind when you have a bounty of fresh garden produce.

—Yvonne Krantz, Mount Upton, NY

PREP: 25 min. • **COOK:** 1½ hours • **MAKES:** 8 servings

1 lb. Italian sausage links,
  cut into ½-in. slices
1 Tbsp. olive oil
1 cup finely chopped onion
1 cup sliced fresh carrots
1 garlic clove, finely minced
1 tsp. dried basil
2 cups shredded cabbage
2 small zucchini, sliced
2 cans (10½ oz. each) condensed
  beef broth, undiluted or 3 beef
  bouillon cubes plus 1½ cups water
1 can (14½ oz.) diced tomatoes,
  undrained
¼ tsp. salt
¼ tsp. pepper
1 can (15½ oz.) great northern beans,
  rinsed and drained
  Minced fresh parsley

1. In a Dutch oven, brown sausage in oil. Add onion, carrots, garlic and basil; cook for 5 minutes. Stir in cabbage, zucchini, broth, tomatoes, salt and pepper.

2. Bring to a boil. Reduce heat; cover and simmer for 1 hour. Add beans; cook 20 minutes longer. Garnish with parsley.

FREEZE OPTION Freeze cooled soup in freezer containers. To use, partially thaw in refrigerator overnight. Heat through in a saucepan, stirring occasionally; add broth or water if necessary.

1 SERVING 236 cal., 14g fat (4g sat. fat), 31mg chol., 1329mg sod., 16g carb. (4g sugars, 5g fiber), 12g pro.

BASIL TOMATO SOUP WITH ORZO

This soup is so scrumptious that it's worth the time it takes to chop the fresh onion, garlic and basil. It's even better the next day after the flavors have had a chance to blend.
—*Tonia Billbe, Elmira, NY*

PREP: 15 min. • **COOK:** 25 min. • **MAKES:** 16 servings (4 qt.)

1 large onion, chopped
¼ cup butter, cubed
2 garlic cloves, minced
3 cans (28 oz. each) crushed tomatoes
1 carton (32 oz.) chicken broth
1 cup loosely packed basil leaves, chopped
1 Tbsp. sugar
½ tsp. pepper
1¼ cups uncooked orzo pasta
1 cup heavy whipping cream
½ cup grated Romano cheese

1. In a Dutch oven, saute onion in butter for 3 minutes. Add garlic; cook until onion is tender, 1-2 minutes longer. Stir in tomatoes, broth, basil, sugar and pepper. Bring to a boil. Reduce heat; cover and simmer for 15 minutes.

2. Meanwhile, cook orzo according to the package directions; drain. Add orzo and cream to soup; heat through (do not boil). Sprinkle each serving with cheese.

1 CUP 208 cal., 10g fat (6g sat. fat), 27mg chol., 607mg sod., 25g carb. (9g sugars, 3g fiber), 7g pro.

SWEET ONION BREAD SKILLET

Because there are just a few ingredients in this recipe, you'll get the best results if you use the finest-quality foods, like a fresh Vidalia onion and aged Parmesan cheese.

—*Lisa Speer, Palm Beach, FL*

PREP: 25 min. • **BAKE:** 10 min. • **MAKES:** 4 servings

1 large sweet onion, thinly sliced
2 Tbsp. butter
2 Tbsp. olive oil, divided
1 can (13.8 oz.) refrigerated pizza crust
¼ cup grated Parmesan cheese

1. In a large cast-iron or other ovenproof skillet, saute onion in butter and 1 Tbsp. oil until softened. Reduce heat to medium-low; cook, stirring occasionally, until golden brown, 15-20 minutes. Set aside.

2. Brush inside of skillet with remaining oil. Unroll crust into skillet; flatten crust and build up edge slightly. Top with onion mixture and cheese. Bake at 450° until golden brown, 10-12 minutes. Cut into 4 wedges.

1 WEDGE 415 cal., 17g fat (5g sat. fat), 19mg chol., 776mg sod., 53g carb. (9g sugars, 2g fiber), 11g pro.

SOFT GARLIC BREADSTICKS

I rely on the convenience of my bread machine to mix the dough for these buttery golden breadsticks that are mildly seasoned with garlic and basil. I like to use this dough when making pizza, too. It yields two 12-inch crusts.
—*Charles Smith, Baltic, CT*

PREP: 30 min. + rising • **BAKE:** 20 min. • **MAKES:** 20 breadsticks

1 cup plus 2 Tbsp. water (70° to 80°)
2 Tbsp. olive oil
3 Tbsp. grated parmesan cheese
2 Tbsp. sugar
3 tsp. garlic powder
1½ tsp. salt
¾ tsp. minced fresh basil or
   ¼ tsp. dried basil
3 cups bread flour
2 tsp. active dry yeast
1 Tbsp. butter, melted

1. In bread machine pan, place the first 9 ingredients in order suggested by manufacturer. Select dough setting (check dough after 5 minutes of mixing; add 1-2 Tbsp. water or flour if needed).

2. When cycle is completed, turn dough onto a lightly floured surface. Divide into 20 portions. Shape each into a ball; roll each ball into a 9-in. rope. Place on greased baking sheets. Cover and let rise in a warm place for 40 minutes or until doubled.

3. Bake at 350° for 18-22 minutes or until golden brown. Remove to wire racks to cool. Brush warm breadsticks with butter. If desired, sprinkle with additional grated Parmesan cheese.

1 BREADSTICK 88 cal., 2g fat (1g sat. fat), 2mg chol., 196mg sod., 15g carb., 1g fiber), 3g pro.

STORING BREADSTICKS

You can wrap these breadsticks in foil and store them at room temperature—use within four days for best results. You can also freeze them for 1-2 months.

⏱ GREAT GARLIC BREAD

Garlic bread may be the go-to accompaniment to any pasta dish or Italian-style soup—but there's no reason it has to be run-of-the-mill! This tasty garlic bread topped with cheese adds the wow factor to any entree.
—Taste of Home *Test Kitchen*

TAKES: 15 min. • **MAKES:** 8 servings

½ cup butter, melted
¼ cup grated Romano cheese
4 garlic cloves, minced
1 loaf (1 lb.) French bread, halved lengthwise
2 Tbsp. minced fresh parsley

1. Preheat oven to 350°. In a small bowl, mix butter, cheese and garlic; brush over cut sides of bread. Place on a baking sheet, cut sides up. Sprinkle with parsley.

2. Bake 7-9 minutes or until light golden brown. Cut into pieces; serve warm.

1 PIECE 283 cal., 14g fat (8g sat. fat), 34mg chol., 457mg sod., 33g carb. (1g sugars, 1g fiber), 8g pro.

WHITE BEAN SOUP WITH ESCAROLE

Pantry staples make this healthy soup oh, so simple to prepare. When I can't find escarole,
I use fresh spinach, just adding it to the soup pot moments before serving.
—*Gina Samokar, North Haven, CT*

PREP: 15 min. • **COOK:** 35 min. • **MAKES:** 8 servings (2 qt.)

1   Tbsp. olive oil
1   small onion, chopped
5   garlic cloves, minced
3   cans (14½ oz. each) reduced-sodium chicken broth
1   can (14½ oz.) diced tomatoes, undrained
½   tsp. Italian seasoning
¼   tsp. crushed red pepper flakes
1   cup uncooked whole wheat orzo pasta
1   bunch escarole, coarsely chopped (about 8 cups)
1   can (15 oz.) cannellini beans, rinsed and drained
¼   cup shredded Parmesan cheese

1. In a Dutch oven, heat oil over medium heat. Add onion and garlic; cook and stir until tender. Add broth, tomatoes, Italian seasoning and pepper flakes; bring to a boil. Reduce heat; simmer, uncovered, 15 minutes.

2. Stir in orzo and escarole. Return to a boil; cook until orzo is tender, 12-14 minutes. Add beans; heat through, stirring occasionally. Sprinkle servings with cheese.

1 CUP SOUP WITH 1½ TSP. CHEESE 174 cal., 3g fat (1g sat. fat), 2mg chol., 572mg sod., 28g carb. (3g sugars, 8g fiber), 9g pro. **DIABETIC EXCHANGES** 1 starch, 1 vegetable, 1 lean meat, ½ fat.

CREAMY TORTELLINI SOUP

Rich and mild, this creamy, indulgent soup gets added "oomph" from red pepper flakes and wine. If you like, you can add Italian sausage—sliced or crumbled—either cooked in the skillet as part of the first step or cooked separately and added at the end.

—Taste of Home *Test Kitchen*

PREP: 15 min. • **COOK:** 15 min. • **MAKES:** 6 cups (1½ qt.)

2 Tbsp. olive oil
3 medium carrots, chopped
1 large onion, chopped
4 garlic cloves, minced
¼ cup all-purpose flour
½ cup dry white wine
2 cans (14½ oz. each) vegetable broth
1 pkg. (9 oz.) refrigerated cheese tortellini
1 tsp. Italian seasoning
¾ tsp. salt
½ tsp. pepper
   Crushed red pepper flakes, optional
1 cup heavy whipping cream
4 cups chopped fresh spinach
   Grated Parmesan cheese, optional

1. In a Dutch oven, heat oil over medium heat. Add carrots and onion; cook and stir until crisp-tender, 6-8 minutes. Add garlic; cook and stir 1 minute longer. Stir in flour until blended; add white wine. Increase heat to medium-high and cook, stirring occasionally, until wine is reduced by half, 2-3 minutes. Gradually whisk in broth. Bring to a boil, stirring constantly; cook and stir until slightly thickened, 3-5 minutes.

2. Add tortellini, Italian seasoning, salt and pepper and, if desired, crushed red pepper flakes. Reduce heat and simmer, uncovered, just until tortellini are tender, 3-5 minutes.

3. Stir in cream and spinach; cook and stir just until spinach is wilted, 1-2 minutes longer. If desired, serve with grated Parmesan cheese and top with additional crushed red pepper flakes.

1 CUP 345 cal., 21g fat (11g sat. fat), 64mg chol., 720mg sod., 33g carb. (6g sugars, 3g fiber), 9g pro.

ROSEMARY FOCACCIA

The savory aroma of rosemary as this classic bread bakes is irresistible.
Try this bread as a side with any meal, as a snack or as a pizza crust.
—*Debrah Peoples, Calgary, AB*

PREP: 30 min. + rising • **BAKE:** 25 min. • **MAKES:** 2 loaves (8 pieces each)

¼ cup plus 3 Tbsp. olive oil, divided
2 medium onions, chopped
1½ tsp. active dry yeast
1½ cups warm water (110° to 115°), divided
½ tsp. sugar
½ tsp. salt
3 to 4 cups all-purpose flour
2 Tbsp. snipped fresh rosemary or 2 tsp. dried rosemary, crushed, divided
   Cornmeal
   Coarse salt

1. In a large skillet, heat ¼ cup oil over medium heat. Add onions; cook and stir until tender, 6-8 minutes.

2. In a large bowl, dissolve yeast in ¼ cup warm water. Add sugar; let stand 5 minutes. Add 2 Tbsp. oil, salt and remaining water. Add 2 cups flour. Beat until smooth. Stir in enough remaining flour to form a soft dough.

3. Turn dough onto a floured surface; knead 6-8 minutes or until smooth and elastic. Add onions and 1 Tbsp. rosemary. Knead 1 minute longer. Place in a greased bowl, turning once to grease top. Cover and let rise in a warm place until doubled, about 40 minutes.

4. Punch dough down. Turn onto a lightly floured surface; divide in half. Pat each piece flat. Let rest for 5 minutes. Grease 2 round baking pans and sprinkle with cornmeal. Stretch each portion of dough into a 10-in. circle on prepared pans. Cover and let rise until doubled, about 40 minutes. Preheat oven to 375°.

5. Brush dough with remaining 1 Tbsp. oil. Sprinkle with coarse salt and remaining 1 Tbsp. rosemary. Bake until golden brown, 25-30 minutes. Remove from pans to wire racks. Serve warm.

1 PIECE 147 cal., 6g fat (1g sat. fat), 0 chol., 75mg sod., 20g carb. (2g sugars, 1g fiber), 3g pro.

USING INSTANT YEAST

You can use instant yeast instead of active dry yeast for this recipe. If you go this route, skip the step of proofing the yeast in water with the sugar—instead, add the instant yeast and sugar along with the flour.

⏱ CHICKEN GNOCCHI PESTO SOUP

After tasting a similar soup at a restaurant, I created this quick
and tasty version. It's rich and creamy, and couldn't be easier to make!
—*Deanna Smith, Des Moines, IA*

TAKES: 25 min. • **MAKES:** 4 servings

1 jar (15 oz.) roasted garlic
    Alfredo sauce
2 cups water
2 cups rotisserie chicken,
    roughly chopped
1 tsp. Italian seasoning
¼ tsp. salt
¼ tsp. pepper
1 pkg. (16 oz.) potato gnocchi
3 cups coarsely chopped
    fresh spinach
4 tsp. prepared pesto

In a large saucepan, combine first
6 ingredients; bring to a gentle boil,
stirring occasionally. Stir in gnocchi
and spinach; cook until gnocchi float,
3-8 minutes. Top each serving with
1 tsp. pesto.

NOTE Look for potato gnocchi in the
pasta or frozen foods section.

1½ CUPS 586 cal., 26g fat (11g sat. fat),
158mg chol., 1650mg sod., 56g carb.
(3g sugars, 4g fiber), 31g pro.

SUN-DRIED TOMATO FOCACCIA

This bread looks inviting and doesn't disappoint when you take a bite. The sun-dried tomatoes
and red onions give it an extra-special appearance, making it fit for any celebratory meal.

—*Kathy Katz, Ocala, FL*

PREP: 1 hour 40 min. + rising • **BAKE:** 20 min. • **MAKES:** 2 loaves (8 servings each)

¼ cup chopped sun-dried tomatoes
   (not packed in oil)
½ cup boiling water
1¼ cups warm V8 juice (70° to 80°)
2 Tbsp. olive oil
¼ cup grated Parmesan cheese
1 Tbsp. dried parsley flakes
2 tsp. sugar
1 tsp. salt
1 tsp. dried basil
½ tsp. garlic powder
2 cups whole wheat flour
1½ cups all-purpose flour
3 tsp. active dry yeast

TOPPING

2 Tbsp. slivered sun-dried tomatoes
   (not packed in oil)
¼ cup boiling water
12 thin slices red onion, halved
1 Tbsp. olive oil
   Minced fresh parsley, optional

1. In a small bowl, combine chopped sun-dried tomatoes and boiling water.
Let stand for 5 minutes; drain.

2. In bread machine pan, place V8 juice, oil, softened tomatoes, cheese, parsley
flakes, sugar, salt, basil, garlic powder, flours and yeast in order suggested by
manufacturer. Select dough setting (check dough after 5 minutes of mixing;
add 1-2 Tbsp. water or flour if needed).

3. In a small bowl, combine slivered tomatoes and boiling water. Let stand for
5 minutes; drain and pat dry with paper towels.

4. When cycle is completed, turn dough onto a lightly floured surface. Punch
down. Divide in half; roll each portion into a 9-in. circle. Place in 2 greased
9-in. cast-iron skillets or round baking pans.

5. Using end of a wooden spoon handle, make ¼-in. indentations in dough.
Arrange tomato slivers and onion slices over dough; press down lightly. Cover
and let rise in a warm place until doubled, about 30 minutes. Brush with oil.

6. Preheat oven to 375°. Bake until golden brown, 20-25 minutes. Remove to
wire racks. If desired, top with additional Parmesan cheese and minced parsley.

1 PIECE 135 cal., 3g fat (1g sat. fat), 1mg chol., 247mg sod., 23g carb. (2g sugars,
3g fiber), 4g pro. **DIABETIC EXCHANGES** 1½ starch, ½ fat.

TO PREPARE DOUGH BY HAND

Combine the chopped sun-dried tomatoes and boiling water. Let
stand for 5 minutes; drain. Dissolve yeast in warm V8 juice (110°
to 115°). Combine olive oil, cheese, parsley, sugar, salt, basil and garlic
powder. Stir in yeast mixture and softened chopped tomatoes; mix
well. Stir in enough flour to form a soft dough. Turn onto a floured
surface; knead until smooth and elastic, 6-8 minutes. Place in a
greased bowl, turning once to grease the top. Cover and let rise in
a warm place until doubled, 1 hour. Proceed with recipe as directed.

TUSCAN PORTOBELLO STEW

Here's a healthy one-skillet meal that's quick and easy to prepare yet elegant enough for company.
I often take this stew to my school's potlucks, where it is devoured by teachers and students alike.

—Jane Siemon, Viroqua, WI

PREP: 20 min. • **COOK:** 20 min. • **MAKES:** 4 servings (1¼ qt.)

2 large portobello mushrooms, coarsely chopped
1 medium onion, chopped
3 garlic cloves, minced
2 Tbsp. olive oil
½ cup white wine or vegetable broth
1 can (28 oz.) diced tomatoes, undrained
2 cups chopped fresh kale
1 bay leaf
1 tsp. dried thyme
½ tsp. dried basil
½ tsp. dried rosemary, crushed
¼ tsp. salt
¼ tsp. pepper
2 cans (15 oz. each) cannellini beans, rinsed and drained

1. In a large skillet, saute mushrooms, onion and garlic in oil until tender. Add wine. Bring to a boil; cook until liquid is reduced by half. Stir in tomatoes, kale, bay leaf, thyme, basil, rosemary, salt and pepper. Bring to a boil. Reduce heat; cover and simmer 8-10 minutes.

2. Add beans; heat through. Discard bay leaf.

1¼ CUPS 309 cal., 8g fat (1g sat. fat), 0 chol., 672mg sod., 46g carb. (9g sugars, 13g fiber), 12g pro. **DIABETIC EXCHANGES** 2 starch, 2 vegetable, 1½ fat, 1 lean meat.

ABOUT PORTOBELLOS

Because of their meaty texture, portobello mushrooms are popular in vegetarian recipes like this one. Baby portobellos are also known as cremini mushrooms; they can be used instead of white mushrooms for a flavor boost.

ITALIAN PINWHEEL ROLLS

Parmesan cheese, garlic and oregano make these rolls hard to resist. My family
gets hungry when they smell them baking and can't wait for them to be done!
—*Patricia Fitzgerald, Candor, NY*

PREP: 35 min. + rising • **BAKE:** 25 min. • **MAKES:** 1 dozen

1   pkg. (¼ oz.) active dry yeast
1   cup warm water (110° to 115°)
1½ tsp. sugar
1½ tsp. butter, softened
1   tsp. salt
2¼ to 2½ cups bread flour

FILLING
2   Tbsp. butter, melted
¼   cup grated Parmesan cheese
2   Tbsp. minced fresh parsley
6   garlic cloves, minced
1   tsp. dried oregano

1. In a large bowl, dissolve yeast in warm water. Add sugar, butter, salt and 1 cup flour; beat until smooth. Stir in enough remaining flour to form a soft dough.

2. Turn onto a floured surface; knead until smooth and elastic, 6-8 minutes. Place in a bowl coated with cooking spray, turning once to coat top. Cover and let rise in a warm place until doubled, about 1 hour.

3. Punch dough down. Turn onto a lightly floured surface. Roll into a 12x10-in. rectangle. Brush with melted butter; sprinkle cheese, parsley, garlic and oregano to within ½ in. of edges. Roll up jelly-roll style, starting with a long side; pinch seam to seal. Cut into 12 rolls.

4. Place rolls cut side up in a 13x9-in. baking pan coated with cooking spray. Cover and let rise until doubled, about 30 minutes.

5. Bake at 350° until golden brown, 25-30 minutes. Remove from pan to a wire rack.

1 ROLL 110 cal., 3g fat (2g sat. fat), 8mg chol., 253mg sod., 18g carb. (1g sugars, 1g fiber), 4g pro.

TRADITIONAL ITALIAN WEDDING SOUP

You don't have to be Italian to love this easy-to-make soup with tiny round pasta! Homemade meatballs pair beautifully with ready-made stock and rotisserie chicken.

—*Mary Sheetz, Carmel, IN*

PREP: 30 min. • **COOK:** 40 min. • **MAKES:** 9 servings (2¼ qt.)

2 large eggs, lightly beaten
½ cup dry bread crumbs
¼ cup minced fresh parsley
2 Tbsp. grated Parmesan cheese
1 Tbsp. raisins, finely chopped
3 garlic cloves, minced
¼ tsp. crushed red pepper flakes
½ lb. lean ground beef (90% lean)
½ lb. bulk spicy pork sausage
2 cartons (32 oz. each) reduced-sodium chicken broth
½ tsp. pepper
1½ cups cubed rotisserie chicken
⅔ cup uncooked acini di pepe pasta
½ cup fresh baby spinach, cut into thin strips
Shredded Parmesan cheese, optional

1. In a large bowl, combine first 7 ingredients. Crumble beef and sausage over mixture and mix lightly but thoroughly. Shape into ½-in. balls.

2. In a Dutch oven, brown meatballs in small batches; drain. Add broth and pepper; bring to a boil. Reduce heat; simmer, uncovered, for 10 minutes. Stir in chicken and pasta; cook 5-7 minutes longer or until pasta is tender. Stir in spinach; cook until wilted. Sprinkle with shredded Parmesan cheese if desired.

FREEZE OPTION Before adding cheese, cool soup. Freeze in freezer containers. To use, partially thaw in refrigerator overnight. Heat through in a saucepan, stirring occasionally; add broth or water if necessary. Sprinkle each serving with cheese.

1 CUP 253 cal., 10g fat (4g sat. fat), 94mg chol., 797mg sod., 18g carb. (3g sugars, 1g fiber), 21g pro.

"My family loved this recipe. We used mild sausage as that's what I had on hand. I did increase the amount of chicken stock and I made extra meatballs as that's their favorite part. Very easy and good."
—LORIMARKLE, TASTEOFHOME.COM

RUSTIC ITALIAN TORTELLINI SOUP

This is my favorite soup recipe. It's quick to fix on a busy night and full of healthy, tasty ingredients. It originally called for spicy sausage links, but I've found that turkey sausage, or even ground turkey breast, is just as good.
—*Tracy Fasnacht, Irwin, PA*

PREP: 20 min. • **COOK:** 20 min. • **MAKES:** 6 servings (2 qt.)

¾ lb. Italian turkey sausage links, casings removed
1 medium onion, chopped
6 garlic cloves, minced
2 cans (14½ oz. each) reduced-sodium chicken broth
1¾ cups water
1 can (14½ oz.) diced tomatoes, undrained
1 pkg. (9 oz.) refrigerated cheese tortellini
1 pkg. (6 oz.) fresh baby spinach, coarsely chopped
2¼ tsp. minced fresh basil or ¾ tsp. dried basil
¼ tsp. pepper
 Dash crushed red pepper flakes
 Shredded Parmesan cheese, optional

1. Crumble sausage into a Dutch oven; add onion. Cook and stir over medium heat until meat is no longer pink. Add garlic; cook 1 minute longer. Stir in broth, water and tomatoes. Bring to a boil.

2. Add tortellini; return to a boil. Cook for 5-8 minutes or until almost tender, stirring occasionally. Reduce heat; add spinach, basil, pepper and pepper flakes. Cook 2-3 minutes longer or until spinach is wilted and tortellini are tender. Serve with cheese if desired.

FREEZE OPTION Place individual portions of cooled soup in freezer containers and freeze. To use, partially thaw in refrigerator overnight. Heat through in a saucepan, stirring occasionally; add broth if necessary.

1⅓ CUPS 203 cal., 8g fat (2g sat. fat), 40mg chol., 878mg sod., 18g carb. (5g sugars, 3g fiber), 16g pro.

WHY BABY SPINACH?

Baby spinach is simply spinach that has been harvested before it is fully grown, and so has a milder flavor. Using baby spinach saves prep time because you don't have to remove the tough stems of mature spinach. You can certainly use less-expensive regular spinach in this soup; its stronger flavor will hold up well to cooking. However, be sure it is rinsed well and that you've removed the stems.

⏱ ITALIAN-STYLE CRESCENTS

This is one of my best easy breads. Pesto and Italian seasoning quickly doctor up
ready-to-bake refrigerated crescent dough, so you're ready to roll.
—*Ann Marie Barber, Oakland Park, FL*

TAKES: 25 min. • **MAKES:** 8 servings

1 tube (8 oz.) refrigerated
   crescent rolls
8 tsp. prepared pesto
1 large egg white, lightly beaten
1½ tsp. Italian seasoning

1. Preheat oven to 375°. Unroll crescent dough; separate into triangles. Spread each piece of dough with 1 tsp. pesto. Roll up from wide end and place pointed side down 2 in. apart on ungreased baking sheets. Curve ends down to form a crescent shape.

2. Brush with egg white; sprinkle with Italian seasoning. Bake until lightly browned, 10-13 minutes.

1 CROISSANT 140 cal., 8g fat (2g sat. fat), 2mg chol., 269mg sod., 12g carb. (2g sugars, 0 fiber), 3g pro.

● PULL-APART HERB BREAD

The ingredients for this recipe are so simple and the results so spectacular that I'm always willing to share the secret. It's actually a variation of a doughnut recipe I made years ago, using refrigerated biscuits. The best part of having this bread is tearing it apart and eating it warm.
—*Evelyn Kenney, Hamilton, NJ*

TAKES: 30 min. • **MAKES:** 10 servings

1 garlic clove, minced
¼ cup butter, melted
2 tubes (10.2 oz. each) refrigerated biscuits
1 cup shredded cheddar cheese
¼ tsp. dried basil
¼ tsp. fennel seed
¼ tsp. dried oregano

1. In a 10-in. cast-iron or other ovenproof skillet, saute garlic in butter for 1 minute; remove from pan and set aside. Separate biscuits; cut in half horizontally. Place half in an even layer in skillet, overlapping as necessary. Brush with garlic mixture; sprinkle with half the cheese and herbs. Repeat layers.

2. Bake at 375° until bread is golden brown, 20-25 minutes. Place pan on a wire rack; serve warm.

1 PIECE 257 cal., 14g fat (8g sat. fat), 23mg chol., 569mg sod., 25g carb. (4g sugars, 1g fiber), 6g pro.

NO CAST-IRON SKILLET?

If you don't have a cast-iron skillet, prepare in a 9-in. springform pan. Just melt the butter and combine with the garlic beforehand. Proceed with the recipe as directed.

NEW YORK-STYLE
PIZZA (PAGE 99)

PIZZA PIES & FLATBREADS

FAVORITE DEEP-DISH PIZZA

My kids love to get pizza delivered, but it's expensive and not very healthy. I came up with a make-at-home pizza that is healthier than delivery and allows the kids to add the toppings of their choice.

—*Sara LaFountain, Rockville, MD*

PREP: 20 min. • **BAKE:** 20 min. • **MAKES:** 8 servings

1¾ cups whole wheat flour
1¾ cups all-purpose flour
2 pkg. (¼ oz. each) quick-rise yeast
4 tsp. sugar
1 tsp. salt
1½ cups warm water (120° to 130°)
¼ cup olive oil
1 can (8 oz.) pizza sauce
8 oz. fresh mozzarella cheese, sliced
2 cups shredded Italian cheese blend
½ tsp. dried oregano
½ tsp. Italian seasoning
Optional: Sliced red onion, chopped green pepper, fresh oregano and crushed red pepper flakes

1. In a large bowl, combine wheat flour, 1 cup all-purpose flour, yeast, sugar and salt. Add water and oil; beat until smooth. Stir in enough remaining flour to form a soft dough. Press dough onto the bottom and up the sides of a greased 13x9-in. baking dish.

2. Spread with pizza sauce. Top with mozzarella slices. Sprinkle with shredded cheese, oregano and Italian seasoning. If desired, top with sliced red onion and green pepper. Bake, uncovered, at 400° for 20-25 minutes or until golden brown. Top with fresh oregano leaves and crushed red pepper flakes if desired.

1 PIECE 449 cal., 20g fat (9g sat. fat), 42mg chol., 646mg sod., 47g carb. (4g sugars, 5g fiber), 19g pro.

🕐 PIZZA CAPRESE

One of my favorite pizzas is so simple to make and comes together so quickly. Pizza Caprese is simply heirloom tomatoes, fresh mozzarella and really good extra virgin olive oil. I could have this every day!

—*Beth Berlin, Oak Creek, WI*

TAKES: 30 min. • **MAKES:** 6 servings

1 pkg. (6½ oz.) pizza crust mix
2 Tbsp. extra virgin olive oil, divided
2 garlic cloves, thinly sliced
1 large tomato, thinly sliced
4 oz. fresh mozzarella cheese, sliced
⅓ cup loosely packed basil leaves

1. Preheat oven to 425°. Prepare pizza dough according to package directions. With floured hands, press dough onto a greased 12-in. pizza pan.

2. Drizzle 1 Tbsp. olive oil over dough and sprinkle with sliced garlic. Bake until crust is lightly browned, 10-12 minutes. Top with tomato and fresh mozzarella; bake until cheese is melted, 5-7 minutes longer. Drizzle with remaining 1 Tbsp. olive oil and top with basil. Serve immediately.

1 PIECE 208 cal., 9g fat (3g sat. fat), 15mg chol., 196mg sod., 23g carb. (3g sugars, 1g fiber), 7g pro.

CRUST OPTIONS

This pizza recipe starts with uncooked dough, so you can substitute a homemade pizza dough without changing the recipe at all. You can also start with a precooked crust, French bread or a soft flatbread, such as naan—just skip the prebaking step and start by adding the toppings.

🕐 BACON, LETTUCE & TOMATO PIZZA

I combine two all-time favorites in this recipe: pizza and BLT sandwiches.
I brought this fun mashup to a ladies lunch and was met with lots of oohs and aahs.
—*Bonnie Hawkins, Elkhorn, WI*

TAKES: 30 min. • **MAKES:** 6 servings

1   tube (13.8 oz.) refrigerated
    pizza crust
2   Tbsp. olive oil
2   Tbsp. grated Parmesan cheese
1   tsp. garlic salt
½   cup mayonnaise
2   tsp. ranch dip mix
4   cups shredded romaine
3   to 4 plum tomatoes, chopped
½   lb. bacon strips, cooked and
    crumbled

1. Preheat oven to 425°. Unroll and press dough onto bottom of a greased 15x10x1-in. baking pan. Brush with oil; top with cheese and garlic salt. Bake until golden brown, 15-18 minutes; cool slightly.

2. Meanwhile, combine mayonnaise and ranch dip mix. Spread over pizza crust; top with romaine, tomatoes and bacon.

1 SERVING 389 cal., 23g fat (5g sat. fat), 16mg chol., 1236mg sod., 34g carb. (5g sugars, 2g fiber), 11g pro.

GRILLED ELOTE FLATBREAD

Here's a fun twist on a classic Mexican dish! Keep your kitchen cooled down
during the summer by grilling this fresh flatbread outdoors.
—*Amanda Phillips, Portland, OR*

PREP: 20 min. • **GRILL:** 15 min. • **MAKES:** 12 servings

2 medium ears sweet corn, husked
3 Tbsp. olive oil, divided
1 lb. fresh or frozen pizza dough, thawed
½ cup mayonnaise
⅓ cup crumbled Cotija cheese, divided
⅓ cup chopped fresh cilantro, divided
1 Tbsp. lime juice
½ tsp. chili powder
⅛ tsp. pepper

1. Brush corn with 1 Tbsp. oil. Grill corn, covered, over medium heat until lightly browned and tender, 10-12 minutes, turning occasionally. Cool slightly. Cut corn from cobs; transfer to a large bowl.

2. On a lightly floured surface, roll or press dough into a 15x10-in. oval (about ¼ in. thick); place on a greased sheet of foil. Brush top with 1 Tbsp. oil.

3. Carefully invert crust onto grill rack, removing foil. Brush top with remaining 1 Tbsp. oil. Grill, covered, over medium heat until golden brown, 2-3 minutes on each side. Remove from grill; cool slightly.

4. Add mayonnaise, 3 Tbsp. cheese, 3 Tbsp. cilantro, lime juice, chili powder and pepper to corn; stir to combine. Spread over warm crust. Sprinkle with remaining cheese and cilantro.

1 PIECE 211 cal., 13g fat (2g sat. fat), 4mg chol., 195mg sod., 20g carb. (2g sugars, 1g fiber), 5g pro.

CREOLE SHRIMP PIZZA

Pizza and the flavors of Creole cuisine blend amazingly well in this hearty dish with a crispy crust.
Add more hot sauce to boost the heat if you like things spicy. If you prefer pasta to pizza,
try tossing the toppings with hot cooked fettucine instead.

—Robin Haas, Cranston, RI

PREP: 15 min. • **BAKE:** 25 min. • **MAKES:** 6 servings

1   prebaked 12-in. pizza crust
1   Tbsp. olive oil, divided
1½ cups shredded part-skim
    mozzarella cheese, divided
1   Tbsp. lemon juice
1½ tsp. reduced-sodium Creole
    seasoning, divided
1   lb. uncooked shrimp (31-40 per lb.),
    peeled and deveined
1   large onion, chopped
½   tsp. coarsely ground pepper
¼   tsp. celery seed
2   garlic cloves, minced
1   cup pizza sauce
¼   tsp. Louisiana-style hot sauce
1   large green pepper, thinly sliced

1. Preheat oven to 425°. Place crust on an ungreased baking sheet. Brush with 1½ tsp. oil; sprinkle with ½ cup mozzarella cheese. Set aside. Combine lemon juice and ½ tsp. Creole seasoning. Add shrimp; toss to coat.

2. In a small skillet, heat remaining 1½ tsp. oil over medium heat. Add onion, pepper, celery seed and remaining 1 tsp. Creole seasoning; saute until onion is tender. Add garlic; cook 1 minute longer. Stir in pizza sauce and hot sauce. Remove from heat.

3. Drain shrimp. Spread the sauce mixture over crust. Top with shrimp and green pepper; sprinkle with remaining 1 cup cheese.

4. Bake until shrimp turn pink and cheese is melted, 25-30 minutes.

1 PIECE 378 cal., 13g fat (4g sat. fat), 110mg chol., 969mg sod., 39g carb. (6g sugars, 3g fiber), 27g pro.

HOMEMADE CREOLE SEASONING

Creole seasoning is commercially available, but you can make your own at home—for each teaspoon of Creole seasoning, mix ¼ tsp. each salt, garlic powder and paprika, and a pinch each dried thyme, ground cumin and cayenne pepper.

NEW YORK-STYLE PIZZA

This is a no-nonsense pizza. Since the crust is pliable, cut the pie into larger pieces if you want to eat your slices in the traditional New York way—folded! Who says pizza isn't portable?

—*Mariam Ishaq, Buffalo, NY*

PREP: 1 hour + rising • **BAKE:** 15 min. • **MAKES:** 8 servings

- 1 tsp. active dry yeast
- ⅔ cup warm water (110° to 115°)
- 2 Tbsp. olive oil
- 1 tsp. salt
- 1¾ to 2¼ cups all-purpose flour
- 1 can (8 oz.) tomato sauce
- 2 cups shredded mozzarella cheese
- ½ cup grated Romano cheese
- ¼ cup chopped fresh basil
- 2 tsp. dried oregano
- 1 tsp. crushed red pepper flakes

1. In a small bowl, dissolve yeast in warm water. In a large bowl, combine oil, salt, yeast mixture and 1 cup flour; beat on medium speed until smooth. Stir in enough remaining flour to form a soft dough (dough will be sticky). Turn dough onto a floured surface; knead until smooth and elastic, 6-8 minutes. Place in a greased bowl, turning once to grease the top. Cover and let rise in a warm place until doubled, about 1 hour.

2. Preheat oven to 475°. Grease a 14-in. pizza pan. Roll dough to fit pan. Pinch edge to form a rim. Cover and let rest 10 minutes. Spread with tomato sauce; top with cheeses, basil, oregano and pepper flakes. Bake on a lower oven rack until crust is lightly browned and cheese is melted, 15-20 minutes. Let stand 5 minutes before slicing.

1 PIECE 254 cal., 12g fat (6g sat. fat), 24mg chol., 714mg sod., 23g carb. (1g sugars, 2g fiber), 13g pro.

REHEATING PIZZA

We recommend reheating pizza in the oven. Place pizza on a foil-lined baking tray and bake at 375° for about 10 minutes. Another option is to reheat your pizza on the stovetop in a cast-iron skillet. Add a few droplets of water around the pizza, place a lid on the skillet and then cook over medium heat for a few minutes. The steam from the water will warm and perfectly melt the cheese on your slice. We do not recommend reheating pizza in the microwave.

CREAMY CHICKEN ENCHILADA PIZZA

This is a twist on a family favorite. We wanted the taste of my chicken enchilada recipe, but we wanted it even faster. This kicked-up pizza was our fun creation.
—*Crystal Jo Bruns, Iliff, CO*

TAKES: 30 min. • **MAKES:** 6 servings

1 tube (11 oz.) refrigerated thin pizza crust
1 pkg. (8 oz.) cream cheese, softened, cubed
1 cup shredded Mexican cheese blend, divided
2 tsp. ground cumin
1½ tsp. garlic powder
½ tsp. salt
2 cups ready-to-use fajita chicken strips, cubed
½ cup salsa
¼ cup green enchilada sauce
Optional: Shredded lettuce, chopped tomatoes and sliced ripe olives

1. Preheat oven to 400°. Unroll and press dough onto bottom and ½ in. up sides of a greased 15x10x1-in. baking pan. Bake 5 minutes.

2. Meanwhile, in a small saucepan, combine cream cheese, ½ cup Mexican cheese blend, cumin, garlic powder and salt over medium heat; cook and stir 5 minutes or until blended. Remove from heat. Add chicken; toss to coat.

3. Spread chicken mixture over crust. Drizzle with salsa and enchilada sauce; sprinkle with remaining ½ cup cheese. Bake until crust is golden and cheese is melted, 8-12 minutes. Serve with toppings of your choice.

1 PIECE 428 cal., 25g fat (12g sat. fat), 83mg chol., 1061mg sod., 30g carb. (5g sugars, 1g fiber), 20g pro.

DON'T SKIP THE PREBAKE

The super creamy topping on this pizza prevents the bottom of the crust from crisping up as much as a traditional pizza, so prebaking the crust is necessary.

PRETZEL CRUST PIZZA

In our house, we love pizza and pretzel bread! When Little Caesar's came out with their pretzel crust pizza, we fell in love but also knew it was unrealistic to be buying it all the time. The next best thing was to make it ourselves, and it came out even better than the restaurant's version! This thick-crusted copycat pizza is bound to blow your socks off!

—Mary Lou Timpson, Centennial Park, AZ

PREP: 25 in. + rising • **BAKE:** 20 min. • **MAKES:** 8 servings

1½ cups warm water (110° to 115°)
2 Tbsp. sugar
1 Tbsp. active dry yeast
4 cups all-purpose flour
1 tsp. salt
½ cup hot water
2 Tbsp. baking soda
¼ tsp. pretzel or coarse salt

PIZZA
½ cup salsa con queso dip, such as Tostitos
2 cups shredded Mexican cheese blend
½ cup sliced pepperoni
1 Tbsp. butter, melted

1. In a stand mixer, stir together warm water, sugar and yeast; let stand until foamy, 4-5 minutes. Add flour and 1 tsp. salt. Using a dough hook, mix on low speed until dough comes together, 1-2 minutes. Increase speed to medium and mix for an additional 5 minutes. Place dough in a greased bowl, turning once to grease the top. Cover and let rise in a warm place until doubled, about 45 minutes.

2. Preheat oven to 425°. Punch down dough; press into a 12-in. circle onto an ungreased 14-in. pizza pan. Let stand 10 minutes. Stir together the hot water and baking soda; brush mixture over outer 1 in. Let stand 5 minutes; repeat. Sprinkle coarse salt over edge.

3. Spread queso dip over inside of crust. Top with cheese and pepperoni. Bake until crust is golden brown and cheese is melted, 16-18 minutes. Brush crust with melted butter before serving.

1 PIECE 414 cal., 15g fat (7g sat. fat), 36mg chol., 772mg sod., 55g carb. (4g sugars, 3g fiber), 15g pro.

⏱ ARUGULA PIZZA

This pizza is great served as an appetizer when family or friends get together. My girlfriends and I love it because it has that sophisticated gourmet touch, and it's healthy too! This also serves four for a main course.

—*Annette Riva, Naperville, IL*

TAKES: 20 min. • **MAKES:** 8 servings

½ cup pizza sauce
1 prebaked 12-in. pizza crust (14 oz.)
1 cup shaved Parmesan cheese
3 oz. thinly sliced prosciutto
2 cups fresh arugula
   Additional fresh arugula, optional

Preheat oven to 425°. Spread sauce over pizza crust. Layer with ½ cup Parmesan cheese, prosciutto and arugula; top with remaining ½ cup cheese. Bake directly on oven rack until edge is lightly browned, 10-12 minutes. Cut into small squares. If desired, top with additional arugula.

2 PIECES 204 cal., 7g fat (3g sat. fat), 17mg chol., 689mg sod., 23g carb. (2g sugars, 1g fiber), 12g pro.

SUGGESTED ADDITIONS

You can add whatever your pizza-loving heart desires to this pizza! We recommend tomatoes (either heirloom or sundried), mushrooms and/or pesto.

SICILIAN PIZZA (SFINCIONE)

My favorite pizza from childhood is still my favorite today. The crunchy bread-crumb topping sets it apart from its American counterpart. I like to top this pie with torn fresh basil.
—*Susan Falk, Sterling Heights, MI*

PREP: 20 min. • **BAKE:** 20 min. • **MAKES:** 12 servings

2 loaves (1 lb. each) fresh or frozen pizza dough, thawed
3 Tbsp. olive oil, divided
1 can (28 oz.) whole tomatoes, drained and crushed
1 medium onion, finely chopped
1 can (2 oz.) anchovy fillets, drained and broken into ¼-in. pieces
1 cup shredded mozzarella cheese
½ cup soft bread crumbs
Fresh torn basil leaves

1. Preheat oven to 425°. Grease a 15x10x1-in. baking pan. Press dough to fit bottom and ½ in. up sides of pan. Brush with 2 Tbsp. oil; top with tomatoes, onion and anchovies. Sprinkle with mozzarella. Combine bread crumbs and the remaining 1 Tbsp. oil; sprinkle over pizza.

2. Bake on a lower oven rack until edges are golden brown and cheese is melted, 20-25 minutes. Sprinkle with basil before serving.

1 PIECE 277 cal., 9g fat (2g sat. fat), 11mg chol., 527mg sod., 38g carb. (4g sugars, 3g fiber), 11g pro.

MEATBALL FLATBREAD

As amazing as this flatbread tastes, you would never know how quickly it comes together.
A little hidden carrot, unnoticed by the kids, adds sweet texture. For a crispier crust, bake the flatbread
in the oven until it is slightly crispy on top before applying tomato sauce.

—*Kimberly Berg, North Street, MI*

TAKES: 25 min. • **MAKES:** 4 flatbreads (2 servings each)

1   can (15 oz.) Italian tomato sauce
1   medium carrot, coarsely chopped
3   fresh basil leaves
1   garlic clove, halved
4   naan flatbreads
2   cups shredded mozzarella cheese
14 frozen fully cooked Italian
    meatballs, thawed and halved
    Dash each salt, pepper, dried
    parsley flakes and dried oregano

1. Preheat oven to 400°. Place tomato sauce, carrot, basil and garlic in a food processor; cover and process until pureed.

2. Place flatbreads on an ungreased baking sheet. Spread with tomato sauce mixture; top with cheese and meatballs. Sprinkle with seasonings.

3. Bake on a lower oven rack until cheese is melted, 12-15 minutes.

½ **FLATBREAD** 228 cal., 10g fat (5g sat. fat), 46mg chol., 835mg sod., 21g carb. (3g sugars, 2g fiber), 14g pro.

EASY PESTO PIZZA

Knead basil, oregano and Parmesan cheese into packaged bread dough for a full-flavored crust.
Prepared pesto keeps this pizza big on taste and convenience.
—Taste of Home *Test Kitchen*

PREP: 20 min. • **BAKE:** 20 min. • **MAKES:** 8 servings

1   loaf (1 lb.) frozen bread dough, thawed
½   cup shredded Parmesan cheese, divided
½   tsp. dried basil
½   tsp. dried oregano
¼   cup prepared pesto
1   cup sliced fresh mushrooms
1   cup shredded part-skim mozzarella cheese

1. Preheat oven to 425°. Place dough on a lightly floured surface; let rest for 10 minutes. Knead in ¼ cup cheese, the basil and oregano. Roll into a 12-in. circle; place on a greased 14-in. pizza pan. Prick with a fork. Bake 10 minutes.

2. Spread pesto over crust. Sprinkle with mushrooms, mozzarella cheese and the remaining ¼ cup Parmesan cheese. Bake pizza until golden brown, 8-10 minutes longer.

1 PIECE 259 cal., 11g fat (4g sat. fat), 17mg chol., 513mg sod., 31g carb. (3g sugars, 2g fiber), 12g pro.

WHICH PESTO?

Basil pesto is the traditional choice, but feel free to use any type of pesto. There are some great store-bought options, but if you have the time, it's hard to beat homemade—it allows you to customize the ingredients, making the pizza taste so fresh. See our recipe for pesto on page 158. For more variety, check out our recipes for Creamy Pesto, Nut-Free Pesto and Ramp Pesto in the Sauces & Crusts chapter, starting on page 252.

THE BEST SAUSAGE PIZZAS

What makes this recipe distinctive is the slow overnight fermentation of the dough.
The flour has time to hydrate and relax, which makes the dough so much easier to roll out!
—*Josh Rink, Milwaukee, WI*

PREP: 30 min. • **BAKE:** 15 min. • **MAKES:** 2 pizzas (8 pieces each)

1   batch Best Pizza Dough (p. 270)
1   lb. bulk Italian sausage
1   cup pizza sauce
4   cups shredded part-skim
    mozzarella cheese
1   medium red onion, sliced
1   medium green pepper, chopped
2   cups sliced fresh mushrooms
    Optional: Grated Parmesan
    cheese, crushed red pepper flakes
    and fresh oregano leaves

1. Divide dough in half. With greased fingers, pat each half onto an ungreased 12-in. pizza pan. Prick dough thoroughly with a fork. Bake at 400° until lightly browned, 10-12 minutes. Meanwhile, in a large skillet, cook the sausage over medium heat until no longer pink, breaking it into crumbles; drain.

2. Spread pizza sauce over crusts. Top with cheese, onion, green pepper, mushrooms and sausage. Bake at 400° until golden brown and cheese is bubbling, 12-15 minutes. If desired, top with grated Parmesan cheese, crushed red pepper flakes and fresh oregano leaves.

FREEZE OPTION Wrap unbaked pizzas and freeze for up to 2 months. To use, unwrap and place on pizza pans; thaw in the refrigerator. Bake at 400° until crust is golden brown, 18-22 minutes.

1 PIECE 344 cal., 20g fat (7g sat. fat), 41mg chol., 651mg sod., 26g carb. (2g sugars, 1g fiber), 15g pro.

CHICKEN PARMESAN PIZZA

This tasty pizza is the perfect combo—quick and easy to make, and a winner with even picky eaters. It's a handy option for a family dinner on a busy night or for the center of the table at a kids' party.

—Karen Wittmeier, Parkland, FL

PREP: 25 min. • **BAKE:** 15 min. • **MAKES:** 6 pieces

8   frozen breaded chicken tenders
1   loaf (1 lb.) frozen pizza dough, thawed
½   cup marinara sauce
¼   tsp. garlic powder
2   cups (8 oz.) shredded part-skim mozzarella cheese
¼   cup shredded Parmesan cheese
2   Tbsp. thinly sliced fresh basil
     Additional warmed marinara sauce

1. Bake chicken tenders according to package directions. Remove from oven; increase oven setting to 450°.

2. Meanwhile, grease a 12-in. pizza pan. Roll dough to fit pan. In a small bowl, mix marinara sauce and garlic powder; spread over dough.

3. Cut chicken into 1-in. pieces. Top pizza with chicken and mozzarella cheese. Bake on a lower oven rack 12-15 minutes or until crust is golden brown and cheese is melted. Sprinkle with Parmesan cheese and basil. Serve with additional marinara.

1 PIECE 440 cal., 17g fat (6g sat. fat), 35mg chol., 774mg sod., 48g carb. (4g sugars, 3g fiber), 23g pro.

BARBECUED CHICKEN PIZZAS

So fast and so easy with refrigerated pizza crust, these saucy, smoky pizzas make quick fans with their hot-off-the-grill, rustic flavor. They're perfect for spur-of-the-moment cookouts and summer dinners on the patio.

—*Alicia Trevithick, Temecula, CA*

PREP: 25 min. • **GRILL:** 10 min. • **MAKES:** 2 pizzas (4 pieces each)

2 boneless skinless chicken breast halves (6 oz. each)
¼ tsp. pepper
1 cup barbecue sauce, divided
1 tube (13.8 oz.) refrigerated pizza crust
2 tsp. olive oil
2 cups shredded Gouda cheese
1 small red onion, halved and thinly sliced
¼ cup minced fresh cilantro

1. Sprinkle chicken with pepper; place on an oiled grill rack over medium heat. Grill, covered, until a thermometer reads 165°, 5-7 minutes per side; baste frequently with ½ cup barbecue sauce during the last 4 minutes. Cool slightly. Cut into cubes.

2. Divide dough in half. On a well-greased large sheet of heavy-duty foil, press each portion of dough into a 10x8-in. rectangle; brush lightly with oil. Invert dough onto grill rack; peel off foil. Grill, covered, over medium heat until bottom is lightly browned, 1-2 minutes.

3. Remove from grill. Spread grilled sides with remaining barbecue sauce. Top with cheese, chicken and onion. Grill, covered, until bottom is lightly browned and cheese is melted, 2-3 minutes. Sprinkle with cilantro.

1 PIECE 339 cal., 12g fat (6g sat. fat), 56mg chol., 956mg sod., 39g carb. (15g sugars, 1g fiber), 20g pro.

STEAKHOUSE PIZZA

One of my first jobs was in a steakhouse restaurant. This recipe gives me a chance to celebrate two favorite foods: steak and pizza. I love the addition of eggs baked onto the pizza for a steak and eggs dish.

—Lisa Benoit, Cookeville, TN

PREP: 35 min. • **BAKE:** 10 min. + standing • **MAKES:** 8 servings

1 loaf (1 lb.) frozen pizza dough, thawed
1 pkg. (8 oz.) frozen spinach and artichoke cheese dip, thawed
¾ cup grape tomatoes, halved
1 boneless beef top loin steak (1 lb.), thinly sliced
1½ tsp. Montreal steak seasoning
⅓ cup torn fresh basil
3 Tbsp. pine nuts
2 bacon strips, cooked and crumbled
⅓ cup prepared ranch salad dressing
1 Tbsp. prepared horseradish

1. Preheat oven to 400°. Press dough to fit a greased 14-in. pizza pan. Pinch edge to form a rim. Bake until edge is lightly browned, 10-12 minutes. Let cool 10 minutes.

2. Spread with dip; top with tomatoes. Toss steak with steak seasoning; place over tomatoes. Bake on a lower oven rack until steak reaches desired doneness and crust is golden brown, 10-12 minutes. Let stand 10 minutes. Sprinkle with basil, pine nuts and bacon. Combine dressing and horseradish; serve with pizza.

1 PIECE 290 cal., 12g fat (2g sat. fat), 28mg chol., 434mg sod., 27g carb. (2g sugars, 1g fiber), 18g pro.

CHICAGO-STYLE DEEP-DISH PIZZA

My husband and I tried to duplicate the pizza from a popular Chicago restaurant, and I think our recipe turned out even better. The secret is baking it in a cast-iron skillet.

—Lynn Hamilton, Naperville, IL

PREP: 20 min. + rising • **BAKE:** 40 min. • **MAKES:** 2 pizzas (8 slices each)

3½ cups all-purpose flour
¼ cup cornmeal
1 pkg. (¼ oz.) quick-rise yeast
1½ tsp. sugar
½ tsp. salt
1 cup water
⅓ cup olive oil

TOPPINGS
6 cups shredded part-skim mozzarella cheese, divided
1 can (28 oz.) diced tomatoes, well drained
1 can (8 oz.) tomato sauce
1 can (6 oz.) tomato paste
½ tsp. salt
¼ tsp. each garlic powder, dried oregano, dried basil and pepper
1 lb. bulk Italian sausage, cooked and crumbled
48 slices pepperoni
½ lb. sliced fresh mushrooms
¼ cup grated Parmesan cheese

1. In a large bowl, combine 1½ cups flour, cornmeal, yeast, sugar and salt. In a saucepan, heat water and oil to 120°-130°. Add to dry ingredients; beat just until moistened. Add remaining flour to form a stiff dough.

2. Turn onto a floured surface; knead until smooth and elastic, 6-8 minutes. Place in a greased bowl, turning once to grease top. Cover and let rise in a warm place until doubled, about 30 minutes.

3. Punch dough down; divide in half. Roll each portion into an 11-in. circle. Press dough onto the bottoms and up the sides of two greased 10-in. cast-iron or other ovenproof skillets. Sprinkle each with 2 cups mozzarella cheese.

4. In a large bowl, combine the tomatoes, tomato sauce, tomato paste and seasonings. Spoon 1½ cups over each pizza. Layer each with half of the sausage, pepperoni and mushrooms; 1 cup mozzarella; and 2 Tbsp. Parmesan cheese.

5. Cover and bake at 450° for 35 minutes. Uncover; bake until lightly browned, about 5 minutes longer.

1 PIECE 407 cal., 23g fat (9g sat. fat), 49mg chol., 872mg sod., 32g carb. (4g sugars, 2g fiber), 20g pro.

THE BEST PIZZA PAN

The best pan for deep-dish pizza is a cast-iron skillet. For this recipe, you can also use two 9-in. springform pans. To do so, place the pans on a baking sheet for cooking. When done, run a knife around edges of the pans to loosen the crusts before removing the sides.

PIZZA MARGHERITA

This classic pie starts with a chewy homemade crust, then is topped with tomatoes, mozzarella, oregano and fresh basil. It's so scrumptious!

—*Loretta Lawrence, Myrtle Beach, SC*

PREP: 30 min. + rising • **BAKE:** 15 min. • **MAKES:** 2 pizzas (8 servings each)

3 tsp. active dry yeast
1 cup warm water (110° to 115°)
2 Tbsp. olive oil
1 tsp. sugar
1 tsp. salt
3 cups bread flour

TOPPINGS
2 cans (14½ oz. each) diced tomatoes, drained
8 cups shredded part-skim mozzarella cheese
2 Tbsp. minced fresh oregano or 2 tsp. dried oregano
20 fresh basil leaves, roughly torn
½ tsp. crushed red pepper flakes
⅛ tsp. salt
⅛ tsp. pepper
2 Tbsp. olive oil

1. In a small bowl, dissolve yeast in warm water. In a large bowl, combine the oil, sugar, salt and 1 cup flour; beat until smooth. Stir in enough remaining flour to form a soft dough.

2. Turn onto a floured surface; knead for 6-8 minutes or until smooth and elastic. Place in a greased bowl, turning once to grease the top. Cover and let rise in a warm place until doubled, about 1 hour.

3. Punch dough down; divide in half. Roll each portion into a 13-in. circle. Transfer to 2 greased 14-in. pizza pans; build up edges slightly. Cover with a clean kitchen towel; let rest for 10 minutes.

4. Spoon tomatoes over dough. Top with cheese, oregano, basil, pepper flakes, salt and pepper. Drizzle with oil. Bake at 450° for 15-20 minutes or until crust is golden brown.

1 PIECE 304 cal., 15g fat (7g sat. fat), 36mg chol., 625mg sod., 25g carb. (3g sugars, 2g fiber), 17g pro.

MOZZARELLA SWAP

Using slices of fresh mozzarella is a great way to level up this pizza. It won't be a true margherita pizza if you add more toppings—but feel free to throw pepperoni, sausage or your favorite toppings on as well.

DEEP-DISH SAUSAGE PIZZA

My grandma made the tastiest snacks for us when we stayed the night at her farm. Her wonderful pizza, hot from the oven, was covered with cheese and had fragrant herbs in the crust. Now this pizza is frequently a meal for my husband, our two young daughters and me.
—Michele Madden, Washington Court House, OH

PREP: 30 min. + rising • **BAKE:** 30 min. + standing • **MAKES:** 8 servings

1 pkg. (¼ oz.) active dry yeast
⅔ cup warm water (110° to 115°)
1¾ to 2 cups all-purpose flour
¼ cup vegetable oil
1 tsp. each dried oregano, basil and marjoram
½ tsp. garlic salt
½ tsp. onion salt

TOPPINGS

4 cups shredded part-skim mozzarella cheese, divided
2 medium green peppers, chopped
1 large onion, chopped
½ tsp. each dried oregano, basil and marjoram
1 Tbsp. olive oil
1 cup grated Parmesan cheese
1 lb. bulk pork sausage, cooked and drained
1 can (28 oz.) diced tomatoes, well drained
2 oz. sliced pepperoni

1. In a bowl, dissolve yeast in warm water. Add 1 cup flour, oil and crust seasonings; beat until smooth. Add enough remaining flour to form a soft dough.

2. Turn dough onto a floured surface; knead until smooth and elastic, 6-8 minutes. Place in a greased bowl; turn once to grease top. Cover and let rise in a warm place until doubled, about 1 hour.

3. Punch dough down; roll out into a 15-in. circle. Transfer to a well-greased 12-in. heavy ovenproof skillet or round baking pan, letting crust drape over edge. Sprinkle with 1 cup mozzarella.

4. In a skillet, saute the green peppers, onion and topping seasonings in oil until tender; drain. Layer half the mixture over crust. Layer with half the Parmesan, sausage and tomatoes. Sprinkle with 2 cups mozzarella. Repeat the vegetable mixture, Parmesan, sausage and tomato layers. Fold crust over to form an edge.

5. Bake at 400° for 20 minutes. Sprinkle with pepperoni and remaining 1 cup mozzarella. Bake until crust is browned, 10-15 minutes longer. Let stand 10 minutes before slicing.

1 PIECE 548 cal., 34g fat (14g sat. fat), 68mg chol., 1135mg sod., 32g carb. (8g sugars, 4g fiber), 27g pro.

SANTA FE CHICKEN PIZZA PIE

Give your pie a southwestern twist when you slather on the taco sauce and
top with black beans, green chilies and kicked-up chicken strips.
—Taste of Home *Test Kitchen*

PREP: 15 min. • **BAKE:** 25 min. • **MAKES:** 6 servings

1   tube (13.8 oz.) refrigerated pizza
    crust
1   bottle (16 oz.) taco sauce
1   can (15 oz.) black beans, rinsed and
    drained
1   large tomato, chopped
½   cup chopped green pepper
½   cup chopped red onion
1   can (4 oz.) chopped green chiles,
    drained
1   pkg. (6 oz.) ready-to-use
    southwestern chicken strips,
    chopped
1½ cups shredded Mexican cheese
    blend

1. Press pizza dough into a greased
15x10x1-in. baking pan, building up
edges slightly. Prick dough thoroughly
with a fork. Bake at 400° until lightly
browned, 8-9 minutes.

2. Spread with taco sauce; top with
beans, tomato, green pepper, onion,
chiles and chicken. Sprinkle with
cheese. Bake until crust is golden
brown, 15-18 minutes.

1 SERVING 434 cal., 12g fat (5g sat. fat),
44mg chol., 1218mg sod., 52g carb.
(12g sugars, 5g fiber), 21g pro.

CALIFORNIA CHICKEN CLUB PIZZA

Inspired by the California Club pizza from California Pizza Kitchen, I decided to whip up my own version. It's loaded with tons of fresh veggies, so that means it has to be good for you, right?
—*Robert Pickart, Chicago, IL*

PREP: 25 min. • **BAKE:** 10 min. • **MAKES:** 4 servings

1   Tbsp. cornmeal
1   loaf (1 lb.) frozen pizza dough, thawed
1   cup shredded mozzarella cheese
1   cup ready-to-use grilled chicken breast strips
4   bacon strips, cooked and crumbled
2   cups shredded romaine
1   cup fresh arugula
¼   cup mayonnaise
1   Tbsp. lemon juice
1   tsp. grated lemon zest
½   tsp. pepper
1   medium tomato, thinly sliced
1   medium ripe avocado, peeled and sliced
¼   cup loosely packed basil leaves, chopped

1. Preheat oven to 450°. Grease a 14-in. pizza pan; sprinkle with cornmeal. On a floured surface, roll dough into a 13-in. circle. Transfer to prepared pan; build up edges slightly. Sprinkle with cheese, chicken and bacon. Bake until crust is lightly browned, 10-12 minutes.

2. Meanwhile, place romaine and arugula in a large bowl. In a small bowl, combine mayonnaise, lemon juice, lemon zest and pepper. Pour over lettuces; toss to coat. Arrange over warm pizza. Top with tomato, avocado and basil. Serve immediately.

2 PIECES 612 cal., 30g fat (7g sat. fat), 51mg chol., 859mg sod., 59g carb. (4g sugars, 5g fiber), 29g pro.

ST. LOUIS-STYLE PIZZA

Provel cheese and a cracker-thin crust are the hallmarks of St. Louis-style pizza. Provel is a processed blend of cheddar, Swiss and provolone that originated in St. Louis. It melts at a low temperature, which means it stays ooey-gooey after the pizza is out of the oven and on the dinner table. Don't forget to cut your pizza as they would in Missouri—square pieces only!

—Taste of Home *Test Kitchen*

PREP: 15 min. + standing • **BAKE:** 30 min. • **MAKES:** 2 pizzas (4 servings each)

- 2   cups all-purpose flour
- 2   tsp. baking powder
- ½   tsp. salt
- 8   to 10 Tbsp. water
- 2   Tbsp. olive oil
- ⅔   cup crushed tomatoes in puree
- 2   Tbsp. tomato paste
- ½   tsp. sugar
- ½   tsp. dried basil
- ¼   tsp. dried oregano
- 12 oz. Provel cheese, shredded or 1½ cups shredded white cheddar plus 1 cup shredded provolone plus 1 cup shredded Swiss
- 1   pkg. (3½ oz.) sliced pepperoni
- 1   small green pepper, thinly sliced
- ½   small red onion, thinly sliced

1. In a large bowl, whisk flour, baking powder and salt. Stir in water and oil until combined. Turn onto a lightly floured surface. Gently form into a ball. Cover and let rest 10 minutes. Divide dough in half. On parchment, roll each half into a 10-in. circle. Transfer (leaving dough on parchment) to a 12-in. pizza pan.

2. Preheat oven to 425°. Combine crushed tomatoes, tomato paste, sugar, basil and oregano; spread over pizzas. Top with cheese, pepperoni, green pepper and onion. If desired, sprinkle with additional dried basil and oregano. Bake on a low oven rack, 1 at a time, until bottom of crust is golden and cheese is lightly browned, 15-20 minutes. Cut into squares.

1 SERVING 382 cal., 23g fat (10g sat. fat), 50mg chol., 755mg sod., 28g carb. (2g sugars, 2g fiber), 17g pro.

WHICH TOPPINGS?

Since the crust for this pizza is super thin, we recommend adding just a few lighter pizza toppings, such as pepperoni, green pepper and onion. Too many toppings can create a soggy pizza—so you'll want to avoid this very common pizza mistake. Be sure to sprinkle some Italian herbs on top too.

TURKEY SAUSAGE PIZZA

If pizza night is a must in your home, give this distinctive, lighter pizza a try. It's also great to keep in the freezer for a quick dinner any time.

—*Melissa Jelinek, Apple Valley, MN*

PREP: 20 min. • **BAKE:** 15 min. • **MAKES:** 8 servings

- 1 loaf (1 lb.) frozen bread dough, thawed
- ¾ lb. Italian turkey sausage links, casings removed
- ½ cup sliced onion
- ½ cup sliced fresh mushrooms
- ½ cup chopped green pepper
- ½ cup pizza sauce
- 2 cups shredded part-skim mozzarella cheese

1. Preheat oven to 400°. With greased fingers, press dough onto a 12-in. pizza pan coated with cooking spray. Prick dough thoroughly with a fork. Bake until lightly browned, 10-12 minutes.

2. Meanwhile, in a large skillet, cook the sausage, onion, mushrooms and green pepper over medium heat until sausage is no longer pink, 6-8 minutes, breaking up sausage into crumbles; drain.

3. Spread crust with pizza sauce. Top with sausage mixture; sprinkle with cheese. Bake until crust is golden brown and cheese is melted, 12-15 minutes longer.

FREEZE OPTION Wrap and freeze cooled pizza. To use, thaw overnight in the refrigerator. Unwrap; bake on a pizza pan at 400° until heated through, 18-22 minutes.

1 PIECE 283 cal., 9g fat (4g sat. fat), 32mg chol., 668mg sod., 30g carb. (4g sugars, 3g fiber), 18g pro. **DIABETIC EXCHANGES** 2 starch, 2 lean meat, ½ fat.

FAVORITE CHEESEBURGER PIZZA

My sister-in-law used to own a pizza restaurant and gave me this awesome recipe that features ground beef, cheddar and thousand island dressing. We like it on whole-wheat crust.

—Katie Buckley, Wyoming, DE

TAKES: 25 min. • **MAKES:** 8 servings

1 lb. ground beef
¼ tsp. salt
1 prebaked 12-in. thin pizza crust
½ cup Thousand Island salad dressing
1 small onion, chopped
2 cups shredded cheddar cheese
2 cups shredded lettuce
½ cup sliced dill pickles

1. Preheat oven to 450°. In a large skillet, cook beef over medium heat, until no longer pink, 6-8 minutes, breaking into crumbles; drain. Sprinkle beef with salt.

2. Place crust on an ungreased pizza pan or baking sheet; spread with salad dressing. Top with beef, onion and cheese.

3. Bake 6-8 minutes or until cheese is melted. Top with lettuce and pickles just before serving.

1 PIECE 394 cal., 24g fat (9g sat. fat), 65mg chol., 706mg sod., 22g carb. (3g sugars, 1g fiber), 21g pro.

⏱ CHINESE CASHEW CHICKEN PIZZA

I make this quick weeknight dinner recipe when I'm craving takeout pizza and Chinese food.
I like using shortcuts, such as premade pizza crust and rotisserie chicken, to cut down on my time in the kitchen.
—*Joseph A. Sciascia, San Mateo, California*

TAKES: 30 min. • **MAKES:** 8 servings

- 1 prebaked 12-in. pizza crust or flatbread
- 1 Tbsp. sesame oil
- ¾ cup hoisin sauce
- 2 tsp. chili garlic sauce
- 1½ cups shredded cooked chicken
- ½ cup chopped sweet red pepper
- ⅓ cup shredded carrots
- ½ cup chopped cashews
- 3 Tbsp. chopped fresh cilantro
- 4 green onions, chopped, divided
- 1¼ cups shredded mozzarella cheese

1. Preheat oven to 425°. Place pizza crust on a pizza pan; brush with sesame oil. In small bowl, combine hoisin sauce and chili garlic sauce; brush ⅓ cup over crust. Toss remaining sauce mixture with chicken; sprinkle over crust. Top with red pepper, carrots, cashews, cilantro and half of the green onions. Sprinkle mozzarella over top.

2. Bake until cheese is lightly browned, 12-15 minutes. Let stand 5 minutes; sprinkle with the remaining green onions.

1 PIECE 357 cal., 15g fat (5g sat. fat), 38mg chol., 876mg sod., 37g carb. (9g sugars, 2g fiber), 19g pro.

GARDEN-FRESH GRILLED VEGGIE PIZZA

I have four gardens, including one just for herbs, so I always have a pretty wonderful spread of produce. I created this loaded-up pizza as a fun summer appetizer using some of my top garden goodies. The shredded carrot may seem out of the ordinary, but it adds a subtle, pleasant sweetness to the pizza.

—*Dianna Wara, Washington, IL*

PREP: 30 min. • **GRILL:** 15 min. • **MAKES:** 6 servings

3 Tbsp. olive oil
3 garlic cloves, minced
3 medium tomatoes, cut into ½-in. slices
1 large sweet red pepper, halved, stemmed and seeded
1 small zucchini, cut lengthwise into ¼-in.-thick slices
1 small onion, cut crosswise into ½-in. slices
1 tsp. coarsely ground pepper
1 prebaked 12-in. pizza crust
⅓ cup spreadable garden vegetable cream cheese
8 slices smoked provolone cheese, divided
½ cup minced fresh basil, divided
¼ cup shredded carrots
1 Tbsp. minced fresh oregano
1 tsp. minced fresh thyme

1. Mix oil and garlic; brush onto both sides of vegetables. Sprinkle with pepper. Grill, covered, over medium heat until tender, 4-5 minutes per side for pepper and onion, 3-4 minutes per side for zucchini and 2-3 minutes per side for tomatoes.

2. Coarsely chop grilled pepper, onion and zucchini. Spread pizza crust with cream cheese; layer with 4 slices provolone and the tomato slices. Sprinkle with ¼ cup basil, the carrots, oregano and thyme. Top with grilled vegetables, then remaining 4 slices cheese.

3. Grill pizza, covered, over medium heat until bottom is golden brown and cheese is melted, 5-7 minutes. Top with remaining basil.

1 PIECE 395 cal., 22g fat (8g sat. fat), 23mg chol., 618mg sod., 36g carb. (6g sugars, 3g fiber), 16g pro.

MAKE A CHEESE BARRIER

The fresh, grilled tomatoes will give up a lot of juice, which is great for flavor but not great for the crust. Be sure to layer half the provolone cheese under the tomatoes as directed—it prevents the crust from getting soggy.

GROW A PIZZA GARDEN

Pizzas come in all shapes, colors and flavors! But the basics are usually the same: crust, sauce, cheese and toppings. Gardeners can grow many of the ingredients for sauce and toppings—here's a guide to the vegetable varieties that make for a perfectly flavored pizza.

SAUCE

ROMA TOMATO

Great pizza sauce starts with delicious Roma tomatoes. **Early Resilience** is a rounded Roma with a deep red interior color, uniform maturity and good-quality flesh for cooking, which is great for a pizza sauce. This variety produces determinate, bushy plants that are resistant to blossom end rot, giving you a large yield and less fruit loss.

Early Resilience

OREGANO

Cleopatra oregano's foliage makes this herb worth appreciating for both its ornamental value and flavor. Unlike most Greek and Italian oreganos, it has a mildly spicy, pepperminty flavor. Use it in Mediterranean dishes and sauces. The plentiful leaves of this compact, trailing plant are also flavorful as a dried spice when fresh isn't an option.

Cleopatra

ONION

Super Star is a white sweet onion recommended for all spring gardens in North America. Most onions require either long days with more than 12 hours of sunlight or short days to bulb. But Super Star is widely adaptable and are exceptional when eaten raw or cooked in sauces.

Super Star

TOPPINGS

SWEET PEPPERS

Dragonfly plants yield beautiful peppers that transform from green into purple fruits and are delicious at any stage of maturity. With their robust flavor, they'll add plenty of color and taste to your pizza.

Dragonfly *Just Sweet*

A vivid yellow snacking pepper with four lobes like a larger bell pepper, **Just Sweet** is ideal for smaller pizzas. The 3-inch fruits are deliciously sweet with thick walls, and the plants have been bred to have a strong bushy habit.

Sweetie Pie is a mini bell pepper that's easy to grow, with an excellent fruit set even under hot and humid conditions. It'll also adapt well to a container or small garden. Fruits are thick-walled, sweet and flavorful, and can be harvested when they're green or red.

Sweetie Pie

HOT PEPPERS

For a cayenne pepper with extra-large fruit, try **Wildcat**. The 8-inch peppers have a smoky flavor and peppery sweetness with a mild pungency of 500 to 1,500 Scoville heat units, which means they're in the mild range of the heat scale.

Wildcat

Buffy

Mighty, strong and hot, **Quickfire** peppers deliver plenty of hot Thai-type fruits of 40,000 Scoville units. The compact, sturdy plant is ideal for container gardening.

Buffy has a good yield of juicy, thick-walled green to red fruits at 500,000 Scoville units on strong, upright plants.

Quickfire

COLORFUL TOMATOES

Now you can experience the sweet, mild flavor of an orange heirloom tomato only 75 days from transplant with hybrid **Chef's Choice Orange**. Its disease resistance is an added bonus. This pick has a bright, almost neon, internal color, and superior flesh taste and texture.

Chef's Choice Orange

Pink Delicious

Pink Delicious is an early maturing tomato with a balanced sweet and acidic flavor. The fruit has an heirloom look, flavor and texture, and the plant is easy to grow because of its hybrid disease resistance and improved germination.

For a uniquely colored tomato to top your pizza, look no further than **Chef's Choice Green**. The tomato produces beautiful green fruits with subtle yellow stripes. Enjoy the citruslike flavor and a perfect tomato texture.

Chef's Choice Green

BASIL

Dolce Fresca basil has sweet, tender leaves that maintain an attractive, compact shape. The plant thrives in containers, borders or as a focal point in the garden. Select this basil if you need a drought-tolerant, hardy plant, are searching for a new and better basil or want great Mediterranean taste on your pizza.

Dolce Fresca

GETTY IMAGES; VEGGIES: ALL-AMERICA SELECTIONS

⏰ LOADED MEXICAN PIZZA

My husband is a picky eater, but this healthy pizza has such amazing flavor that he looks forward to it. Leftovers taste even better the next day.
—*Mary Barker, Knoxville, TN*

TAKES: 30 min. • **MAKES:** 6 servings

1 can (15 oz.) black beans, rinsed and drained
1 medium red onion, chopped
1 small sweet yellow pepper, chopped
3 tsp. chili powder
¾ tsp. ground cumin
3 medium tomatoes, chopped
1 jalapeno pepper, seeded and finely chopped
1 garlic clove, minced
1 prebaked 12-in. thin pizza crust
2 cups chopped fresh spinach
2 Tbsp. minced fresh cilantro
   Hot pepper sauce to taste
½ cup shredded reduced-fat cheddar cheese
½ cup shredded pepper jack cheese

1. In a small bowl, mash black beans. Stir in the onion, yellow pepper, chili powder and cumin. In another bowl, combine the tomatoes, jalapeno and garlic.

2. Place crust on an ungreased 12-in. pizza pan; spread with bean mixture. Top with tomato mixture and spinach. Sprinkle with cilantro, pepper sauce, cheddar cheese and pepper Jack cheese.

3. Bake at 400° for 12-15 minutes or until cheese is melted.

NOTE Wear disposable gloves when cutting hot peppers; the oils can burn skin. Avoid touching your face.

1 PIECE 295 cal., 8g fat (3g sat. fat), 17mg chol., 581mg sod., 40g carb. (5g sugars, 6g fiber), 15g pro. **DIABETIC EXCHANGES** 2½ starch, 1 vegetable, 1 lean meat.

SUGGESTED ADDITIONS

If you want to add some protein to this pizza, we suggest sticking with the Mexican theme and adding taco meat or rotisserie chicken tossed with salsa.

AIR-FRYER
PIZZA PUFFS
(PAGE 142)

PIZZA WITH
A TWIST

CALZONE ROLLS

Big pizza flavor comes through in these rolls. My recipe makes two pans
because you'll need 'em! It's so easy to make the dough in my bread machine.
—*Barb Downie, Peterborough, ON*

PREP: 20 min. + rising • **BAKE:** 20 min. • **MAKES:** 2 dozen

1²⁄₃ cups water (70° to 80°)
2 Tbsp. nonfat dry milk powder
2 Tbsp. sugar
2 Tbsp. shortening
1¼ tsp. salt
4½ cups all-purpose flour
2¼ tsp. active dry yeast
½ cup chopped onion
½ cup sliced fresh mushrooms
½ cup chopped green pepper
½ cup chopped sweet red pepper
1 Tbsp. olive oil
⅓ cup pizza sauce
½ cup diced pepperoni
1 cup shredded pizza cheese blend
¼ cup chopped ripe olives
2 Tbsp. grated Parmesan cheese

1. In bread machine pan, place the first 7 ingredients in order suggested by manufacturer. Select dough setting (check dough after 5 minutes of mixing; add 1-2 Tbsp. water or flour if needed).

2. In a small skillet, saute onion, mushrooms and peppers in oil until tender; cool.

3. When bread machine cycle is completed, turn dough onto a lightly floured surface; divide in half. Let rest for 5 minutes. Roll each portion into a 16x10-in. rectangle; spread with pizza sauce. Top with onion mixture, pepperoni, pizza cheese and olives. Roll up each rectangle jelly-roll style, starting with a long side; pinch seam to seal. Cut each into 12 slices (discard end pieces).

4. Place slices cut side down in 2 greased 10-in. cast-iron skillets or 9-in. round baking pans. Sprinkle with Parmesan cheese. Cover and let rise until doubled, about 30 minutes.

5. Bake at 375° until golden brown, 20-30 minutes. Serve warm.

1 ROLL 144 cal., 5g fat (2g sat. fat), 7mg chol., 244mg sod., 21g carb. (2g sugars, 1g fiber), 5g pro.

TO MAKE DOUGH BY HAND

No bread machine? No problem. In a mixing bowl, dissolve yeast in warm water (110°-115°). Add milk powder, sugar, shortening, salt and 3 cups flour. Beat on medium speed until smooth. Stir in enough remaining flour to form a soft dough. Turn dough onto a floured surface; knead until smooth and elastic, 6-8 minutes. Place in a greased bowl, turning once to grease the top. Cover and let rise in a warm place until doubled, about 1 hour. Punch dough down. Proceed as directed.

⏱ PIZZA ON A STICK

My daughter and her friends had fun turning sausage, pepperoni, veggies and pizza dough into these cute kabobs.
—*Charlene Woods, Norfolk, VA*

TAKES: 30 min. • **MAKES:** 5 servings

8 oz. Italian turkey sausage links
2 cups whole fresh mushrooms
2 cups cherry tomatoes
1 medium onion, cut into 1-in. pieces
1 large green pepper, cut into
   1-in. pieces
30 slices turkey pepperoni (2 oz.)
1 tube (13.8 oz.) refrigerated
   pizza crust
1½ cups shredded part-skim
   mozzarella cheese
1¼ cups pizza sauce, warmed

1. Preheat oven to 400°. In a large nonstick skillet, cook sausage over medium heat until no longer pink; drain. When cool enough to handle, cut sausage into 20 pieces. On 10 metal or wooden skewers, alternately thread sausage, vegetables and pepperoni.

2. Unroll pizza dough onto a lightly floured surface; cut widthwise into 1-in.-wide strips. Starting at pointed end of a prepared skewer, pierce skewer through 1 end of dough strip. Spiral-wrap dough strip around skewer, allowing vegetables and meats to peek through. Wrap remaining end of dough strip around skewer above first ingredient. Repeat with remaining dough strips and skewers.

3. Arrange kabobs on a baking sheet coated with cooking spray. Bake until vegetables are tender and pizza crust is golden, 10-12 minutes. Immediately sprinkle with cheese. Serve with pizza sauce.

2 KABOBS WITH ¼ CUP SAUCE 429 cal., 15g fat (6g sat. fat), 52mg chol., 1337mg sod., 52g carb. (13g sugars, 3g fiber), 26g pro.

🕐 PARTY PIZZAS

With the irresistible combination of creamy cheese and lightly seasoned meat
on crispy toast, these snacks get cleared away quickly.

—Carolyn Snow, Sedalia, MO

TAKES: 30 min. • **MAKES:** 3 dozen

1   lb. ground beef
1   lb. bulk Italian sausage
1   lb. Velveeta, cubed
3   Tbsp. Worcestershire sauce
3   Tbsp. ketchup
1   tsp. garlic salt
1   tsp. dried oregano
¼   tsp. salt
¼   tsp. pepper
1   loaf (1 lb.) snack rye bread
    Thinly sliced green onions, optional

1. In a large skillet over medium heat, cook beef and sausage until no longer pink; drain. Add cheese, Worcestershire sauce, ketchup and seasonings; stir until cheese is melted. Spread 1-2 Tbsp. hot mixture on each bread slice. Place on ungreased baking sheets.

2. Freeze pizzas or bake at 350° until heated through, 10-15 minutes. If desired, top with green onions.

NOTE To use frozen pizzas, bake at 350° until heated through, 15-20 minutes.

2 MINI PIZZAS 234 cal., 13g fat (6g sat. fat), 39mg chol., 792mg sod., 15g carb. (4g sugars, 2g fiber), 14g pro.

SPICE IT UP

To make this recipe spicier, swap in spicy Italian sausage for the plain stuff. Or sprinkle finished rye bread pizzas with red pepper flakes or finely diced jalapenos.

PIZZA RUSTICA (EASTER PIE)

My nanny (grandma) shared this recipe and always supervised when it came time for me to make it on my own for Easter. My husband and brother love it so much, they now request it on every special occasion, especially Easter! The dough can be made ahead, which cuts the time and wait to eat it in half. You can chose just about any deli meat for the filling, but we always come back to Nanny's basic recipe. If pressed for time, eliminate the dough portion by purchasing refrigerated pie dough.

—*Kristy Pianoforte, Brooklyn, NY*

PREP: 20 min. + chilling • **BAKE:** 1¼ hours + cooling • **MAKES:** 8 servings

3½ cups all-purpose flour
¾ tsp. salt
½ tsp. pepper
1 cup shortening
8 to 10 Tbsp. ice water

FILLING
9 large eggs, divided use
1 container (15 oz.) whole-milk ricotta cheese
1 lb. shredded mozzarella cheese (4 cups)
2 cups cubed dry salami
¼ lb. thinly sliced hard salami, chopped
¼ lb. sliced provolone cheese, chopped
4 thin slices prosciutto, chopped

1. In a large bowl, mix flour, salt and pepper; cut in shortening until crumbly. Gradually add ice water, tossing with a fork until dough holds together when pressed. Divide dough into two-thirds and one-third sized pieces. Shape each into a disk; wrap and refrigerate 1 hour or overnight.

2. Preheat oven to 350°. On a lightly floured surface, roll larger piece of dough to a 12-in. circle; line bottom and press up side of a greased 9-in. springform pan. For filling, in a large bowl, beat 8 eggs and ricotta until smooth. Stir in mozzarella, salamis, provolone and prosciutto. Pour into crust. Roll remaining dough to an 11-in. circle. Place over filling. Trim and seal edge. Cut slits in top.

3. In a small bowl, whisk remaining egg; brush over crust.

4. Bake until crust is golden brown and a knife inserted in center comes out clean, 1¼-1½ hours. Loosen side from pan with a knife; remove rim. Let cool 1-1½ hours; serve warm or at room temperature.

1 PIECE 1010 cal., 69g fat (27g sat. fat), 312mg chol., 1928mg sod., 47g carb. (4g sugars, 2g fiber), 48g pro.

BISTRO TURKEY CALZONE

Turkey, cheddar, bacon and apple harmonize in a sandwich that's perfect for a harvest meal.
—*DonnaMarie Ryan, Topsfield, MA*

PREP: 25 min. • **BAKE:** 20 min. • **MAKES:** 6 servings

1   Tbsp. cornmeal
1   loaf (1 lb.) frozen pizza dough, thawed
¾   lb. thinly sliced cooked turkey
8   slices cheddar cheese
5   bacon strips, cooked and crumbled
1   small tart apple, peeled and thinly sliced
1   large egg, beaten
½   tsp. Italian seasoning

1. Sprinkle cornmeal over a greased baking sheet. On a lightly floured surface, roll dough to a 15-in. circle. Transfer to prepared pan. Arrange half the turkey over half the dough; top with cheese, bacon, apple and remaining turkey. Fold dough over filling and pinch edge to seal.

2. With a sharp knife, cut 3 slashes in top. Brush with egg and sprinkle with Italian seasoning. Bake at 400° until golden brown, 20-25 minutes. Let stand 5 minutes before cutting into wedges.

1 PIECE 481 cal., 20g fat (10g sat. fat), 124mg chol., 756mg sod., 38g carb. (3g sugars, 0 fiber), 34g pro.

🕐 MINI ZUCCHINI PIZZAS

This simple snack is the perfect, low-carb way to satisfy your pizza cravings.
—Taste of Home *Test Kitchen*

TAKES: 20 min. • **MAKES:** about 2 dozen

1   large zucchini (about 11 oz.),
    cut diagonally into ¼-in. slices
⅛   tsp. salt
⅛   tsp. pepper
⅓   cup pizza sauce
¾   cup shredded part-skim
    mozzarella cheese
½   cup miniature pepperoni slices
    Minced fresh basil

1. Preheat broiler. Arrange zucchini in a single layer on a greased baking sheet. Broil 3-4 in. from heat just until crisp-tender, 1-2 minutes per side.

2. Sprinkle zucchini with salt and pepper; top with sauce, cheese and pepperoni. Broil until cheese is melted, about 1 minute. Sprinkle with basil.

1 APPETIZER 29 cal., 2g fat (1g sat. fat), 5mg chol., 108mg sod., 1g carb. (1g sugars, 0 fiber), 2g pro.

🕐 STUFFED PIZZA ROLLS

After trying a similar dish at a local restaurant, I came up with
my own version. It is easy, delicious and fun for potlucks or parties.
—*Sarah Gilbert, Beaverton, OR*

TAKES: 30 min. • **MAKES:** 1 dozen

1 tube (13.80 oz.) refrigerated
   pizza crust
¼ cup prepared ranch salad dressing
6 oz. pepperoni, finely chopped
1 cup shredded pepper jack cheese
¼ cup shredded Romano cheese
¼ cup thinly sliced green onions
¼ cup chopped green pepper
4 cooked bacon strips, chopped
2 tsp. Italian seasoning
1 tsp. garlic powder
   Optional: Marinara sauce or
   Alfredo sauce, warmed

1. Preheat oven to 350°. Grease 12 muffin cups; set aside.

2. On a lightly floured surface, unroll pizza crust. Spread ranch to within ½-in. of edges. Sprinkle with pepperoni, cheeses, green onions, green pepper, bacon and seasonings. Roll up jelly-roll style; pinch the edge closed. Cut crosswise into 12 slices. Place each slice in prepared muffin cups.

3. Bake until lightly browned, 20-25 minutes. Serve rolls warm, with marinara or Alfredo sauce if desired.

1 ROLL 234 cal., 14g fat (6g sat. fat), 28mg chol., 664mg sod., 17g carb. (2g sugars, 1g fiber), 10g pro.

"I didn't have the pizza dough, so I used flaky biscuit dough. It works just great! I love that you can make these rolls with whatever pizza ingredients each person in the family wants. I make them with my kids, they stuff theirs with what they want, and then I make another batch for my husband and me. I love recipes like this where you can involve the kids and make cooking fun!"
—DARLYN29, TASTEOFHOME.COM

AIR-FRYER PIZZA PUFFS

I love pizza in any form, so it seemed only logical to turn my pizza love into an appetizer. These little bundles can be made ahead of time and chilled until you're ready to pop them into the air fryer.

—Vivi Taylor, Middleburg, FL

PREP: 20 min. • **COOK:** 10 min./batch • **MAKES:** 20 servings

1 loaf (1 lb.) frozen pizza dough, thawed
20 slices pepperoni
8 oz. part-skim mozzarella cheese, cut into 20 cubes
¼ cup butter
2 small garlic cloves, minced
Dash salt
Marinara sauce, warmed
Optional: Crushed red pepper flakes and grated Parmesan cheese

1. Preheat air fryer to 350°. Shape dough into 1½-in. balls; flatten into ⅛-in.-thick circles. Place 1 pepperoni slice and 1 cheese cube in center of each circle; wrap dough around pepperoni and cheese. Pinch edges to seal; shape into a ball. Repeat with remaining dough, cheese and pepperoni.

2. In batches, place seam side up in a single layer on greased tray in air-fryer basket; cook until light golden brown, 6-8 minutes. Cool slightly.

3. Meanwhile, in a small saucepan, melt butter over low heat. Add garlic and salt, taking care not to brown butter or garlic; brush over puffs. Serve with marinara sauce; if desired, sprinkle with red pepper flakes and Parmesan.

FREEZE OPTION Cover and freeze unbaked pizza puffs on waxed paper-lined baking sheets until firm. Transfer to a freezer container; seal and return to freezer. To use, preheat air fryer to 350°; cook pizza puffs on greased tray in air-fryer basket as directed, increasing time as necessary until golden brown.

1 PIZZA PUFF 120 cal., 6g fat (3g sat. fat), 15mg chol., 189mg sod., 11g carb. (1g sugars, 0 fiber), 5g pro.

PEPPERY PIZZA LOAVES

I often take these French bread pizzas to church picnics or potluck suppers and there are never any left. When I fix them for the two of us, I freeze two halves in foil to enjoy later.

—*Lou Stasny, Poplarville, MS*

PREP: 20 min. • **BAKE:** 10 min. • **MAKES:** 12 servings

1½ lbs. ground beef
½ tsp. garlic powder
½ tsp. salt
2 loaves (8 oz. each) French bread, halved lengthwise
1 cup cheese dip
1 can (4 oz.) mushroom stems and pieces, drained
1 cup chopped green onions
1 can (4 oz.) sliced jalapenos, drained
1 can (8 oz.) tomato sauce
½ cup grated Parmesan cheese
4 cups shredded part-skim mozzarella cheese

1. Preheat oven to 350°. In a large skillet, cook beef over medium heat until no longer pink, breaking into crumbles; drain. Stir in garlic powder and salt.

2. Arrange bread on a baking sheet, cut side up. Spread with cheese dip. Top with beef mixture, mushrooms, onions and jalapenos. Drizzle with tomato sauce. Top with Parmesan and mozzarella.

3. Bake for 10-15 minutes or until golden brown. Serve warm.

FREEZE OPTION Wrap and freeze loaves. To use, unwrap loaves and thaw on baking sheets in the refrigerator. Bake at 350° for 18 minutes or until cheese is melted. May be frozen for up to 3 months.

1 PIECE 323 cal., 19g fat (11g sat. fat), 71mg chol., 907mg sod., 15g carb. (2g sugars, 1g fiber), 23g pro.

PEPPERONI PIZZA POCKETS

Stuffed with a pizza-style filling, these special sandwiches surprise you with a burst of flavor in every bite.
They were popular at our son's birthday party, but you can be sure adults will love them too!
—*Robin Werner, Brush Prairie, WA*

PREP: 1 hour • **BAKE:** 20 min. • **MAKES:** 16 pockets

2 pkg. (¼ oz. each) active dry yeast
2 cups warm water (110° to 115°)
2 Tbsp. sugar
2 Tbsp. butter, melted
2 tsp. salt
6 to 6½ cups all-purpose flour
1 can (8 oz.) pizza sauce, divided
96 slices turkey pepperoni
4 cups shredded part-skim
   mozzarella cheese
1 large egg, lightly beaten
8 tsp. grated Parmesan cheese
2 tsp. Italian seasoning

1. Preheat oven to 400°. In a large bowl, dissolve yeast in warm water. Add sugar, butter, salt and 4½ cups flour. Beat until smooth. Stir in enough remaining flour to form a soft dough.

2. Turn onto a floured surface; knead until smooth and elastic, 6-8 minutes. Divide dough into 16 pieces. On a lightly floured surface, roll each dough portion into a 6-in. circle. Place 2 tsp. pizza sauce, 6 slices pepperoni and ¼ cup mozzarella on each circle. Lightly brush edge of dough with egg. Bring dough over filling; press firmly, then crimp seams to seal.

3. Place on greased or parchment-lined baking sheets. Brush with egg; sprinkle with Parmesan and Italian seasoning. Bake until golden brown, 18-20 minutes. Warm remaining pizza sauce; serve with pizza pockets.

1 POCKET 316 cal., 9g fat (5g sat. fat), 47mg chol., 751mg sod., 41g carb. (3g sugars, 2g fiber), 16g pro.

STORING AND REHEATING

Leftover pepperoni pizza pockets should be cooled, then kept in an airtight container in the refrigerator. If you don't plan to eat them within 3 days, place the baked, cooled pockets in an airtight container and freeze for up to 3 months. To reheat, bake them at 350° until heated through, 10 to 15 minutes, or microwave until hot throughout.

CHICKEN PARMESAN STROMBOLI

I love chicken Parmesan and my family loves stromboli, so one day I combined the two using a few convenience products. This recipe turned out better than I could have hoped. It's now a staple in our house.

—Cyndy Gerken, Naples, FL

PREP: 20 min. • **BAKE:** 20 min. • **MAKES:** 6 servings

4 frozen breaded chicken tenders (about 1½ oz. each)
1 tube (13.8 oz.) refrigerated pizza crust
8 slices part-skim mozzarella cheese
⅓ cup shredded Parmesan cheese
1 Tbsp. olive oil
½ tsp. garlic powder
¼ tsp. dried oregano
¼ tsp. pepper
Marinara sauce, warmed

1. Prepare chicken tenders according to package directions. Preheat oven to 400°. Unroll pizza crust onto a parchment-lined baking sheet. Layer with mozzarella, chicken tenders and Parmesan to within ½ in. of edges. Roll up jelly-roll style, starting with a short side; pinch seam to seal and tuck ends under. Combine olive oil, garlic powder, oregano and pepper; brush over top.

2. Bake for 18-22 minutes or until crust is dark golden brown. Let stand 5 minutes before slicing. Serve with marinara sauce for dipping.

1 PIECE 408 cal., 18g fat (7g sat. fat), 34mg chol., 859mg sod., 42g carb. (5g sugars, 2g fiber), 21g pro.

MINI MEDITERRANEAN PIZZA

I was on a mini pizza kick and had already served up Mexican and Italian variations, so I opted for a Mediterranean version and came up with these.
—Jenny Dubinsky, Inwood, WV

PREP: 30 min. • **BAKE:** 5 min. • **MAKES:** 4 servings

1 Tbsp. olive oil
8 oz. lean ground beef (90% lean)
¼ cup finely chopped onion
2 garlic cloves, minced
1 can (8 oz.) tomato sauce
1 tsp. minced fresh rosemary or ¼ tsp. dried rosemary, crushed
2 whole wheat pita breads (6 in.), cut in half horizontally
1 medium tomato, seeded and chopped
½ cup fresh baby spinach, thinly sliced
12 Greek pitted olives, thinly sliced
½ cup shredded part-skim mozzarella cheese
¼ cup crumbled feta cheese

1. Preheat oven to 400°. Heat oil in a large nonstick skillet; cook beef, onion and garlic over medium heat until meat is no longer pink, 5-6 minutes, breaking into crumbles; drain. Stir in tomato sauce and rosemary; bring to a boil. Reduce heat; simmer, uncovered, until thickened, 6-9 minutes.

2. Place pita halves, cut side up, on a baking sheet. Top with meat mixture, tomato, spinach and olives. Sprinkle with cheeses. Bake until cheeses are melted, 4-6 minutes.

1 PIZZA 287 cal., 12g fat (5g sat. fat), 47mg chol., 783mg sod., 25g carb. (3g sugars, 4g fiber), 21g pro. **DIABETIC EXCHANGES** 2 lean meat, 1½ starch, 1 fat.

BAKED MACARONI & CHEESE PIZZA

Here's a fun and flavorful way to combine pizza and macaroni and cheese.
Experiment with other pizza toppings such as sausage or diced green peppers.
—*Andrew McDowell, Lake Villa, IL*

PREP: 25 min. • **BAKE:** 10 min. + standing • **MAKES:** 8 servings

1   pkg. (7¼ oz.) macaroni and cheese
    dinner mix
2   large eggs, beaten
½   lb. ground beef
¾   cup chopped onion
1¼ cups pizza sauce
1   can (4 oz.) mushroom stems and
    pieces, drained
28 pepperoni slices
1   cup shredded Mexican cheese
    blend

1. Preheat oven to 375°. Prepare macaroni and cheese according to package directions; gradually stir in eggs.

2. Spread onto a greased 12-in. pizza pan. Bake for 10 minutes. Meanwhile, in a large skillet, cook beef and onion over medium heat until meat is no longer pink, breaking into crumbles; drain. Stir in pizza sauce.

3. Spread over macaroni crust. Sprinkle with mushrooms, pepperoni and cheese blend. Bake for 10-15 minutes or until a thermometer inserted in crust reads 160° and cheese is melted.

1 PIECE 332 cal., 20g fat (10g sat. fat), 108mg chol., 723mg sod., 22g carb. (5g sugars, 1g fiber), 17g pro.

⏱ WAFFLE-MAKER PIZZAS

These little pizza pockets put together using the waffle maker are a fun mashup.
Try your favorite toppings or even breakfast fillings like ham and eggs.
—*Amy Lents, Grand Forks, ND*

TAKES: 30 min. • **MAKES:** 4 servings

1   pkg. (16.3 oz.) large refrigerated
    buttermilk biscuits
1   cup shredded part-skim
    mozzarella cheese
24 slices turkey pepperoni
    (about 1½ oz.)
2   ready-to-serve fully cooked
    bacon strips, chopped
    Pizza sauce, warmed

1. Roll or press biscuits to fit waffle
iron. On 1 biscuit, place ¼ cup cheese,
6 slices pepperoni and 1 scant Tbsp.
chopped bacon to within ½ in. of edges.
Top with a second biscuit, folding
bottom edge over top edge and
pressing to seal completely.

2. Bake in a preheated waffle iron
according to manufacturer's directions
until golden brown, 4-5 minutes.
Repeat with remaining ingredients.
Serve with pizza sauce.

1 PIZZA 461 cal., 21g fat (8g sat. fat), 28mg
chol., 1650mg sod., 50g carb. (5g sugars,
2g fiber), 19g pro.

REHEATING OPTIONS

To reheat waffle pizza, bake in a single layer on a baking sheet at 300° until
heated through. You can also pop the pizzas back into the waffle maker for
a few minutes to warm them up.

CORNED BEEF PIZZA SWIRLS

Offer these fun little bites that taste like a Reuben for St. Patrick's Day.
Even better, don't wait—deli meat and cheese make them doable all year long.
—*Colleen Delawder, Herndon, VA*

PREP: 30 min. + rising • **BAKE:** 35 min. • **MAKES:** 12 servings

2 tsp. sugar
1 tsp. active dry yeast
1 cup warm whole milk (110° to 115°)
1 Tbsp. olive oil
2 tsp. kosher salt
2 tsp. caraway seeds
2½ cups all-purpose flour

THOUSAND ISLAND SAUCE
½ cup mayonnaise
3 Tbsp. finely diced dill pickles
2 Tbsp. ketchup
1 tsp. brown sugar
½ tsp. onion powder
¼ tsp. pepper
2 dashes Louisiana-style hot sauce
Dash garlic powder

PIZZA SWIRLS
¾ lb. thinly sliced corned beef
½ lb. thinly sliced lacy Swiss cheese

1. Add sugar and yeast to warm milk; let stand for 15 minutes. Beat yeast mixture, oil, kosher salt and caraway seeds until blended. Beat in flour, ½ cup at a time, just until combined. With oiled hands, place dough in a greased bowl, turning once to grease top. Cover and let rise in a warm place until doubled, about 2 hours.

2. Meanwhile, mix all ingredients for Thousand Island sauce; refrigerate.

3. Punch down dough. To assemble pizza swirls, turn dough onto a well-floured surface; roll into a 15x10-in. rectangle. Arrange corned beef and cheese slices to within ¾ in. of edges. Roll up jelly-roll style, starting with a long side; pinch seam to seal and tuck ends under. Cut crosswise into 1-in. slices. Place slices, sides touching, on a parchment-lined baking sheet.

4. Preheat oven to 375°. Cover pizza swirls with greased foil; let stand 20 minutes. Bake, covered, 20 minutes; remove foil and bake until golden brown, 15-20 minutes longer. Serve warm with Thousand Island sauce.

1 PIZZA SWIRL 290 cal., 16g fat (6g sat. fat), 36mg chol., 807mg sod., 23g carb. (3g sugars, 1g fiber), 13g pro.

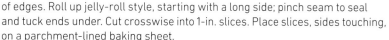

PEPPERONI & SAUSAGE DEEP-DISH PIZZA QUICHE

Try this savory quiche for a hearty change-of-pace breakfast. Needless to say, it's wonderful for lunch and dinner too.
—Donna Chesney, Naples, FL

PREP: 20 min. • **COOK:** 40 min. • **MAKES:** 8 servings

2 cups shredded mozzarella cheese, divided
1 cup shredded sharp cheddar cheese
4 large eggs
4 oz. cream cheese, softened
⅓ cup 2% milk
¼ cup grated Parmesan cheese
½ tsp. garlic powder
½ tsp. Italian seasoning
½ lb. bulk Italian sausage
½ cup pizza sauce
1 cup chopped pepperoni
Fresh basil, optional

1. Preheat oven to 350°. Sprinkle 1 cup mozzarella and cheddar cheese in a greased 13x9-in. baking dish. In a small bowl, beat eggs, cream cheese, milk, Parmesan, garlic powder and Italian seasoning; pour into dish. Bake 30 minutes.

2. Meanwhile, in a small skillet, cook sausage over medium heat until no longer pink, 5-6 minutes, breaking into crumbles; drain. Spread pizza sauce over egg mixture; top with sausage, pepperoni and remaining 1 cup mozzarella cheese. Bake until golden brown and bubbly, 10-15 minutes longer. Let stand 5 minutes before serving. Top with fresh basil if desired.

1 PIECE 409 cal., 34g fat (16g sat. fat), 177mg chol., 971mg sod., 5g carb. (2g sugars, 0 fiber), 21g pro.

"Perfect and so tasty. This is by far the best keto pizza I've ever had. It's is a keeper."
—JANET59, TASTEOFHOME.COM

MINI PIZZA MUFFIN CUPS

I just baked these mini pizzas and the kids are already demanding more.
The no-cook pizza sauce and refrigerated dough make this meal a snap.
—*Melissa Haines, Valparaiso, IN*

PREP: 25 min. • **BAKE:** 10 min. • **MAKES:** 8 servings

1 can (15 oz.) tomato sauce
1 can (6 oz.) tomato paste
1 tsp. dried basil
½ tsp. garlic salt
¼ tsp. onion powder
¼ tsp. sugar
1 tube (11 oz.) refrigerated thin pizza crust
1½ cups shredded part-skim mozzarella cheese

OPTIONAL TOPPINGS
Pepperoni, olives, sausage, onion, green pepper, Canadian bacon, pineapple, tomatoes, fresh basil and crushed red pepper flakes

1. Preheat oven to 425°. In a small bowl, mix first 6 ingredients.

2. Unroll pizza crust; cut into 16 squares. Press squares onto bottoms and up sides of 16 ungreased muffin cups, allowing corners to hang over edges.

3. Spoon 1 Tbsp. sauce mixture into each cup. Top with cheese; add toppings as desired. Bake for 10-12 minutes or until crust is golden brown. Serve remaining sauce mixture with pizzas.

FREEZE OPTION Freeze cooled baked pizzas in a resealable freezer container. To use, reheat pizzas on a baking sheet in a preheated 425° oven until heated through.

2 PIZZAS WITH 2 TBSP. SAUCE 209 cal., 8g fat (3g sat. fat), 14mg chol., 747mg sod., 26g carb. (5g sugars, 2g fiber), 10g pro.

GARLIC PIZZA WEDGES

Our pastor made this for a get-together, and my husband and i just couldn't stay away from the hors d'oeuvres table. The cheesy slices taste great served warm, but they're still wonderful when they've cooled slightly.
—*Krysten Johnson, Simi Valley, CA*

TAKES: 25 min. • **MAKES:** 2 dozen

1 prebaked 12-in. pizza crust
1 cup grated Parmesan cheese
1 cup mayonnaise
1 small red onion, chopped
3½ tsp. minced garlic
1 Tbsp. dried oregano
  Alfredo sauce, optional

Place crust on an ungreased 14-in. pizza pan. In a small bowl, combine Parmesan cheese, mayonnaise, onion, garlic and oregano; spread over crust. Bake at 450° until edge is lightly browned, 8-10 minutes. Cut into wedges. If desired, serve wedges with Alfredo sauce.

1 PIECE 119 cal., 8g fat (2g sat. fat), 4mg chol., 193mg sod., 8g carb. (0 sugars, 0 fiber), 3g pro.

SAUSAGE &
SWISS CHARD
PASTA (PAGE 164)

LOTSA PASTA

⏱ PESTO PASTA

My husband loves this fresh-tasting side dish that's as good as it is easy.
The appetizing aroma of basil is sure to whet guests' appetites.
—Karen Behrend, Newport, WA

TAKES: 20 min. • **MAKES:** 6 servings

8 oz. uncooked spaghetti
⅓ cup minced fresh basil
¼ cup minced fresh parsley
¼ cup grated Parmesan cheese
½ tsp. salt
1 garlic clove, quartered
⅛ tsp. ground nutmeg
⅓ cup olive oil

1. Cook pasta according to package directions.

2. Meanwhile, in a blender or food processor, place basil, parsley, Parmesan cheese, salt, garlic and nutmeg. Cover and process on low for 1 minute or until very finely chopped. While processing, gradually add oil in a steady stream.

3. Drain pasta; top with pesto and toss to coat.

¾ CUP 263 cal., 14g fat (2g sat. fat), 3mg chol., 261mg sod., 29g carb. (1g sugars, 1g fiber), 6g pro.

WHICH PASTA?

Besides spaghetti, pesto pairs best with long, thin noodles like linguine, fettuccine, cappellini and bucatini. However, it also works with shorter textured noodles like gemelli or orecchiette.

HOMEMADE POTATO GNOCCHI

My Italian mother remembers her mother making these dumplings for special occasions.
She still has the bowl Grandma mixed the dough in, which will be passed down to me some day.
—*Tina Mirilovich, Johnstown, PA*

PREP: 30 min. • **COOK:** 10 min./batch • **MAKES:** 8 servings

4   medium potatoes, peeled and quartered
1   egg, lightly beaten
1½ tsp. salt, divided
1¾ to 2 cups all-purpose flour
    Spaghetti sauce, warmed
    Optional: Grated Parmesan cheese, crushed red pepper flakes, and fresh herbs, such as basil, oregano or parsley

1. Place potatoes in a saucepan and cover with water. Bring to a boil. Reduce heat; cover and cook for 15-20 minutes or until tender. Drain and mash.

2. Place 2 cups mashed potatoes in a large bowl (save any remaining mashed potatoes for another use). Stir in egg and 1 tsp. salt. Gradually beat in flour until blended (dough will be firm and elastic).

3. Turn onto a lightly floured surface; knead 15 times. Roll into ½-in.-wide ropes. Cut ropes into 1-in. pieces. Press down on each piece with a lightly floured fork.

4. In a Dutch oven, bring 3 qt. water and remaining salt to a boil. Add gnocchi in small batches; cook 8-10 minutes or until gnocchi float to top and are cooked through. Remove with a slotted spoon. Serve immediately with spaghetti sauce. Add toppings as desired.

1 SERVING 159 cal., 1g fat (0 sat. fat), 27mg chol., 674mg sod., 33g carb. (1g sugars, 2g fiber), 5g pro.

TROUBLESHOOTING GNOCCHI

If your gnocchi are mushy, it could be for a couple of reasons. You might not have drained the potatoes thoroughly after boiling, so excess moisture made it into the dough. Otherwise, the issue could be with the dough prep. Make sure you don't skip (or skimp) on the kneading step—this helps develop the gluten to give it some tooth.

CARAMELIZED ONION & GARLIC PASTA

This full-flavored recipe is the result of my mom's love of pasta and our love of cooking together. With a bit of pepper heat and smoky bacon, the entree is excellent alone or paired with grilled chicken.

—*Lacy Jo Matheson, Sault Ste. Marie, MI*

PREP: 20 min. • **COOK:** 35 min. • **MAKES:** 6 servings

¼   cup butter, cubed
2   large sweet onions, thinly sliced
¼   tsp. crushed red pepper flakes
⅛   tsp. salt
8   garlic cloves, minced
2   cups grape tomatoes, halved
¼   cup balsamic vinegar
¼   cup olive oil, divided
1   pkg. (16 oz.) uncooked
     angel hair pasta
9   bacon strips, cooked and crumbled
⅔   cup shredded Parmesan cheese
½   tsp. coarsely ground pepper
     Fresh basil leaves, optional

1. In a large skillet over medium-high heat, melt butter. Add onions, pepper flakes and salt; saute until onions are tender. Stir in garlic. Reduce heat to medium-low; cook, stirring occasionally, 30-40 minutes or until onions are deep golden brown.

2. Add tomatoes, vinegar and 2 Tbsp. oil to skillet. Cook pasta according to package directions. Drain pasta; toss with onion mixture.

3. Drizzle with remaining 2 Tbsp. oil. Sprinkle with bacon, cheese and pepper; heat through. Garnish with basil if desired.

1½ CUPS 587 cal., 25g fat (9g sat. fat), 39mg chol., 496mg sod., 71g carb. (12g sugars, 4g fiber), 19g pro.

🕐 SAUSAGE & SWISS CHARD PASTA

I whipped up lunch with fresh produce from the farmers market, and the result was amazing.
The pasta absorbs the cooking liquid quickly, so serve immediately to guarantee the best texture.
—Kate Stiltner, Grand Rapids, MI

TAKES: 30 min. • **MAKES:** 6 servings

12 oz. uncooked orecchiette or small tube pasta (about 2½ cups)
1 Tbsp. olive oil
½ lb. bulk Italian sausage
½ cup chopped red onion
1 medium fennel bulb, chopped
½ lb. baby portobello mushrooms, chopped
3 garlic cloves, minced
1 bunch Swiss chard, trimmed and chopped
½ tsp. salt
¼ tsp. pepper
¾ cup grated Parmesan cheese, divided
½ cup pine nuts or chopped walnuts, toasted

1. Cook pasta according to package directions for al dente. Meanwhile, in a large skillet, heat oil over medium heat. Cook sausage and red onion until no longer pink, 3-4 minutes, breaking sausage into crumbles. Add fennel, mushrooms and garlic; cook until tender, 6-8 minutes. Add Swiss chard; cook and stir until wilted, 4-5 minutes longer.

2. Drain pasta, reserving 1 cup pasta water. In a large bowl, combine pasta, sausage mixture, salt, pepper and ½ cup Parmesan cheese, adding enough reserved pasta water to coat pasta and create a creamy texture. Serve with remaining ¼ cup cheese and toasted pine nuts.

1⅓ CUPS 487 cal., 25g fat (6g sat. fat), 34mg chol., 726mg sod., 51g carb. (5g sugars, 4g fiber), 19g pro.

SUGGESTED ADDITIONS

Spicy Italian sausage would complement the flavors in this dish nicely. You can also lighten it up by using turkey Italian sausage, and add fiber with whole wheat orecchiette instead of white pasta.

KNOW YOUR PASTA SHAPES

Do you know your fettuccini from your farfalle and your orzo from your oricchiette? Here's a quick guide to which pasta is which.

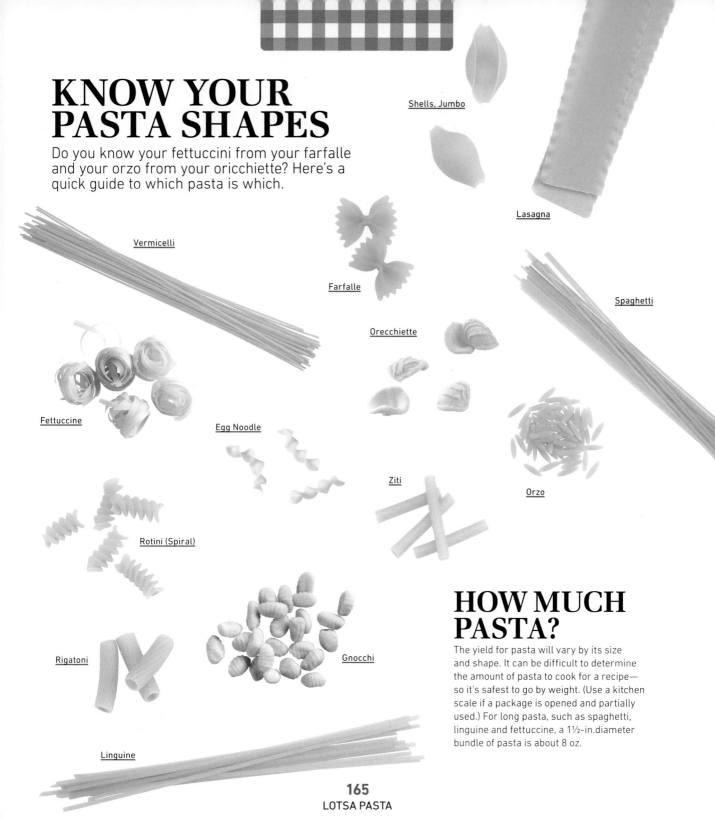

Shells, Jumbo

Lasagna

Vermicelli

Farfalle

Spaghetti

Orecchiette

Fettuccine

Egg Noodle

Ziti

Orzo

Rotini (Spiral)

Rigatoni

Gnocchi

Linguine

HOW MUCH PASTA?

The yield for pasta will vary by its size and shape. It can be difficult to determine the amount of pasta to cook for a recipe—so it's safest to go by weight. (Use a kitchen scale if a package is opened and partially used.) For long pasta, such as spaghetti, linguine and fettuccine, a 1½-in.diameter bundle of pasta is about 8 oz.

LEMONY SCALLOPS WITH ANGEL HAIR PASTA

This delicate dish tastes so bright with a touch of lemon and tender sauteed scallops. Serve with crusty whole grain bread, and you have an impressive dinner that comes together in a flash.
—*Thomas Faglon, Somerset, NJ*

TAKES: 25 min. • **MAKES:** 4 servings

8 oz. uncooked multigrain angel hair pasta
3 Tbsp. olive oil, divided
1 lb. sea scallops, patted dry
2 cups sliced radishes (about 1 bunch)
2 garlic cloves, sliced
½ tsp. crushed red pepper flakes
6 green onions, thinly sliced
½ tsp. kosher salt
1 Tbsp. grated lemon zest
¼ cup lemon juice

1. In a 6-qt. stockpot, cook pasta according to package directions; drain and return to pot.

2. Meanwhile, in a large skillet, heat 2 Tbsp. oil over medium-high heat; sear scallops in batches until opaque and edges are golden brown, about 2 minutes per side. Remove from skillet; keep warm.

3. In same skillet, saute radishes, garlic and pepper flakes in remaining 1 Tbsp. oil until radishes are tender, 2-3 minutes. Stir in green onions and salt; cook for 1 minute longer. Add to pasta; toss to combine. Sprinkle with lemon zest and juice. Top with scallops to serve.

1½ CUPS 404 cal., 13g fat (2g sat. fat), 27mg chol., 737mg sod., 48g carb. (4g sugars, 6g fiber), 25g pro.

CUT THE CARBS

Create a satisfying low-carb version of this dish by swapping cauliflower rice or shirataki noodles for the angel hair pasta.

⏱ ONE-POT BLACK BEAN ENCHILADA PASTA

I love this cozy dish because it is ready in 30 minutes and is full of healthy ingredients—it has everything a busy weeknight meal calls for.
—*Nora Rushev, Reitnau, Switzerland*

TAKES: 30 min. • **MAKES:** 6 servings

- 4 cups uncooked mini penne or other small pasta
- 4 cups vegetable broth or water
- 1 can (15 oz.) black beans, rinsed and drained
- 1 can (14½ oz.) diced tomatoes, undrained
- 1 medium sweet yellow pepper, chopped
- 1 medium sweet red pepper, chopped
- 1 cup fresh or frozen corn, thawed
- 1 can (10 oz.) enchilada sauce
- 2 Tbsp. taco seasoning
- ½ cup shredded cheddar cheese
  Optional: Fresh cilantro leaves, cherry tomatoes and lime wedges

In a Dutch oven or large skillet, combine first 9 ingredients. Bring to a boil; reduce heat. Simmer, uncovered, until pasta is al dente and sauce has thickened slightly, 12-15 minutes. Add cheese; stir until melted. Serve with desired toppings.

1¾ CUPS 444 cal., 5g fat (2g sat. fat), 9mg chol., 1289mg sod., 84g carb. (8g sugars, 8g fiber), 18g pro.

SUGGESTED ADDITIONS

You could also top this pasta with sliced avocado, sour cream, olives and green onions. Try adding a protein, like shredded chicken, ground beef or ground turkey. If you have gluten sensitivities or an allergy, replace the pasta with a gluten-free pasta alternative. You'll also want to make sure that the sauces and seasonings you're using are gluten-free too.

⏱ SUMMER ZUCCHINI PASTA

I'm always experimenting when my garden is cranking out zucchini and summer squash. This simple and healthy pasta dish is one of my latest wins. It's meatless, but you can add shredded chicken or grilled salmon for a heartier dish.
—Beth Berlin, Oak Creek, WI

TAKES: 25 min. • **MAKES:** 10 servings

1 pkg. (16 oz.) pappardelle
   or tagliatelle pasta
¼ cup olive oil
2 small zucchini, cut into thin ribbons
2 small yellow summer squash,
   cut into thin ribbons
4 garlic cloves, thinly sliced
2 cans (14½ oz. each) diced tomatoes
   with roasted garlic, undrained
⅓ cup loosely packed basil leaves,
   torn
1 Tbsp. coarsely chopped
   fresh rosemary
½ tsp. salt
¼ tsp. crushed red pepper flakes

Cook pasta according to package directions. Meanwhile, in a Dutch oven, heat oil over medium-high heat. Add zucchini and yellow squash; cook and stir until crisp-tender, 3-4 minutes. Add garlic; cook 1 minute longer. Add tomatoes, basil, rosemary, salt and pepper flakes; heat through. Drain pasta; serve with zucchini mixture. If desired, top with additional basil.

1 CUP 254 cal., 7g fat (1g sat. fat), 0 chol., 505mg sod., 42g carb. (8g sugars, 3g fiber), 7g pro.

"I enjoyed this simple pasta dish. Instead of extra basil, I sprinkled it with grated Parmesan cheese to serve."
—AUG2295, TASTEOFHOME.COM

COPYCAT PASTA DA VINCI

I fell in love with this dish at the Cheesecake Factory and experimented with the ingredients until I could duplicate it. I think mine is just as good if not better! The sauce can be made ahead and refrigerated or frozen. Thaw if frozen and then warm gently in a large skillet. Cook pasta and you have a delicious dinner on a weeknight.

—Trisha Kruse, Eagle, ID

PREP: 25 min. • **COOK:** 35 min. • **MAKES:** 8 servings

1 pkg. (16 oz.) penne pasta
1 large red onion, diced
2 Tbsp. olive oil
3 garlic cloves, minced
1½ lbs. boneless skinless chicken breasts, cubed
½ lb. sliced fresh mushrooms
2 cups dry white wine
1 can (14½ oz.) beef broth
1 pkg. (8 oz.) cream cheese, softened
½ cup butter, softened
½ cup half-and-half cream, room temperature
½ tsp. salt
¼ tsp. pepper
½ cup grated Parmesan cheese, divided
  Minced fresh parsley, optional

1. Cook pasta according to package directions for al dente. Meanwhile, in a large skillet, cook onion in oil over medium heat until softened, 4-5 minutes. Add garlic; cook 1 minute longer. Stir in chicken and mushrooms. Cook, stirring frequently, until chicken is no longer pink, 5-7 minutes. With a slotted spoon, remove mixture.

2. To the same skillet, add wine and broth; bring to a simmer. Cook until liquid is reduced by half, 15-20 minutes. Reduce heat to low; add cream cheese and butter, whisking until melted. Whisk in cream, salt and pepper. Add chicken mixture to pan; heat through on low. Toss with pasta and ¼ cup Parmesan cheese. Top with remaining ¼ cup Parmesan cheese and, if desired, parsley.

1½ CUPS 634 cal., 31g fat (16g sat. fat), 118mg chol., 706mg sod., 49g carb. (5g sugars, 3g fiber), 30g pro.

WINE OPTIONS

If you don't have a dry white wine like pinot grigio or chardonnay, feel free to use a different type. Madeira is a great option, as it has a ton of flavor and just a splash will bring any dish to life. Or try using Marsala or another semisweet wine you have on hand.

CAJUN CHICKEN & PASTA

This kicked-up pasta dish is a family favorite and my most-requested recipe. It's easy to adapt too. Substitute shrimp for the chicken, add your favorite veggies and adjust the spice level to your family's taste—you can't go wrong!
—*Dolly Kragel, Sloan, IA*

PREP: 10 min. + standing • **COOK:** 35 min. • **MAKES:** 6 servings

1 lb. boneless skinless chicken breasts, cut into 2x½-in. strips
3 tsp. Cajun seasoning
8 oz. uncooked penne pasta (about 2⅓ cups)
2 Tbsp. butter, divided
1 small sweet red pepper, diced
1 small green pepper, diced
½ cup sliced fresh mushrooms
4 green onions, chopped
1 cup heavy whipping cream
½ tsp. salt
¼ tsp. dried basil
¼ tsp. lemon-pepper seasoning
¼ tsp. garlic powder
Pepper to taste
Chopped plum tomatoes
Minced fresh basil
Shredded Parmesan cheese

1. Toss chicken with Cajun seasoning; let stand for 15 minutes. Cook pasta according to package directions; drain.

2. In a large skillet, heat 1 Tbsp. butter over medium-high heat; saute chicken until no longer pink, 5-6 minutes. Remove from pan.

3. In same pan, heat remaining 1 Tbsp. butter over medium-high heat; saute peppers, mushrooms and onions until peppers are crisp-tender, 6-8 minutes. Stir in cream and seasonings; bring to a boil. Cook, stirring, until slightly thickened, 4-6 minutes. Stir in pasta and chicken; heat through. Top with tomatoes and basil. Sprinkle with Parmesan cheese.

1 SERVING 398 cal., 21g fat (12g sat. fat), 97mg chol., 357mg sod., 31g carb. (4g sugars, 2g fiber), 22g pro.

THE BEST CAJUN SEASONING

The best Cajun seasoning is the one you like best! There are lots of spice blends on the market—everything from major spice labels to smaller independent merchants. What they'll all have in common is peppers (black pepper, cayenne and potentially more), garlic and paprika. You can make your own basic blend and then add different spices to suit your preference.

🕐 RAVIOLI WITH CREAMY SQUASH SAUCE

Store-bought ravioli speeds assembly of this cozy, restaurant-quality dish that tastes so good your family won't notice it's meatless.
—Taste of Home *Test Kitchen*

TAKES: 20 min. • **MAKES:** 4 servings

1   pkg. (9 oz.) refrigerated
    cheese ravioli
3   garlic cloves, minced
2   Tbsp. butter
1   pkg. (10 oz.) frozen cooked
    winter squash, thawed
1   pkg. (6 oz.) fresh baby spinach
1   cup heavy whipping cream
⅓   cup vegetable broth
¼   tsp. salt
1   cup chopped walnuts, toasted

1. Cook ravioli according to package directions. Meanwhile, in a Dutch oven, saute garlic in butter for 1 minute. Add squash and spinach; cook until spinach is wilted, 2-3 minutes longer. Stir in cream, broth and salt. Bring to a gentle boil; cook until slightly thickened, 6-8 minutes.

2. Drain ravioli; add to squash mixture. Toss to coat. Sprinkle with walnuts.

1¼ CUPS 671 cal., 51g fat (22g sat. fat), 122mg chol., 578mg sod., 42g carb. (2g sugars, 7g fiber), 18g pro.

SHRIMP SPAGHETTI WITH CHERRY TOMATOES

This is a very tasty pasta dish, full of umami flavors and, if done properly,
an insanely silky sauce. Shut your eyes and you will swear you're in Sicily.
—*Hassan Nurullah, Hapeville, GA*

PREP: 15 min. • **COOK:** 25 min. • **MAKES:** 6 servings

1 lb. uncooked spaghetti
3 Tbsp. olive oil
2 garlic cloves, smashed
1 tsp. crushed red pepper flakes
4 cups heirloom cherry tomatoes
2 shallots, thinly sliced
1 can anchovy fillets (2 oz.)
¾ cup muffuletta mix or
olive bruschetta topping
4 Tbsp. unsalted butter
1 lb. uncooked shrimp (26-30 per lb.),
peeled and deveined
1½ cups grated Romano cheese
2 Tbsp. minced fresh parsley

1. In a Dutch oven, cook pasta according to package directions; drain, reserving 1 cup cooking liquid. Set aside.

2. In same Dutch oven, heat oil over medium-high heat. Add garlic and pepper flakes until fragrant. Discard garlic cloves; add tomatoes, shallots, anchovy fillets, muffuletta mix and butter. Cook until tomatoes begin to burst, 4-5 minutes. Add shrimp; cook until shrimp turn pink, 4-5 minutes. Add pasta, reserved pasta water and Romano to pan; stir until creamy. Garnish with parsley and additional Romano.

1¾ CUPS 726 cal., 35g fat (13g sat. fat), 150mg chol., 1163mg sod., 66g carb. (5g sugars, 4g fiber), 38g pro.

GREEN SPAGHETTI

A fun alternative to other pasta sauces, this southwestern-style mix of peppers,
cilantro and sour cream brings an unexpected zing to your dinner table.

—Taste of Home *Test Kitchen*

PREP: 25 min. + standing • **COOK:** 5 min. • **MAKES:** 6 servings

4   poblano peppers
12   oz. uncooked spaghetti
4   oz. cream cheese, cubed
1   small onion, chopped
½   cup sour cream
¼   cup fresh cilantro leaves
¼   cup chicken stock
2   garlic cloves, minced
½   tsp. salt
¼   tsp. pepper
2   Tbsp. butter
     Crumbled Cotija cheese or
     queso fresco

1. Place peppers on a foil-lined baking sheet. Broil 4 in. from heat until skins blister, about 5 minutes. With tongs, rotate peppers a quarter turn. Broil and rotate until all sides are blistered and blackened. Immediately place peppers in a large bowl; let stand, covered, 20 minutes.

2. Cook spaghetti according to package directions. Meanwhile, peel off charred skin from peppers and remove stems and seeds; discard. Chop peppers. Transfer to a blender. Add cream cheese, onion, sour cream, cilantro, stock, garlic, salt and pepper. Cover and blend until smooth.

3. Melt butter in a large skillet over medium heat; add pepper mixture. Cook and stir until heated through, about 3 minutes. Drain spaghetti; stir into sauce. Serve with Cotija cheese and additional cilantro.

NOTE Wear disposable gloves when cutting hot peppers; the oils can burn skin. Avoid touching your face.

1 CUP 374 cal., 15g fat (9g sat. fat), 43mg chol., 321mg sod., 49g carb. (5g sugars, 3g fiber), 10g pro.

⏱ HEARTY PENNE BEEF

This is comfort food at its finest! The best of everything is found here—it's tasty,
easy and a smart way to sneak in some spinach for extra nutrition.
—Taste of Home *Test Kitchen*

TAKES: 30 min. • **MAKES:** 4 servings

1¾ cups uncooked penne pasta
1 lb. ground beef
1 tsp. minced garlic
1 can (15 oz.) tomato puree
1 can (14½ oz.) beef broth
1½ tsp. Italian seasoning
1 tsp. Worcestershire sauce
¼ tsp. salt
¼ tsp. pepper
2 cups chopped fresh spinach
2 cups shredded part-skim
   mozzarella cheese

1. Cook pasta according to package directions. Meanwhile, in a Dutch oven, cook beef over medium heat until no longer pink, 6-8 minutes, breaking into crumbles. Add garlic; cook 1 minute longer. Drain. Stir in tomato puree, broth, Italian seasoning, Worcestershire sauce, salt and pepper.

2. Bring to a boil. Reduce heat; simmer, uncovered, until slightly thickened, 10-15 minutes. Add spinach; cook until wilted, 1-2 minutes.

3. Drain pasta; stir into beef mixture. Sprinkle with cheese; cover and cook until cheese is melted, 3-4 minutes.

FREEZE OPTION Freeze cooled pasta mixture in freezer containers. To use, partially thaw in refrigerator overnight. Heat through in a saucepan, stirring occasionally; add broth or water if necessary.

1½ CUPS 482 cal., 20g fat (10g sat. fat), 88mg chol., 1001mg sod., 33g carb. (5g sugars, 2g fiber), 41g pro.

🕐 CHICKEN & BOWS

I first made this recipe when I was a professional nanny. It comes
together quickly at dinnertime when the kids are hungry.
—Danette Forbes, Overland Park, KS

TAKES: 25 min. • **MAKES:** 8 servings

1   pkg. (16 oz.) bow tie pasta
2   lbs. boneless skinless chicken
    breasts, cut into strips
1   cup chopped sweet red pepper
¼   cup butter, cubed
2   cans (10¾ oz. each) condensed
    cream of chicken soup, undiluted
2   cups frozen peas
1½ cups 2% milk
1   tsp. garlic powder
¼   to ½ tsp. salt
¼   tsp. pepper
⅔   cup grated Parmesan cheese
    Crushed red pepper flakes,
    optional

1. Cook pasta according to package
directions. Meanwhile, in a Dutch oven,
cook chicken and red pepper in butter
over medium heat until chicken is no
longer pink, 5-6 minutes.

2. Stir in the soup, peas, milk, garlic
powder, salt and pepper; heat through.
Stir in cheese.

3. Drain pasta; add to chicken mixture
and toss to coat. If desired, sprinkle
with red pepper flakes.

FREEZE OPTION Transfer individual
portions of cooled mixture into freezer
containers. Freeze up to 3 months. To
use, thaw in the refrigerator overnight.
Transfer to an ungreased shallow microwave-safe dish. Cover and microwave
on high until heated through, stirring occasionally.

1¼ CUPS 536 cal., 18g fat (8g sat. fat), 94mg chol., 908mg sod., 57g carb. (7g sugars,
5g fiber), 37g pro. **DIABETIC EXCHANGES** 3 lean meat, 3 very lean meat, 2 starch,
2 fat.

FETTUCCINE WITH BLACK BEAN SAUCE

When my husband needed to go on a heart-smart diet, I had to come up with new ways to get more vegetables into our daily meals. This meatless spaghetti sauce is a winner; it's especially delicious with spinach fettuccine.

—Marianne Neuman, East Troy, WI

TAKES: 30 min. • **MAKES:** 5 servings

6 oz. uncooked fettuccine
1 small green pepper, chopped
1 small onion, chopped
1 Tbsp. olive oil
2 cups garden-style pasta sauce
1 can (15 oz.) black beans, rinsed and drained
2 Tbsp. minced fresh basil or 2 tsp. dried basil
1 tsp. dried oregano
½ tsp. fennel seed
¼ tsp. garlic salt
1 cup shredded part-skim mozzarella cheese
Additional chopped fresh basil, optional

1. Cook fettuccine according to package directions. Meanwhile, in a large saucepan, saute green pepper and onion in oil until tender. Stir in pasta sauce, black beans and seasonings.

2. Bring to a boil. Reduce heat; simmer, uncovered, 5 minutes. Drain fettuccine. Top with pasta sauce. Sprinkle with cheese and, if desired, fresh basil on top.

¾ CUP SAUCE WITH ¾ CUP PASTA 350 cal., 10g fat (3g sat. fat), 17mg chol., 761mg sod., 51g carb. (12g sugars, 8g fiber), 16g pro. **DIABETIC EXCHANGES** 2½ starch, 2 vegetable, 1 lean meat, 1 fat.

MAKE IT EVEN HEALTHIER

As long as you're eating a healthy dinner, switch up your noodle game too. Try this dish with whole wheat, buckwheat, quinoa, chickpea or multigrain pasta.

BURRATA RAVIOLI

Using burrata cheese as ravioli filling is easy and really delivers on flavor. Instead of mixing up ingredients for the filling, this quicker version uses chunks of burrata and fresh basil to create a luscious interior. Serve the ravioli with your favorite sauce.
—Taste of Home *Test Kitchen*

PREP: 45 min. + standing • **COOK:** 10 min. • **MAKES:** 4 servings (3½ cups sauce)

2½ to 3 cups all-purpose flour
3 large eggs
¼ cup water
1½ tsp. olive oil

SAUCE
1½ tsp. olive oil
¼ cup finely chopped onion
1 garlic clove, minced
1 can (28 oz.) Italian crushed tomatoes
1½ tsp. Italian seasoning
2 to 3 tsp. sugar
¼ tsp. salt
¼ tsp. pepper

FILLING
8 oz. burrata cheese, cut into 30 quarter-sized pieces
¼ cup minced fresh basil

1. Place 2½ cups flour in a large bowl. Make a well in center. Beat eggs, water and oil; pour into well. Stir together, forming a ball. Turn onto a floured surface; knead until smooth and elastic, 4-6 minutes, adding remaining flour if necessary to keep dough from sticking. Cover and let rest 30 minutes.

2. Meanwhile, in a small saucepan, heat oil over medium heat. Add onion; cook and stir until tender, 2-3 minutes. Add garlic; cook and stir 1 minute longer. Stir in remaining sauce ingredients. Bring to a boil. Reduce heat; cover and simmer until flavors are blended, about 30 minutes, stirring occasionally. Keep warm.

3. Divide pasta dough in half; on a lightly floured surface (or using a pasta roller) roll 1 portion to 1/16-in. thickness. (Keep pasta covered until ready to use.) Working quickly, arrange burrata pieces 1 in. apart over half of pasta sheet. Top each piece of burrata with a scant ½ tsp. basil. Fold sheet over; press down to seal. Cut into squares with a pastry wheel. Repeat with remaining dough and filling.

4. In a Dutch oven, bring salted water to a boil; add ravioli. Reduce heat to a gentle simmer; cook until ravioli float to top and are tender, 1-2 minutes. Drain. Serve with sauce.

8 RAVIOLI WITH ABOUT ¾ CUP SAUCE 607 cal., 20g fat (10g sat. fat), 180mg chol., 781mg sod., 75g carb. (11g sugars, 6g fiber), 26g pro.

WHAT SAUCE?

As here, a simple marinara sauce would work with burrata ravioli. You can also serve this pasta with a bright pesto sauce, a creamy Alfredo sauce or a red clam sauce.

🕐 GORGONZOLA SHRIMP PASTA

This creamy pasta dish is so quick and easy to make. It's perfect
for weeknights, but feels special enough for company.
—*Robin Haas, Hyde Park, MA*

TAKES: 30 min. • **MAKES:** 6 servings

12 oz. uncooked penne pasta
2   Tbsp. olive oil
1   lb. uncooked shrimp (31-40 per lb.),
    peeled and deveined
3   garlic cloves, minced
½   cup dried cranberries
½   cup dry white wine or
    reduced-sodium chicken broth
6   oz. fresh baby spinach
    (about 3 cups)
4   oz. reduced-fat cream cheese,
    cubed
½   cup crumbled Gorgonzola cheese
3   Tbsp. minced fresh parsley
¼   tsp. salt
⅓   cup chopped walnuts

1. Cook penne according to package directions for al dente. Meanwhile, in a large cast-iron skillet or Dutch oven, heat oil over medium heat. Add shrimp and garlic; cook until shrimp are pink, 5-10 minutes. Remove from pan and keep warm.

2. Stir cranberries and wine into same pan. Bring to a boil; cook until liquid is almost evaporated, about 5 minutes.

3. Drain penne, reserving 1 cup pasta water; add penne to pan. Stir in spinach, cream cheese, Gorgonzola cheese, parsley, salt and shrimp. Cook, stirring, until mixture is heated through and cheeses have melted, about 5 minutes, adding enough reserved pasta water to reach desired consistency. Top with chopped walnuts.

2 CUPS 486 cal., 18g fat (6g sat. fat), 114mg chol., 422mg sod., 57g carb. (13g sugars, 4g fiber), 26g pro.

🕐 PENNE ALLA VODKA

This easy and impressive pasta is always on the menu when my husband and I invite first-time guests over for dinner. Many friends have asked me to make the recipe again years after they first tried it.
—*Cara Langer, Overland Park, KS*

TAKES: 30 min. • **MAKES:** 6 servings

1 pkg. (16 oz.) penne pasta
3 Tbsp. butter
2 garlic cloves, minced
4 oz. thinly sliced prosciutto,
  cut into strips
1 can (28 oz.) whole plum tomatoes,
  drained and chopped
¼ cup vodka
½ tsp. salt
½ tsp. crushed red pepper flakes
½ cup heavy whipping cream
½ cup shredded Parmesan cheese

1. Cook pasta according to package directions.

2. Meanwhile, in a large skillet, heat butter over medium-high heat. Add garlic; cook and stir 1 minute. Add prosciutto; cook 2 minutes longer. Stir in tomatoes, vodka, salt and pepper flakes. Bring to a boil. Reduce heat; simmer, uncovered, 5 minutes. Stir in cream; cook 2-3 minutes longer, stirring occasionally.

3. Drain pasta. Add pasta and cheese to sauce; toss to combine.

1⅓ CUPS 504 cal., 19g fat (11g sat. fat), 64mg chol., 966mg sod., 62g carb. (6g sugars, 4g fiber), 19g pro.

BEST SPAGHETTI & MEATBALLS

One evening we had unexpected company. Since I had some of these meatballs left over in the freezer, I warmed them up as appetizers. Everyone raved! This classic recipe makes a big batch and is perfect for entertaining.

—Mary Lou Koskella, Prescott, AZ

PREP: 30 min. • **COOK:** 2 hours • **MAKES:** 16 servings

2   Tbsp. olive oil
1½ cups chopped onions
3   garlic cloves, minced
2   cans (12 oz. each) tomato paste
3   cups water
1   can (29 oz.) tomato sauce
⅓ cup minced fresh parsley
1   Tbsp. dried basil
2   tsp. salt
½ tsp. pepper

MEATBALLS
4   large eggs, lightly beaten
2   cups soft bread cubes (cut into ¼-in. pieces)
1½ cups 2% milk
1   cup grated Parmesan cheese
3   garlic cloves, minced
2   tsp. salt
½ tsp. pepper
3   lbs. ground beef
2   Tbsp. canola oil
2   lbs. spaghetti, cooked

1. In a Dutch oven, heat olive oil over medium heat. Add onions; saute until softened. Add garlic; cook 1 minute longer. Stir in tomato paste; cook for 3-5 minutes. Add next 6 ingredients. Bring to a boil. Reduce heat; simmer, covered, for 50 minutes.

2. Combine first 7 meatball ingredients. Add beef; mix lightly but thoroughly. Shape into 1½-in. balls.

3. In a large skillet, heat canola oil over medium heat. Add meatballs; brown in batches until no longer pink. Drain. Add to sauce; bring to a boil. Reduce heat; simmer, covered, until flavors are blended, about 1 hour, stirring occasionally. Serve with hot cooked spaghetti.

½ CUP SAUCE WITH 4 MEATBALLS AND 1¼ CUPS SPAGHETTI 519 cal., 18g fat (6g sat. fat), 106mg chol., 1043mg sod., 59g carb. (8g sugars, 4g fiber), 30g pro.

COOKING MEATBALLS

Instead of frying, you can also bake the meatballs: Place them on a rack over a rimmed baking sheet and bake at 400° until golden brown, about 20 minutes.

LEMONY SHRIMP & ARUGULA ORZO

What I love about this recipe is that it's so tasty and it can be eaten hot or cold.
If you're allergic to shrimp, it tastes great with chicken too.
—Aleni Salcedo, East Elmhurst, NY

TAKES: 30 min. • **MAKES:** 8 servings

2 Tbsp. olive oil
1 small onion, chopped
2 garlic cloves, minced
3½ cups reduced-sodium chicken broth
1 lb. uncooked whole wheat orzo pasta
1 cup water
1 lb. uncooked shrimp (31-40 per lb.), peeled and deveined
4 cups fresh arugula
3 Tbsp. lemon juice
½ tsp. salt
¼ tsp. pepper
½ cup pitted Greek olives, halved
1½ cups crumbled feta cheese
Chopped fresh basil leaves

1. In a large skillet, heat oil over medium-high heat. Add onion; cook and stir until crisp-tender, 3-4 minutes. Add garlic; cook 1 minute longer. Stir in broth, orzo and water. Bring to a boil; reduce heat. Simmer, uncovered, until orzo is al dente, 8-10 minutes.

2. Stir in shrimp, arugula, lemon juice, salt and pepper. Cook and stir until shrimp turn pink, 4-5 minutes. Stir in olives. Sprinkle with feta cheese and fresh basil.

1 CUP 367 cal., 11g fat (3g sat. fat), 80mg chol., 808mg sod., 44g carb. (1g sugars, 10g fiber), 22g pro.

"This recipe is delicious and fresh. Every ingredient is a favorite of mine. I didn't change a thing. It'll be a staple in our home!"
—JENNT1981, TASTEOFHOME.COM

TORTELLINI WITH SAUSAGE & MASCARPONE

When I crave Italian comfort food on a busy night and don't have a lot of time to cook, this dish is a lifesaver. It's fast and yummy and starts with a premade jarred sauce, but then makes it much more special with just a few key additions. You can have it on the table in less time than a takeout order.
—*Gerry Vance, Millbrae, CA*

TAKES: 20 min. • **MAKES:** 6 servings

1 pkg. (20 oz.) refrigerated cheese tortellini
8 oz. bulk Italian sausage
1 jar (24 oz.) pasta sauce with mushrooms
½ cup shredded Parmesan cheese
1 carton (8 oz.) mascarpone cheese
Crushed red pepper flakes, optional

1. Prepare tortellini according to package directions. Meanwhile, in a large cast-iron or other heavy skillet, cook sausage over medium heat until no longer pink, 6-8 minutes, breaking into crumbles; drain. Stir in pasta sauce; heat through.

2. Drain tortellini, reserving 1 cup cooking water. Add tortellini to sauce with enough reserved cooking water to reach desired consistency; toss to coat. Stir in Parmesan cheese; dollop with mascarpone cheese. If desired, sprinkle with red pepper flakes.

1 CUP 637 cal., 37g fat (17g sat. fat), 113mg chol., 1040mg sod., 57g carb. (11g sugars, 4g fiber), 24g pro.

HOMEMADE PASTA DOUGH

Go for it. Once you try homemade pasta, you're hooked.
—*Kathryn Conrad, Milwaukee, WI*

PREP: 15 min. + standing • **MAKES:** 6 servings

2 large eggs
1 large egg yolk
¼ cup water
1 Tbsp. olive oil
¼ tsp. salt
½ tsp. coarsely ground pepper, optional
1½ cups all-purpose flour
½ cup semolina flour

1. In a small bowl, whisk first 5 ingredients and, if desired, pepper. On a clean work surface, mix all-purpose and semolina flours, forming a mound. Make a large well in center. Pour egg mixture into well. Using a fork or your fingers, gradually mix flour mixture into egg mixture, forming a soft dough (dough will be slightly sticky).

2. Lightly dust work surface with all-purpose flour; knead dough gently 5 times. Divide into 6 portions; cover and let rest 30 minutes.

3. To make fettuccine, roll each ball into a 10x8-in. rectangle, dusting lightly with flour. Roll up jelly-roll style. Cut into ¼-in.-wide strips. Cook in boiling water 1-3 minutes.

1 SERVING 217 cal., 5g fat (1g sat. fat), 93mg chol., 124mg sod., 34g carb. (0 sugars, 1g fiber), 8g pro.

PASTA BASICS

Whether you're using homemade pasta or store-bought, fresh or dried, here are some simple guidelines to get you started.

STORING

• Store uncooked dried pasta in a cool, dry place for up to 1 year. Store fresh pasta in the refrigerator and cook or, if applicable, freeze by the use-by date.

COOKING

• Follow the directions on the package for preparing the pasta.

• For Italian-style pasta, prepare 2 oz. per person for a main-dish serving.

• If boiling the pasta, use the amount of water called for in the directions in a large pot. Overcrowding the pot will encourage clumping and sticking.

• Cooking times vary with the size and variety of pasta. Thin pasta takes less time to cook than thick. Fresh pasta cooks faster than dried.

• If the pasta will require further cooking, such as in a casserole, boil it for the shortest time listed on the directions.

DONENESS TESTING

• To test for doneness, remove a strand of pasta from the boiling water, rinse it under cold water and bite it. It should be al dente (firm, yet tender).

• As soon as the pasta tests done, pour it into a colander in the sink to drain.

LASAGNA DELIZIOSA
(PAGE 212)

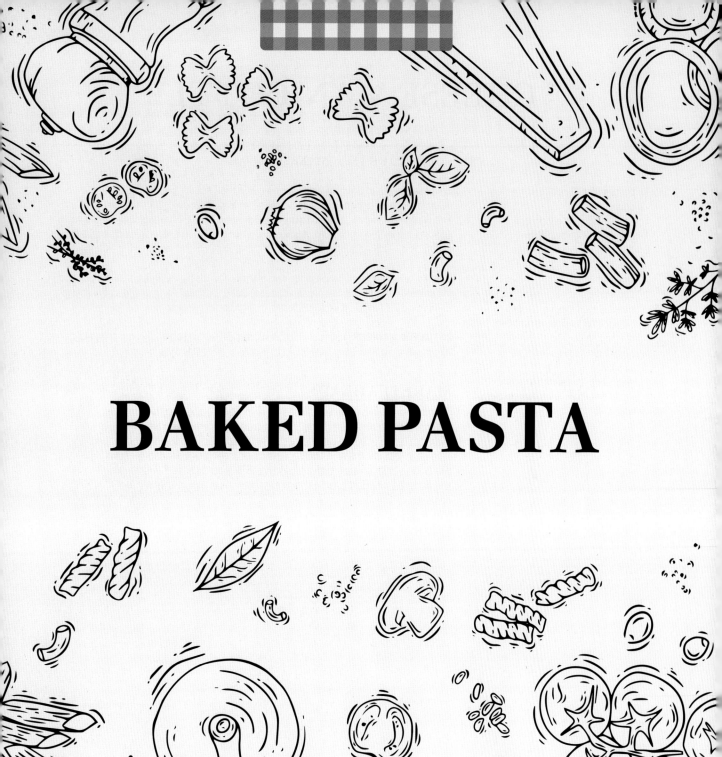

BAKED PASTA

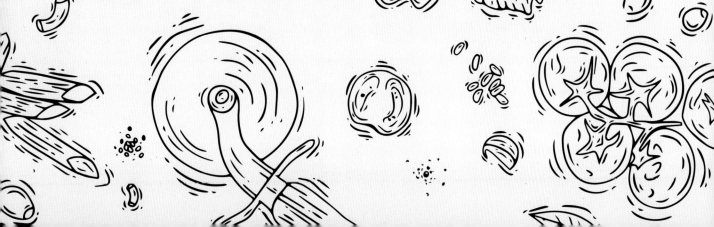

CHEESE MANICOTTI

This is the first meal I ever cooked for my husband, and all these years later he still enjoys my manicotti!
—Joan Hallford, North Richland Hills, TX

PREP: 25 min. • **BAKE:** 1 hour • **MAKES:** 7 servings

- 1 carton (15 oz.) reduced-fat ricotta cheese
- 1 small onion, finely chopped
- 1 large egg, lightly beaten
- 2 Tbsp. minced fresh parsley
- ½ tsp. pepper
- ¼ tsp. salt
- 1 cup shredded part-skim mozzarella cheese, divided
- 1 cup grated Parmesan cheese, divided
- 4 cups marinara sauce
- ½ cup water
- 1 pkg. (8 oz.) manicotti shells
  Additional minced fresh parsley, optional

1. Preheat oven to 350°. In a small bowl, mix the first 6 ingredients; stir in ½ cup mozzarella and ½ cup Parmesan cheese. In another bowl, mix marinara sauce and water; spread ¾ cup sauce onto bottom of a 13x9-in. baking dish coated with cooking spray. Fill uncooked manicotti shells with ricotta mixture; arrange over sauce. Top with remaining sauce.

2. Bake, covered, until pasta is tender, 50 minutes. Sprinkle with remaining ½ cup mozzarella and ½ cup Parmesan cheese. Bake, uncovered, until cheese is melted, 10-15 minutes longer. If desired, top with additional parsley.

2 STUFFED MANICOTTI 361 cal., 13g fat (6g sat. fat), 64mg chol., 1124mg sod., 41g carb. (12g sugars, 4g fiber), 19g pro.

MAKE IT AHEAD

This recipe can be assembled and refrigerated for up to 3 days; just remove from the fridge 30 minutes before baking as directed. Manicotti can also be assembled and frozen for up to 2 months. To use, partially thaw in the refrigerator overnight. Remove from the fridge 30 minutes before baking. Bake as directed, increasing the time as needed until a thermometer inserted in the center reads 165°F.

BAKED FETA PASTA

There's a reason this recipe went viral on TikTok! It's simple to throw together and incredibly creamy and delicious.
—*Sarah Tramonte, Milwaukee, WI*

PREP: 15 min. • **BAKE:** 30 min. • **MAKES:** 8 servings

2 pints cherry tomatoes
3 garlic cloves, halved
½ cup olive oil
1 pkg. (8 oz.) block feta cheese
1 tsp. sea salt
¼ tsp. coarsely ground pepper
1 pkg. (16 oz.) rigatoni or other short pasta
  Fresh basil leaves, coarsely chopped

1. Preheat oven to 400°. In a 13x9-in. baking dish, combine tomatoes, garlic and ¼ cup olive oil. Place the block of feta in the center, moving tomatoes so the cheese is sitting on the bottom of the dish. Drizzle feta with remaining ¼ cup oil and sprinkle with salt and pepper. Bake until tomato skins start to split and the garlic has softened, 30-40 minutes.

2. Meanwhile, cook pasta according to package directions for al dente. Drain, reserving 1 cup pasta water.

3. Stir the feta mixture, lightly pressing tomatoes, until combined. Add pasta; toss to combine. Stir in enough of the reserved pasta water to reach desired consistency. Sprinkle with basil.

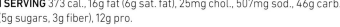

1 SERVING 373 cal., 16g fat (6g sat. fat), 25mg chol., 507mg sod., 46g carb. (5g sugars, 3g fiber), 12g pro.

STICK WITH BLOCK FETA

We recommend against substituting pre-crumbled feta cheese for the block in this recipe. Just like other cheeses, feta melts better if you start with a block. Plus, crumbled feta may burn and stick to the bottom of the baking dish. Even if it means running to the store to pick up a block just for this recipe, it's worth the effort! If you want to experiment, greens like spinach would be a health-conscious and colorful addition. You could finish the dish with red pepper flakes for a little zip, or stir in spicy ground Italian sausage at the same time as the noodles.

SPAGHETTI PIE

A classic combination is remade into a creamy, family-pleasing casserole in this quick and easy dish. This recipe was given to me several years ago, and my family never gets tired of it.

—*Ellen Thompson, Springfield, OH*

PREP: 30 min. • **BAKE:** 25 min. • **MAKES:** 6 servings

6   oz. uncooked spaghetti
1   lb. lean ground beef (90% lean)
½   cup finely chopped onion
¼   cup chopped green pepper
1   cup undrained canned diced tomatoes
1   can (6 oz.) tomato paste
1   tsp. dried oregano
¾   tsp. salt
½   tsp. garlic powder
¼   tsp. pepper
¼   tsp. sugar
2   large egg whites, lightly beaten
1   Tbsp. butter, melted
¼   cup grated Parmesan cheese
1   cup (8 oz.) 2% cottage cheese
½   cup shredded part-skim mozzarella cheese

1. Preheat oven to 350°. Cook spaghetti according to package directions for al dente; drain.

2. In a large skillet, cook beef, onion and green pepper over medium heat, breaking up beef into crumbles, until beef is no longer pink, 5-7 minutes; drain. Stir in tomatoes, tomato paste, seasonings and sugar.

3. In a large bowl, whisk egg whites, melted butter and Parmesan cheese until blended. Add spaghetti and toss to coat. Press spaghetti mixture onto bottom and up side of a greased 9-in. deep-dish pie plate, forming a crust. Spread cottage cheese onto bottom; top with beef mixture.

4. Bake, uncovered, 20 minutes. Sprinkle with mozzarella cheese. Bake until heated through and cheese is melted, 5-10 minutes longer. Let stand 5 minutes before serving.

1 PIECE 348 cal., 10g fat (5g sat. fat), 52mg chol., 690mg sod., 33g carb. (9g sugars, 4g fiber), 29g pro. **DIABETIC EXCHANGES** 3 lean meat, 2 vegetable, 1½ starch, 1 fat.

CHEESE-STUFFED SHELLS

When I was living in California, I tasted this rich cheesy pasta dish at a neighborhood Italian restaurant.
I got the recipe and made a few changes to it, to suit our tastes—now it's even better!
—*Lori Mecca, Grants Pass, OR*

PREP: 35 min. • **BAKE:** 50 min. • **MAKES:** 2 casseroles (6 servings each)

1   lb. bulk Italian sausage
1   large onion, chopped
1   pkg. (10 oz.) frozen chopped spinach, thawed and squeezed dry
1   pkg. (8 oz.) cream cheese, cubed
1   large egg, lightly beaten
2   cups shredded part-skim mozzarella cheese, divided
2   cups shredded cheddar cheese
1   cup 4% cottage cheese
1   cup grated Parmesan cheese
¼   tsp. salt
¼   tsp. pepper
⅛   tsp. ground cinnamon, optional
24 jumbo pasta shells, cooked and drained

SAUCE
1   can (29 oz.) tomato sauce
1   Tbsp. dried minced onion
1½   tsp. dried basil
1½   tsp. dried parsley flakes
2   garlic cloves, minced
1   tsp. sugar
1   tsp. dried oregano
½   tsp. salt
¼   tsp. pepper

1. In a large skillet, cook sausage and onion over medium heat until meat is no longer pink; drain. Transfer to a large bowl. Stir in the spinach, cream cheese and egg. Add 1 cup mozzarella cheese and the cheddar cheese, cottage cheese, Parmesan cheese, salt, pepper and, if desired, cinnamon.

2. Stuff pasta shells with sausage mixture. Arrange in 2 shallow 2-qt. or 11x7-in. baking dishes coated with cooking spray. Combine the sauce ingredients; spoon over shells.

3. Cover and bake at 350° for 45 minutes. Uncover; sprinkle with remaining 1 cup mozzarella. Bake until bubbly and cheese is melted, 5-10 minutes longer. Let stand for 5 minutes before serving.

FREEZE OPTION Cool unbaked casseroles; cover and freeze. To use, partially thaw in refrigerator overnight. Remove from refrigerator 30 minutes before baking. Preheat oven to 350°. Cover casserole with foil; bake 50 minutes. Uncover; bake 15-20 minutes longer or until heated through and a thermometer inserted in center reads 165°.

2 STUFFED SHELLS 397 cal., 23g fat (14g sat. fat), 94mg chol., 1097mg sod., 24g carb. (5g sugars, 2g fiber), 24g pro.

SICILIAN MAC & CHEESE

To give our mac and cheese a Sicilian touch, we mix sausage, basil and fennel
with three cheeses to make an awesome comfort casserole.

—Michael Cohen, Los Angeles, CA

PREP: 45 min. • **BAKE:** 20 min. • **MAKES:** 8 servings

1   pkg. (16 oz.) elbow macaroni
4   Italian sausage links (4 oz. each)
½   cup water
½   cup butter
¼   cup all-purpose flour
2   cups half-and-half cream
2   cups shredded part-skim
    mozzarella cheese
2   cups grated Parmesan cheese
2   large eggs
2   cups 2% milk
2   cups loosely packed basil leaves,
    chopped
1   Tbsp. fennel seed, toasted
2   garlic cloves, minced
1   tsp. salt
½   tsp. pepper
1   cup shredded Romano cheese
    Additional chopped fresh basil

1. Preheat oven to 350°. Cook pasta according to package directions for al dente.

2. In a Dutch oven, brown sausages on all sides, about 5 minutes. Reduce heat to medium-low; add water. Cook, covered, until a thermometer inserted in sausages reads 160°, 10-15 minutes. Remove from pan; slice sausages.

3. In the same pot, melt butter over medium heat. Stir in flour until smooth; gradually whisk in cream. Bring to a boil, stirring constantly; cook and stir until thickened, 1-2 minutes. Stir in mozzarella and Parmesan cheese until melted; remove from heat.

4. Meanwhile, in a large bowl, whisk eggs and milk until blended. Stir in basil, fennel seed, garlic, salt, pepper and cooked sausage. Add to Dutch oven. Drain pasta and add to cheese mixture immediately; toss to coat. Sprinkle with Romano cheese. Bake, uncovered, until a thermometer reads 160°, 20-25 minutes. Sprinkle with additional basil.

1½ CUPS 814 cal., 49g fat (25g sat. fat), 189mg chol., 1610mg sod., 56g carb. (8g sugars, 3g fiber), 37g pro.

CARNITAS WITH ORZO & PEPPERS IN RED MOLE SAUCE

For a tasty way to stretch my grocery dollars, I combine pork shoulder roast with orzo, peppers and mole sauce to make this spicy Mexican comfort food.
—*Kari Wheaton, South Beloit, IL*

PREP: 1 hour 35 min. • **BAKE:** 40 min. • **MAKES:** 5 servings

1   boneless pork shoulder butt roast (1½ to 2 lbs.), cut into ½-in. cubes
1½ tsp. salt, divided
½   tsp. pepper
1   cup uncooked orzo pasta
1   each medium green, sweet red and yellow peppers, chopped
2   jalapeno peppers, seeded and chopped
1   medium onion, chopped
1   Tbsp. olive oil
1   cup chicken broth
¼   cup red mole sauce
2   Tbsp. tomato paste
1   cup quesadilla or Monterey Jack cheese, shredded
    Optional: Chopped cilantro and sour cream

1. Place pork in a 15x10x1-in. baking pan; sprinkle with 1 tsp. salt and the pepper. Bake at 325° until tender, about 1½ hours. Remove pork from oven. Increase oven setting to 350°.

2. Meanwhile, cook pasta according to package directions; drain and set aside. In a large skillet, saute peppers and onion in oil until crisp-tender. In a greased 13x9-in. baking pan, combine the orzo, peppers and onion.

3. In a small saucepan, whisk the chicken broth, mole sauce, tomato paste and remaining ½ tsp. salt. Cook and stir until thickened and bubbly. Pour over orzo and vegetables. Stir in pork; sprinkle with cheese. Cover and bake until heated through, 35-40 minutes. Uncover; broil 3-4 in. from the heat until cheese is golden brown, 4-5 minutes. If desired, top with chopped cilantro and serve with sour cream.

FREEZE OPTION Cool unbaked casserole; cover and freeze. To use, partially thaw in refrigerator overnight. Remove from the refrigerator 30 minutes before baking. Bake casserole as directed, increasing time as necessary to heat through.

NOTE Wear disposable gloves when cutting hot peppers; the oils can burn skin. Avoid touching your face.

1⅓ CUPS 559 cal., 26g fat (9g sat. fat), 105mg chol., 1509mg sod., 45g carb. (8g sugars, 5g fiber), 37g pro.

LASAGNA WITH BECHAMEL

Instead of ricotta, this lasagna layers rich and creamy bechamel sauce between cooked noodles and meat sauce.
For added color, sprinkle with chopped fresh basil or parsley before serving.

—Taste of Home *Test Kitchen*

PREP: 1 hour • **BAKE:** 50 min. + standing • **MAKES:** 12 servings

12 uncooked lasagna noodles
1½ lbs. ground beef
1 large onion, chopped
1 can (14½ oz.) diced tomatoes, undrained
1 can (15 cans) tomato sauce
2 Tbsp. tomato paste
1½ tsp. Italian seasoning
½ tsp. salt
½ tsp. pepper

BECHAMEL SAUCE
¼ cup butter, cubed
¼ cup all-purpose flour
1 tsp. salt
¼ tsp. pepper
2½ cups 2% milk

ADDITIONAL INGREDIENTS
2 cups shredded mozzarella cheese
Minced fresh parsley, optional

1. Preheat oven to 350°. Cook the noodles according to package directions for al dente; drain.

2. In a Dutch oven, cook beef and onion over medium heat until meat is no longer pink, breaking beef into crumbles; drain. Stir in tomatoes, tomato sauce, tomato paste and seasonings. Bring to a boil. Reduce heat; cover and simmer 20 minutes, stirring occasionally.

3. Meanwhile, for the bechamel sauce, melt butter in a large saucepan; stir in flour, salt and pepper until blended. Gradually whisk in milk. Bring to a boil; cook and stir until thickened, about 1 minute. Remove from the heat.

4. Arrange 3 cooked noodles in a single layer in a greased 13x9-in. baking dish. Top with ¼ of the meat sauce and ¼ of the bechamel sauce. Repeat layers 3 times. Sprinkle with mozzarella cheese.

5. Bake, uncovered, until bubbly and cheese is lightly browned, 50-55 minutes. Let stand 10 minutes before cutting. If desired, sprinkle with parsley.

1 PIECE 327 cal., 16g fat (8g sat. fat), 64mg chol., 718mg sod., 25g carb. (6g sugars, 2g fiber), 20g pro.

BAKED ZITI & SAUSAGE

This is my husband's favorite casserole, and he requests it often. He loves
the combination of zesty Italian sausage and three types of cheese.
—*Christina Ingalls, Manhattan, KS*

PREP: 25 min. • **BAKE:** 30 min. • **MAKES:** 6 servings

- 3 cups uncooked ziti or other small tube pasta
- ½ lb. Italian sausage links
- ¼ cup butter, cubed
- ¼ cup all-purpose flour
- 1½ tsp. salt, divided
- ¼ tsp. plus ⅛ tsp. pepper, divided
- 2 cups 2% milk
- ½ cup grated Parmesan cheese, divided
- 1 large egg, room temperature, lightly beaten
- 2 cups 4% cottage cheese
- 1 Tbsp. minced fresh parsley
- 1 cup shredded part-skim mozzarella cheese
  Paprika

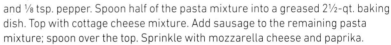

1. Cook pasta according to package directions. Preheat oven to 350°. Drain; place in a large bowl. In a small skillet, cook sausage over medium heat until no longer pink; drain and cut into ½-in. slices.

2. In a large saucepan, melt butter. Stir in the flour, 1 tsp. salt and ¼ tsp. pepper until smooth; gradually add milk. Bring to a boil; cook and stir until thickened, 2 minutes. Remove from the heat; stir in ¼ cup Parmesan cheese. Pour over pasta; toss to coat.

3. In a small bowl, combine the egg, cottage cheese, parsley, and remaining ¼ cup Parmesan cheese, ½ tsp. salt and ⅛ tsp. pepper. Spoon half of the pasta mixture into a greased 2½-qt. baking dish. Top with cottage cheese mixture. Add sausage to the remaining pasta mixture; spoon over the top. Sprinkle with mozzarella cheese and paprika.

4. Bake, uncovered, until a thermometer reads 160°, 30-35 minutes.

1 CUP 523 cal., 28g fat (14g sat. fat), 113mg chol., 1406mg sod., 42g carb. (9g sugars, 1g fiber), 27g pro.

STORING & REHEATING

Baked ziti will last in the refrigerator for 3-4 days. You can also store it in the freezer for up to 3 months. To freeze, cut it into individual portions, place each portion in a freezer bag or freezer-safe container, then reheat them for an instant individual meal.

OLD-FASHIONED MACARONI & CHEESE

Bring back the taste of days gone by with this ooey-gooey mac-and-cheese classic.
A little ground mustard and hot pepper sauce give it just the right spice.

—James Backman, Centralia, WA

PREP: 15 min. • **BAKE:** 45 min. • **MAKES:** 16 servings

3½ cups uncooked elbow macaroni
¼ cup butter, cubed
¼ cup all-purpose flour
1 tsp. salt
¾ tsp. ground mustard
½ tsp. pepper
Few dashes hot pepper sauce
3½ cups whole milk
5 cups shredded cheddar cheese, divided
Optional: Crumbled cooked bacon and coarsely ground pepper

1. Preheat oven to 350°. Cook macaroni in boiling water until almost tender; drain. Meanwhile, in a Dutch oven, melt butter over medium heat. Stir in flour, salt, mustard, pepper and pepper sauce until smooth. Cook and stir until bubbly, about 1 minute. Stir in cooked macaroni, milk and 4 cups cheese.

2. Transfer to an ungreased 13x9-in. baking dish. Cover and bake until bubbly, 45-50 minutes. Uncover; sprinkle with the remaining 1 cup cheese. Let stand for 5 minutes before serving. If desired, top with bacon and pepper.

1 CUP 267 cal., 17g fat (10g sat. fat), 48mg chol., 425mg sod., 17g carb. (3g sugars, 1g fiber), 12g pro.

SUGGESTED ADDITIONS

Use any variety of cheddar you like in this recipe (we recommend sharp), then mix in other smooth or flavorful cheeses such as fontina, muenster, Swiss or Parmesan.

If you like your mac & cheese with a crunchy topping, you can add crushed corn flakes, croutons, potato chips or Ritz crackers. One of the best options is a buttered bread crumb topping—combine 1 Tbsp. of melted butter per 2 Tbsp. dry bread crumbs and sprinkle over the mac and cheese before baking.

MEXICAN-STYLE CHICKEN MANICOTTI

Combining an Italian pasta dish with Tex-Mex ingredients created an exceptional dish.
This recipe is well liked even here in Cajun Country!
—*Larry Phillips, Shreveport, LA*

PREP: 25 min. • **BAKE:** 25 min. • **MAKES:** 2 servings

4 uncooked manicotti shells
1 cup cubed cooked chicken breast
1 cup salsa, divided
½ cup reduced-fat ricotta cheese
2 Tbsp. sliced ripe olives
4 tsp. minced fresh parsley
1 Tbsp. diced pimientos
1 green onion, thinly sliced
1 small garlic clove, minced
¼ to ½ tsp. hot pepper sauce
⅓ cup shredded Monterey Jack
   cheese

1. Cook manicotti according to package directions. In a small bowl, combine the chicken, ¼ cup salsa, ricotta cheese, olives, parsley, pimientos, green onion, garlic and pepper sauce. Drain manicotti; fill with chicken mixture.

2. Spread ¼ cup salsa in an 8-in. square baking dish coated with cooking spray. Top with manicotti shells and the remaining ½ cup salsa.

3. Cover and bake at 400° for 20 minutes. Uncover; sprinkle with Monterey Jack cheese and bake until cheese is melted and filling is heated through, 5-10 minutes longer.

2 SHELLS 352 cal., 10g fat (4g sat. fat), 71mg chol., 708mg sod., 34g carb. (6g sugars, 2g fiber), 30g pro. **DIABETIC EXCHANGES** 4 lean meat, 2 starch.

LASAGNA DELIZIOSA

Everyone loves this lasagna. It's often served as a birthday treat for guests.
I've lightened it up a lot from the original, but no one can tell the difference!
—*Heather O'Neill, Troy, OH*

PREP: 45 min. • **BAKE:** 50 min. + standing • **MAKES:** 12 servings

9   uncooked lasagna noodles
1   pkg. (19½ oz.) Italian turkey
    sausage links, casings removed
½   lb. lean ground beef (90% lean)
1   large onion, chopped
2   garlic cloves, minced
1   can (28 oz.) diced tomatoes,
    undrained
1   can (12 oz.) tomato paste
¼   cup water
2   tsp. sugar
1   tsp. dried basil
½   tsp. fennel seed
¼   tsp. pepper
1   large egg, lightly beaten
1   carton (15 oz.) reduced-fat ricotta
    cheese
1   Tbsp. minced fresh parsley
½   tsp. salt
2   cups shredded part-skim
    mozzarella cheese
¾   cup grated Parmesan cheese
    Torn fresh basil leaves, optional

1. Cook noodles according to package directions. Meanwhile, in a Dutch oven, cook and crumble sausage and beef with onion over medium heat until meat is no longer pink. Add garlic; cook 1 minute longer. Drain.

2. Stir in the tomatoes, tomato paste, water, sugar, basil, fennel and pepper. Bring to a boil. Reduce heat; cover and simmer 15-20 minutes, stirring occasionally.

3. Meanwhile, preheat oven to 375°. In a small bowl, combine the egg, ricotta cheese, parsley and salt. Drain noodles and rinse in cold water. Spread 1 cup meat sauce into a 13x9-in. baking dish coated with cooking spray. Top with 3 noodles, 2 cups meat sauce, ⅔ cup ricotta cheese mixture, ⅔ cup mozzarella and ¼ cup Parmesan cheese. Repeat layers twice.

4. Cover and bake 40 minutes. Uncover; bake 10-15 minutes longer or until bubbly. Let stand 10 minutes before cutting. If desired, top with fresh basil leaves and sprinkle with additional Parmesan cheese.

1 PIECE 323 cal., 12g fat (5g sat. fat), 79mg chol., 701mg sod., 28g carb. (11g sugars, 4g fiber), 25g pro. **DIABETIC EXCHANGES** 3 lean meat, 2 vegetable, 1 starch, 1 fat.

CHICKEN GARDEN MEDLEY

After my family sampled this cozy casserole at a friend's house, it quickly became a favorite—especially with our teenage daughters, who request it at least once a week.
—*Dohreen Winkler, Howell, MI*

PREP: 25 min. • **BAKE:** 20 min. • **MAKES:** 4 servings

1 lb. boneless skinless chicken breasts, cut into strips
1 garlic clove, minced
¼ cup butter, divided
1 small yellow squash, halved lengthwise and sliced
1 small zucchini, halved lengthwise and sliced
½ cup julienned sweet red pepper
½ cup julienned green pepper
¼ cup thinly sliced onion
2 Tbsp. all-purpose flour
½ tsp. salt
¼ tsp. pepper
¾ cup chicken broth
½ cup half-and-half cream
8 oz. angel hair pasta, cooked and drained
2 Tbsp. shredded Parmesan cheese

1. In a large skillet, saute the chicken and garlic in 2 Tbsp. butter for 10-12 minutes or until chicken juices run clear. Add vegetables. Cook until crisp-tender; remove from skillet and set aside.

2. In the same skillet, melt remaining 2 Tbsp. butter. Add flour, salt and pepper; stir to form a smooth paste. Gradually add broth. Bring to a boil; cook and stir for 2 minutes or until thickened. Stir in cream and heat through. Add chicken and vegetables; stir until well mixed.

3. Place pasta in a greased 2-qt. baking dish. Pour chicken mixture over top. Sprinkle with Parmesan cheese. Cover and bake at 350° for 15 minutes; uncover and bake 5 minutes longer.

1½ CUPS 404 cal., 19g fat (11g sat. fat), 111mg chol., 690mg sod., 26g carb. (4g sugars, 2g fiber), 30g pro.

CREAMY CAVATAPPI & CHEESE

Dive fork-first into oodles of noodles coated with a to-die-for sharp cheddar cheese sauce in this grown-up mac and cheese. Hot sauce lends a mild heat that's delectable with the smoky topping.

—*Barbara Colucci, Rockledge, FL*

PREP: 30 min. • **BAKE:** 20 min. • **MAKES:** 10 servings

- 6 cups uncooked cavatappi or spiral pasta
- 3 garlic cloves, minced
- 1/3 cup butter
- 1/4 cup all-purpose flour
- 1 Tbsp. hot pepper sauce
- 4 cups 2% milk
- 6 cups shredded sharp cheddar cheese
- 1 cup cubed Velveeta
- 3 green onions, chopped

TOPPINGS
- 1/2 cup panko bread crumbs
- 3 thick-sliced bacon strips, cooked and coarsely crumbled
- 1 Tbsp. butter, melted
- 1 green onion, chopped
  Coarsely ground pepper, optional

1. Cook cavatappi according to package directions.

2. Meanwhile, saute garlic in butter in a Dutch oven. Stir in flour and pepper sauce until blended; gradually add milk. Bring to a boil; cook and stir until thickened, about 2 minutes.

3. Stir in cheeses until melted; add green onions. Drain cavatappi; stir into cheese mixture.

4. Transfer to a greased 13x9-in. baking dish. Combine the bread crumbs, bacon and melted butter; sprinkle over top.

5. Bake, uncovered, at 350° until bubbly, 20-25 minutes. Sprinkle with green onion and, if desired, pepper.

1 CUP 706 cal., 38g fat (21g sat. fat), 110mg chol., 782mg sod., 60g carb. (8g sugars, 3g fiber), 32g pro.

PASTA SUBSTITUTION

Cavatappi is a thick, hollow, corkscrew-shaped pasta. An easy substitute for cavatappi would be large or medium elbow macaroni.

CRAB-STUFFED MANICOTTI

I love pasta, and my husband loves seafood. I combined them to create this dish, and he raved that it's the best meal ever!
—*Sonya Polfliet, Anza, CA*

PREP: 25 min. • **BAKE:** 25 min. • **MAKES:** 2 servings

4 uncooked manicotti shells
1 Tbsp. butter
4 tsp. all-purpose flour
1 cup fat-free milk
1 Tbsp. grated Parmesan cheese
1 cup lump crabmeat, drained
⅓ cup reduced-fat ricotta cheese
¼ cup shredded part-skim mozzarella cheese
¼ tsp. lemon-pepper seasoning
¼ tsp. pepper
⅛ tsp. garlic powder
  Minced fresh parsley

1. Preheat oven to 350°. Cook the manicotti shells according to package directions; drain. Meanwhile, in a small saucepan, melt butter. Stir in flour until smooth; gradually add milk. Bring to a boil; cook and stir until thickened, about 2 minutes. Remove from heat; stir in Parmesan cheese.

2. In a small bowl, combine crab, ricotta, mozzarella, lemon pepper, pepper and garlic powder. Stuff shells with the crab mixture. Spread ¼ cup sauce in an 8-in. square baking dish coated with cooking spray. Top with stuffed manicotti. Pour the remaining sauce over top.

3. Bake, covered, for 25-30 minutes or until heated through. Just before serving, sprinkle with parsley and, if desired, additional grated Parmesan cheese.

2 STUFFED SHELLS 359 cal., 12g fat (7g sat. fat), 98mg chol., 793mg sod., 38g carb. (11g sugars, 1g fiber), 26g pro. **DIABETIC EXCHANGES** 2 starch, 2 lean meat, 1 fat, ½ fat-free milk.

FIVE-CHEESE ZITI AL FORNO

After having the five-cheese ziti at Olive Garden, I tried to make my own homemade version—and
I think I got pretty close. I always double this and freeze the second one for another meal.
—*Keri Whitney, Castro Valley, CA*

PREP: 20 min. • **BAKE:** 30 min. + standing • **MAKES:** 12 servings

1½ lbs. (about 7½ cups) uncooked ziti
    or small tube pasta
2   jars (24 oz. each) marinara sauce
1   jar (15 oz.) Alfredo sauce
2   cups shredded part-skim
    mozzarella cheese, divided
½   cup reduced-fat ricotta cheese
½   cup shredded provolone cheese
½   cup grated Romano cheese

TOPPING
½   cup grated Parmesan cheese
½   cup panko bread crumbs
3   garlic cloves, minced
2   Tbsp. olive oil
    Optional: Minced fresh parsley
    or basil

1. Preheat oven to 350°. Cook the pasta according to the package directions for al dente; drain.

2. Meanwhile, in a large Dutch oven, combine the marinara sauce, Alfredo sauce, 1 cup mozzarella and the ricotta, provolone and Romano. Cook over medium heat until sauce begins to simmer and cheeses are melted. Stir in cooked pasta; pour mixture into a greased 13x9-in. baking dish. Top with remaining 1 cup mozzarella cheese.

3. For the topping, in a small bowl, stir together the Parmesan, bread crumbs, garlic and olive oil; sprinkle over the pasta.

4. Bake, uncovered, until mixture is bubbly and topping is golden brown, 30-40 minutes. Let stand 10 minutes before serving. Garnish with fresh parsley or basil if desired.

1 CUP 449 cal., 15g fat (8g sat. fat), 32mg chol., 960mg sod., 59g carb. (11g sugars, 4g fiber), 21g pro.

EASY CHICKEN TETRAZZINI

This easy chicken tetrazzini is made with leftover cooked chicken and canned soup. It's the perfect recipe for busy weeknights because it's so easy to assemble. Once you pop the dish in the oven, you'll have time to take care of other things on your to-do list.

—Martha Sue Stroud, Clarksville, TX

PREP: 15 min. • **BAKE:** 1 hour • **MAKES:** 8 servings

1 pkg. (16 oz.) uncooked spaghetti
2 Tbsp. butter
1 medium green pepper, chopped
1 medium onion, chopped
2 cups cubed cooked chicken
2 cans (4 oz. each) mushrooms, drained
1 jar (2 oz.) diced pimiento, drained
1 can (10¾ oz.) condensed cream of mushroom soup, undiluted
2 cups 2% milk
½ tsp. garlic powder
½ tsp. salt
1 to 1½ cups shredded cheddar cheese

1. Preheat oven to 350°. Cook spaghetti according to package directions.

2. Meanwhile, melt butter in a large Dutch oven over medium-high heat; add green pepper and onion. Cook and stir until vegetables are crisp-tender, 4-5 minutes. Stir in chicken, mushrooms, pimientos, soup, milk, garlic powder and salt. Drain spaghetti; add to pan and toss to coat.

3. Pour into a greased 13x9-in. baking dish. Cover and bake until hot and bubbly, 50-60 minutes. Uncover; sprinkle with cheese. Bake, uncovered, until cheese is melted, about 10 minutes.

1¼ CUPS 438 cal., 14g fat (6g sat. fat), 59mg chol., 686mg sod., 52g carb. (6g sugars, 3g fiber), 24g pro.

MAKE-AHEAD OPTIONS

You can do the prep work for this casserole in advance, and then freeze it until you're ready to bake it. After adding the spaghetti, tightly wrap the dish in foil and place it in the freezer. To use, thaw it in the refrigerator the night before and then bake as directed. Chicken tetrazzini will last in the freezer for up to 6 months.

To reheat already cooked tetrazzini, bake it in the oven at 350° until it is warm all the way through, about 20 minutes.

MOSTACCIOLI

Even though we're not Italian, this rich, cheesy pasta dish is a family tradition in our house for holidays and other special occasions. It tastes just like lasagna without the layering work.
—*Nancy Mundhenke, Kinsley, KS*

PREP: 15 min. • **BAKE:** 45 min. • **MAKES:** 12 servings

1   lb. uncooked mostaccioli
1½ lbs. bulk Italian sausage
1   jar (28 oz.) meatless spaghetti sauce
1   large egg, lightly beaten
1   carton (15 oz.) ricotta cheese
2   cups shredded part-skim mozzarella cheese
½   cup grated Romano cheese

1. Cook pasta according to package directions; drain.

2. Meanwhile, in a Dutch oven over medium heat, cook sausage until no longer pink, breaking into crumbles; drain. Stir in spaghetti sauce and pasta. In a large bowl, combine egg, ricotta cheese and mozzarella cheese.

3. Spoon half the pasta mixture into a greased shallow 3-qt. baking dish; layer with cheese mixture and remaining pasta mixture.

4. Bake, covered, at 375° for 40 minutes or until a thermometer reads 160°. Uncover; top with Romano cheese. Bake until heated through, about 5 minutes longer.

1 CUP 386 cal., 18g fat (9g sat. fat), 74mg chol., 747mg sod., 36g carb. (8g sugars, 2g fiber), 22g pro.

SEAFOOD LASAGNA

This rich, satisfying dish is loaded with scallops, shrimp and crab in a creamy sauce.
I consider it the crown jewel in my repertoire of recipes.
—*Elena Hansen, Ruidoso, NM*

PREP: 35 min. • **BAKE:** 35 min. + standing • **MAKES:** 12 servings

1   green onion, finely chopped
2   Tbsp. canola oil
2   Tbsp. plus ½ cup butter, divided
½   cup chicken broth
1   bottle (8 oz.) clam juice
1   lb. bay scallops
1   lb. uncooked shrimp (41-50 per lb.),
    peeled and deveined
1   pkg. (8 oz.) imitation crabmeat,
    chopped
¼   tsp. white pepper, divided
½   cup all-purpose flour
1½ cups 2% milk
½   tsp. salt
1   cup heavy whipping cream
½   cup shredded Parmesan cheese,
    divided
9   lasagna noodles, cooked and
    drained

1. In a large skillet, saute onion in oil and 2 Tbsp. butter until tender. Stir in broth and clam juice; bring to a boil. Add scallops, shrimp, crab and ⅛ tsp. pepper; return to a boil. Reduce heat; simmer, uncovered, for 4-5 minutes or until shrimp turn pink and scallops are firm and opaque, stirring gently. Drain, reserving cooking liquid; set seafood mixture aside.

2. In a large saucepan, melt the remaining ½ cup butter; stir in the flour until smooth. Combine milk and reserved cooking liquid; gradually add to the saucepan. Add salt and remaining ⅛ tsp. pepper. Bring to a boil; cook and stir for 2 minutes or until thickened.

3. Remove from the heat; stir in cream and ¼ cup cheese. Stir ¾ cup white sauce into the seafood mixture.

4. Preheat oven to 350°. Spread ½ cup white sauce in a greased 13x9-in. baking dish. Top with 3 noodles; spread with half of the seafood mixture and 1¼ cups sauce. Repeat layers. Top with remaining noodles, sauce and cheese.

5. Bake, uncovered, until golden brown, 35-40 minutes. Let stand 15 minutes before cutting. If desired, top with additional chopped green onions and shredded Parmesan cheese.

1 PIECE 367 cal., 22g fat (12g sat. fat), 111mg chol., 628mg sod., 24g carb. (3g sugars, 1g fiber), 19g pro.

SPINACH & SQUASH PIEROGI CASSEROLE

This recipe is tasty and quick to make—you use prepackaged ingredients for ease and then credit the cooking to yourself! The variations are endless: Choose any savory pierogi you prefer, add fresh vegetables or add spice if you want some heat. This makes a nice vegetarian meal, but you can add sliced sausage or cubed chicken if you'd like.
—*Susan Skrtich, Hamilton, ON*

PREP: 35 min. • **BAKE:** 55 min. + standing • **MAKES:** 6 servings

1 tsp. olive oil
1 medium onion, chopped
1 Tbsp. minced garlic
1 Tbsp. minced fresh basil
½ tsp. salt
½ tsp. pepper
1 cup meatless pasta sauce
1 pkg. (14 oz.) frozen potato and cheese pierogi, thawed
1½ cups frozen chopped spinach, thawed and squeezed dry
1 large egg, lightly beaten
1 cup frozen cubed butternut squash (about 5 oz.)
1½ cups shredded part-skim mozzarella cheese
½ cup sour cream, optional

1. Preheat oven to 350°. Line a 9x5-in. loaf pan with foil, letting ends extend up sides; grease foil.

2. In a small skillet, heat oil over medium-high heat. Add onion; cook and stir until tender, 6-8 minutes. Add garlic, basil, salt and pepper; cook 1 minute longer. Remove from the heat.

3. Spread ½ cup pasta sauce into prepared pan. Top with pierogi; press firmly. Top with onion mixture. Mix spinach and egg; spoon over onion mixture. Spread squash evenly over spinach; spoon remaining ½ cup pasta sauce over top. Sprinkle with cheese.

4. Bake until bubbly and cheese is golden brown, 55-65 minutes. Let stand 10 minutes. Lifting with foil, remove from pan. Cut into slices. Serve with sour cream if desired.

1 SERVING 269 cal., 9g fat (4g sat. fat), 54mg chol., 855mg sod., 33g carb. (10g sugars, 4g fiber), 14g pro.

MAKE-AHEAD SPICY OLIVE PASTA

This is a fancied-up version of my grandchildren's favorite baked spaghetti.
It feels like such a special dinner, and it's so cozy for winter.
—Louise Miller, Westminster, MD

PREP: 25 min. • **BAKE:** 1 hour + standing • **MAKES:** 10 servings

1   pkg. (16 oz.) spaghetti
1   lb. ground beef
1   medium onion, chopped
1   Tbsp. minced garlic
1   jar (24 oz.) pasta sauce
1   cup pitted ripe olives
3   Tbsp. capers, drained
3   anchovy fillets, minced
½   to ¾ tsp. crushed red pepper
    flakes
½   tsp. seasoned salt
2   large eggs
⅓   cup grated Parmesan cheese
5   Tbsp. butter, melted
2   cups 4% cottage cheese, divided
4   cups shredded part-skim
    mozzarella cheese, divided
    Optional: Minced fresh basil,
    sliced olives and capers

1. Preheat oven to 350°. Cook spaghetti according to package directions for al dente. Meanwhile, in a large skillet, cook beef, onion and garlic over medium heat until meat is no longer pink and onion is tender, 6-8 minutes, breaking up beef into crumbles; drain. Stir in pasta sauce, olives, capers, anchovies, pepper flakes and seasoned salt; set aside.

2. In a large bowl, whisk eggs, Parmesan cheese and butter. Drain spaghetti; add to egg mixture and toss to coat.

3. Place half the spaghetti mixture in a greased 13x9-in. or 3-qt. baking dish. Top with 1 cup cottage cheese, half the meat sauce and 2 cups mozzarella cheese. Repeat layers. Place baking dish on a rimmed baking sheet.

4. Cover and bake for 40 minutes. Uncover; bake until heated through, 20-25 minutes longer. Let stand 15 minutes before serving. If desired, sprinkle with basil, olives and capers.

1¼ CUPS 563 cal., 27g fat (13g sat. fat), 116mg chol., 1104mg sod., 48g carb. (10g sugars, 4g fiber), 33g pro.

WARM CHICKEN TORTELLINI AU GRATIN

I have a number of easy, planned leftover recipes in my arsenal, which are especially useful when I'm busy. This is one of my favorites: Pasta from Monday plus roasted chicken from Tuesday equals this delicious dish on Wednesday. When paired with a green salad and toasty bread, you have a meal that's fancy enough for company.

—*Brenda Cole, Reisterstown, MD*

PREP: 15 min. • **BAKE:** 30 min. • **MAKES:** 6 servings

2 cans (14 oz. each) water-packed artichoke hearts
3 cups shredded cooked chicken
3 cups refrigerated spinach tortellini, cooked
1½ cups mayonnaise
1½ cups grated Asiago cheese, divided
Fresh basil, optional

1. Preheat oven to 350°. Drain artichoke hearts, reserving ¼ cup juice. Coarsely chop; combine with chicken, tortellini, mayonnaise, 1 cup cheese and the reserved artichoke liquid. Place mixture in a greased 13x9-in. baking dish; sprinkle with remaining ½ cup cheese.

2. Bake for 30 minutes or until bubbly and starting to brown. If desired, garnish with basil.

1⅓ CUPS 709 cal., 54g fat (13g sat. fat), 101mg chol., 859mg sod., 19g carb. (1g sugars, 2g fiber), 34g pro.

PESTO LASAGNA

The bright flavor of basil takes center stage in this pesto lasagna. Paired with a rich cheese sauce and layers of noodles, it's a potluck dish that will have guests asking you for the recipe.
—Taste of Home *Test Kitchen*

PREP: 25 min. • **BAKE:** 35 min. + standing • **MAKES:** 12 servings

⅓ cup butter, cubed
1 medium onion, chopped
1 garlic clove, minced
½ cup all-purpose flour
1 tsp. salt
3½ cups 2% milk
4 cups shredded part-skim mozzarella cheese, divided
1 cup grated Parmesan cheese, divided
1 tsp. dried basil
1 tsp. dried oregano
½ tsp. white pepper
1 carton (15 oz.) whole-milk ricotta cheese
1 Tbsp. minced fresh parsley
9 lasagna noodles, cooked and drained
1 jar (8.1 oz.) prepared pesto
2 pkg. (10 oz. each) frozen chopped spinach, thawed and squeezed dry

1. Preheat oven to 350°. In a large saucepan melt butter over medium heat; add onion. Cook and stir until tender, 4-6 minutes. Add garlic; cook 1 minute longer. Stir in flour and salt until blended. Gradually whisk in milk. Bring to a boil; cook and stir until thickened, about 1 minute. Stir in 2 cups mozzarella cheese, ½ cup Parmesan cheese, basil, oregano and pepper; set aside.

2. In a large bowl, combine ricotta cheese, parsley and remaining 2 cups mozzarella; set aside. Spread about 1½ cup cheese sauce into a greased 13x9-in. baking dish; top with 3 noodles and half of each of the following: ricotta mixture, pesto and spinach. Repeat layers. Top with remaining noodles and cheese sauce. Sprinkle with remaining ½ cup Parmesan.

3. Bake, uncovered, until heated through and cheese is melted and sauce is bubbly, 35-40 minutes. Let stand 15 minutes before serving.

1 PIECE 452 cal., 27g fat (13g sat. fat), 65mg chol., 903mg sod., 31g carb. (7g sugars, 3g fiber), 23g pro.

HOMEMADE PESTO

Instead of store-bought pesto, you can make your own. To make classic pesto, place 4 cups loosely packed basil leaves, ½ cup grated Parmesan cheese, 2 garlic cloves (halved) and ¼ tsp. salt in a food processor; cover and pulse until chopped. Add ½ cup toasted pine nuts; cover and process until blended. While processing, gradually add ½ cup olive oil in a steady stream.

If you like, you can use a different type of pesto—see our recipes for Creamy Pesto, Nut-Free Pesto and Ramp Pesto in the Sauces & Crusts chapter, starting on page 252.

SASSY SOUTHWEST STUFFED SHELLS

When I was a child, my mom made this dish quite often. When I came across her recipe on an index card, I quickly copied it. Over the years, I have made very few changes because I wanted to retain that taste-of-home memory.
—*Kellie Braddell, West Point, CA*

PREP: 45 min. • **BAKE:** 35 min. • **MAKES:** 8 servings

24 uncooked jumbo pasta shells
½ lb. lean ground beef (90% lean)
½ lb. lean ground pork
1 large carrot, shredded
3 green onions, chopped
3 garlic cloves, minced
2 cans (4 oz. each) chopped green chiles
2 cups shredded Mexican cheese blend, divided
1 can (6 oz.) french-fried onions, divided
¼ cup minced fresh cilantro
1 jar (16 oz.) picante sauce
2 cans (8 oz. each) tomato sauce
1 cup water

1. Preheat oven to 350°. Cook pasta according to package directions for al dente. Drain and rinse in cold water.

2. Meanwhile, in a large skillet, cook beef and pork over medium heat until no longer pink, breaking into crumbles, 8-10 minutes; drain. Add carrot, green onions and garlic; cook 1 minute longer. Stir in chiles, 1 cup cheese, half of the french-fried onions and the cilantro. In a large bowl combine picante sauce, tomato sauce and water; stir 1 cup picante mixture into pan.

3. Spread 1 cup of the remaining picante mixture into a greased 13x9-in. baking dish. Fill pasta shells with meat mixture; place in baking dish, overlapping ends slightly. Top with remaining sauce. Cover and bake 30 minutes. Uncover; top with remaining 1 cup of cheese and remaining french-fried onions. Bake until cheese is melted, 5-10 minutes longer.

3 STUFFED SHELLS 487 cal., 26g fat (10g sat. fat), 59mg chol., 1181mg sod., 41g carb. (5g sugars, 3g fiber), 22g pro.

CHICKEN RANCH MAC & CHEESE

Prep once, feed the family twice when you double this marvelous mac to freeze half for another day.
I created it for people I love most, using ingredients they love best.
—*Angela Spengler, Niceville, FL*

PREP: 15 min. • **BAKE:** 30 min. • **MAKES:** 8 servings

3 cups uncooked elbow macaroni
3 Tbsp. butter
2 Tbsp. all-purpose flour
½ tsp. salt
¼ tsp. pepper
1 cup 2% milk
1½ cups shredded cheddar cheese
½ cup grated Parmesan cheese
½ cup shredded Swiss cheese
¾ cup ranch salad dressing
1 cup coarsely chopped cooked chicken

TOPPING

⅓ cup seasoned bread crumbs
2 Tbsp. butter, melted
10 bacon strips, cooked and crumbled
1 Tbsp. minced fresh parsley

1. Preheat oven to 350°. In a 6-qt. stockpot, cook macaroni according to package directions for al dente; drain and return to pot.

2. Meanwhile, in a medium saucepan, melt butter over medium heat. Stir in flour, salt and pepper until smooth; gradually whisk in milk. Bring to a boil, stirring constantly; cook and stir until thickened, 1-2 minutes. Stir in cheeses until blended. Stir in dressing.

3. Add chicken and sauce to macaroni, tossing to combine. Transfer to a greased 13x9-in. baking dish.

4. For topping, toss bread crumbs with melted butter; sprinkle over macaroni. Top with bacon. Bake, uncovered, 30-35 minutes or until topping is golden brown. Sprinkle with parsley.

FREEZE OPTION Prepare recipe as directed, increasing milk to 1⅓ cups. Cool unbaked casserole; cover and freeze. To use, partially thaw in refrigerator overnight. Remove from refrigerator 30 minutes before baking. Preheat oven to 350°. Cover casserole with foil; bake 30 minutes. Uncover; continue baking as directed or until heated through and a thermometer inserted in center reads 165°.

1 CUP 586 cal., 37g fat (15g sat. fat), 84mg chol., 889mg sod., 40g carb. (4g sugars, 2g fiber), 25g pro.

TUSCAN-STYLE
ROASTED
ASPARAGUS
(PAGE 247)

SIDE DISHES

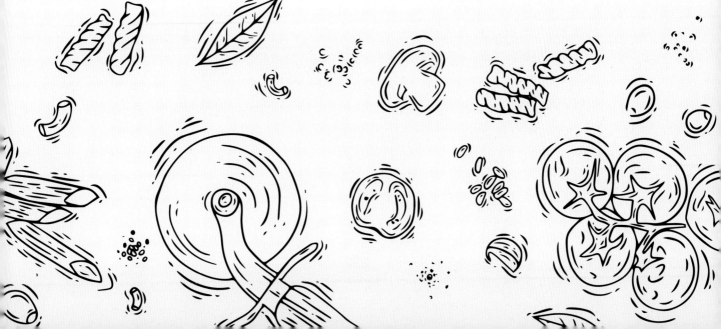

FAVORITE MARINATED MUSHROOMS

Here's a great way to prepare mushrooms. I'll serve them as a side dish, an appetizer on their own, as part of an antipasto platter or add them to salads for a tangy flavor.
—*Brenda Snyder, Hesston, PA*

PREP: 15 min. + marinating • **MAKES:** 4 cups

2   lbs. fresh mushrooms
1   envelope (0.7 oz.) Italian salad dressing mix
1   cup water
½   cup olive oil
⅓   cup cider vinegar
2   Tbsp. lemon juice
1   Tbsp. sugar
1   Tbsp. minced fresh parsley
1   Tbsp. reduced-sodium soy sauce
2   tsp. crushed red pepper flakes
3   garlic cloves, minced
½   tsp. salt
⅛   tsp. pepper

1. Remove mushroom stems (discard or save for another use). Place caps in a large saucepan and cover with water. Bring to a boil. Reduce heat; cook for 3 minutes, stirring occasionally. Drain and cool.

2. In a small bowl, whisk salad dressing mix and the next 11 ingredients. Place mushrooms in a large bowl; add dressing and stir to coat. Refrigerate, covered, 8 hours or overnight.

½ **CUP** 166 cal., 14g fat (2g sat. fat), 0 chol., 602mg sod., 9g carb. (5g sugars, 2g fiber), 4g pro.

HOW LONG WILL THEY LAST?

This is a great recipe to make in advance. Make sure the mushrooms you use are fresh when you start, and marinated mushrooms will last in the refrigerator in an airtight container for up to 10 days.

🕐 GNOCCHI WITH MUSHROOMS & ONION

Tender potato gnocchi are so delicious with the earthy, rich flavors of sauteed mushrooms and onions. It's one of my family's go-to side dishes.

—*Kris Berezansky, Clymer, PA*

TAKES: 20 min. • **MAKES:** 5 servings

1   pkg. (16 oz.) potato gnocchi
½   lb. sliced fresh mushrooms
¾   cup chopped sweet onion
¼   cup butter, cubed
¼   tsp. salt
¼   tsp. Italian seasoning
¼   tsp. crushed red pepper flakes
    Grated Parmesan cheese

1. Cook gnocchi according to package directions. Meanwhile, in a large cast-iron skillet, saute mushrooms and onion in butter until tender.

2. Drain gnocchi. Add gnocchi, salt, Italian seasoning and pepper flakes to the skillet; heat through. Sprinkle with cheese.

NOTE Look for potato gnocchi in pasta or frozen foods section.

¾ CUP 287 cal., 11g fat (6g sat. fat), 31mg chol., 583mg sod., 41g carb. (7g sugars, 3g fiber), 8g pro.

ADJUST THE HEAT

The crushed red pepper flakes add a pleasant kick—but you can easily just skip them if your family prefers mild flavors.

PRESSURE-COOKER SICILIAN STEAMED LEEKS

I love the challenge of developing recipes for the fresh leeks from my garden, a delicious but underused vegetable. This Italian-flavored dish is a family favorite.
—*Roxanne Chan, Albany, CA*

PREP: 10 min. • **COOK:** 5 min. • **MAKES:** 6 servings

1 large tomato, chopped
1 small navel orange, peeled, sectioned and chopped
2 Tbsp. minced fresh parsley
2 Tbsp. sliced Greek olives
1 tsp. capers, drained
1 tsp. red wine vinegar
1 tsp. olive oil
½ tsp. grated orange zest
½ tsp. pepper
6 medium leeks (white portion only), halved lengthwise, cleaned
Crumbled feta cheese

1. Combine first 9 ingredients; set aside. Place trivet insert and 1 cup water in a 6-qt. electric pressure cooker. Set leeks on trivet. Lock lid; close pressure-release valve. Adjust to pressure-cook on high 2 minutes. Quick-release pressure.

2. Transfer leeks to a serving platter. Spoon tomato mixture on top; sprinkle with cheese.

1 SERVING 83 cal., 2g fat (0 sat. fat), 0 chol., 77mg sod., 16g carb. (6g sugars, 3g fiber), 2g pro. **DIABETIC EXCHANGES** 1 starch, ½ fat.

ROASTED ARTICHOKES WITH LEMON AIOLI

Petals of savory artichoke leaves are so delicious dipped into a creamy lemon aioli.
It may seem intimidating to roast whole artichokes, but the steps couldn't be simpler—
and the earthy, comforting flavor is a definite payoff.
—Taste of Home *Test Kitchen*

PREP: 20 min. • **BAKE:** 50 min. • **MAKES:** 4 servings

4   medium artichokes
2   Tbsp. olive oil
½   medium lemon
½   tsp. salt
¼   tsp. pepper

AIOLI
¼   cup mayonnaise
¼   cup plain Greek yogurt
½   tsp. minced fresh garlic
¼   tsp. grated lemon zest
     Dash pepper

1. Preheat oven to 400°. Using a sharp knife, cut 1 in. from top of each artichoke. Using kitchen scissors, cut off tips of outer leaves. Cut each artichoke lengthwise in half. With a spoon, carefully scrape and remove fuzzy center of artichokes.

2. Drizzle oil into a 15x10x1-in. baking pan. Rub cut surfaces of artichokes with lemon half; sprinkle with salt and pepper. Place in pan, cut side down. Squeeze lemon juice over artichokes. Cover pan with foil; bake on a lower oven rack until tender and a leaf near center pulls out easily, 50-55 minutes.

3. Meanwhile, mix aioli ingredients; refrigerate until serving. Serve with artichokes.

2 HALVES WITH 2 TBSP. AIOLI 233 cal., 19g fat (3g sat. fat), 5mg chol., 446mg sod., 16g carb. (2g sugars, 7g fiber), 4g pro.

CLEANING ARTICHOKES

To clean an artichoke, rinse under cold water. Use a soft kitchen brush to gently remove a natural, light film that can give artichokes a bitter taste. The edible parts of an artichoke are the base of the petals, the center core of the stem and the heart. The fuzzy choke at the center is not edible.

SPICY POTATOES WITH GARLIC AIOLI

These potatoes are tossed in a flavorful spice mix and then finished to a crispy golden brown. The garlic aioli takes it over the top for an unconventional potato appetizer or side that'll be a hit at any party.
—*John Stiver, Bowen Island, BC*

PREP: 35 min. • **BAKE:** 25 min. • **MAKES:** 10 servings (1¾ cups aioli)

3 lbs. medium Yukon Gold potatoes, cut into 1½-in. cubes (about 8 potatoes)
2 Tbsp. olive oil
2 garlic cloves, minced
2 Tbsp. smoked paprika
2 tsp. garlic powder
1½ tsp. chili powder
1½ tsp. ground cumin
¼ tsp. salt
¼ tsp. crushed red pepper flakes
⅛ tsp. pepper

AIOLI
1½ cups mayonnaise
3 Tbsp. lemon juice
3 garlic cloves, minced
1 Tbsp. minced fresh chives plus additional for topping
1 tsp. red wine vinegar
¼ tsp. salt
¼ tsp. pepper

1. Preheat oven to 375°. Place potatoes in a Dutch oven; add water to cover. Bring to a boil. Reduce heat; cook, uncovered, 8-10 minutes or until just tender. Drain; pat dry with paper towels. Transfer potatoes to a mixing bowl. Toss potatoes in oil and minced garlic to coat evenly.

2. Combine paprika, garlic powder, chili powder, cumin, salt, pepper flakes and pepper; sprinkle over potatoes. Gently toss to coat. Transfer potatoes to 2 greased 15x10x1-in. baking pans, spreading into a single layer. Bake until crispy, about 25 minutes, stirring potatoes and rotating pans halfway through cooking.

3. For aioli, combine ingredients until blended. Transfer potatoes to a serving platter; sprinkle with chives. Serve warm with aioli.

¾ CUP POTATOES WITH ABOUT 3 TBSP. AIOLI 469 cal., 34g fat (5g sat. fat), 3mg chol., 396mg sod., 37g carb. (3g sugars, 4g fiber), 5g pro.

SAVE THE SPICE BLEND

The seasoning blend gives these potatoes a nice kick; smoked paprika makes them taste as if they were cooked over an open fire. Remember this spice mix the next time you're prepping Tater Tots, fries, or another plain potato, and sprinkle some on for an upgrade.

OVEN-ROASTED TOMATOES

I love tomatoes, as they're both healthy and versatile. You can use
these roasted ones in sandwiches or omelets, or to top broiled chicken.

—*Julie Tilney (Gomez), Downey, CA*

PREP: 20 min. • **BAKE:** 3 hours + cooling • **MAKES:** 16 servings (4 cups)

20 plum tomatoes (about 5 lbs.)
¼ cup olive oil
5 tsp. Italian seasoning
2½ tsp. salt

1. Cut tomatoes into ½-in. slices. Brush with oil; sprinkle with Italian seasoning and salt.

2. Place on racks coated with cooking spray in foil-lined 15x10x1-in. baking pans. Bake, uncovered, at 325° for 3-3½ hours or until tomatoes start to turn dark brown around edges and are shriveled. Cool for 10-15 minutes. Serve warm or at room temperature.

3. Store in an airtight container in the refrigerator for up to 1 week.

FREEZE OPTION Place in airtight freezer container; freeze for up to 3 months. Bring tomatoes to room temperature before using.

¼ CUP 45 cal., 4g fat (0 sat. fat), 0 chol., 373mg sod., 3g carb. (2g sugars, 1g fiber), 1g pro.

"My oven is convection and they cooked much quicker, but still were so delicious. I used only salt and pepper since I was using them in another recipe that called for a heavy seasoning."
—JMARTINELLI13, TASTEOFHOME.COM

RUSTIC TOMATO PIE

Perk up your plate with this humble tomato pie. We like to use fresh-from-the-garden tomatoes and herbs, but store-bought produce will work in a pinch.
—Taste of Home *Test Kitchen*

PREP: 15 min. Bake 30 min. + standing • **MAKES:** 8 servings

Dough for single-crust pie
1¾ lbs. mixed tomatoes, seeded and cut into ½-in. slices
¼ cup thinly sliced green onions
½ cup mayonnaise
½ cup shredded cheddar cheese
2 Tbsp. minced fresh basil
¼ tsp. salt
¼ tsp. pepper
2 bacon strips, cooked and crumbled
2 Tbsp. grated Parmesan cheese

1. Preheat oven to 400°. On a lightly floured surface, roll dough to a ⅛-in.-thick circle; transfer to a 9-in. pie plate. Trim crust to ½ in. beyond rim of plate.

2. Place half the tomatoes and half the onions in crust. Combine mayonnaise, cheddar cheese, basil, salt and pepper; spread over tomatoes. Top with remaining onions and tomatoes. Fold crust edge over filling, pleating as you go and leaving an 8-in. opening in center. Sprinkle with bacon and Parmesan cheese. Bake on a lower oven rack until crust is golden and filling is bubbly, 30-35 minutes. Let stand 10 minutes before cutting. If desired, sprinkle with additional basil.

DOUGH FOR SINGLE-CRUST PIE Combine 1¼ cups all-purpose flour and ¼ tsp. salt; cut in ½ cup cold butter until crumbly. Gradually add 3-5 Tbsp. ice water, tossing with a fork until dough holds together when pressed. Shape into a disk; wrap and refrigerate 1 hour.

1 PIECE 325 cal., 25g fat (11g sat. fat), 41mg chol., 409mg sod., 19g carb. (3g sugars, 2g fiber), 6g pro.

SICILIAN BRUSSELS SPROUTS

I love to make this dish because the flavors jumping around in your mouth keep you coming back bite after bite. Other nuts can be used in place of the pine nuts.
—Marsha Gillett, Yukon, OK

PREP: 30 min. • **BAKE:** 15 min. • **MAKES:** 12 servings

12 oz. pancetta, diced
2 lbs. fresh Brussels sprouts, halved
3 Tbsp. capers, drained
¼ cup olive oil
3 Tbsp. champagne vinegar
1 tsp. lemon juice
¼ tsp. salt
¼ tsp. pepper
¾ cup golden raisins
½ cup pine nuts, toasted
1 tsp. grated lemon zest

1. In a large cast-iron or other ovenproof skillet, cook pancetta over medium heat until browned. Remove to paper towels with a slotted spoon.

2. Add Brussels sprouts to pan; cook and stir until lightly browned. Remove from heat. Stir in capers, oil, vinegar, lemon juice, salt and pepper.

3. Bake, uncovered, at 350° until caramelized, stirring occasionally, 15-20 minutes. Add raisins, pine nuts, lemon zest and pancetta; toss to coat.

¾ CUP 235 cal., 17g fat (4g sat. fat), 23mg chol., 723mg sod., 15g carb. (8g sugars, 4g fiber), 9g pro.

ABOUT CAPERS

Capers are the immature buds from a small bush native to the Middle East and Mediterranean regions; the buds are either brined in vinegar or packed in coarse salt to preserve them. Capers are best rinsed before using and are often used in French-, Italian- and Greek-style dishes.

⏱ ROASTED FENNEL & PEPPERS

Fennel makes for a tasty change of pace in this versatile side that goes nicely with grilled meats.
Best of all, it's full of flavor and easy to do—and it doesn't seem light at all!
—Taste of Home *Test Kitchen*

TAKES: 30 min. • **MAKES:** 6 servings

2 fennel bulbs, halved and sliced
2 medium sweet red peppers,
　cut into 1-in. pieces
1 medium onion, cut into 1-in. pieces
3 garlic cloves, minced
1 Tbsp. olive oil
½ tsp. salt
½ tsp. pepper
½ tsp. rubbed sage
　Fresh sage leaves, thinly sliced,
　optional

1. Place fennel, peppers, onion and garlic in a 15x10x1-in. baking pan coated with cooking spray. Drizzle with oil; sprinkle with salt, pepper and rubbed sage. Toss to coat.

2. Bake, uncovered, at 425° until tender, 20-25 minutes, stirring twice. Garnish with fresh sage if desired.

⅔ CUP 67 cal., 3g fat (0 sat. fat), 0 chol., 240mg sod., 10g carb. (5g sugars, 4g fiber), 2g pro. **DIABETIC EXCHANGES** 1 vegetable, ½ fat.

"I sauteed this in the summer, when it was too hot to turn the oven on. It was wonderful!"
—JOANRCOOK, TASTEOFHOME.COM

EGGPLANT PARMESAN

We really like eggplant and would rather have it baked than fried.
This can be served as a side or a main dish.
—*Donna Wardlow-Keating, Omaha, NE*

PREP: 10 min. • **BAKE:** 45 min. + cooling • **MAKES:** 2 servings

2 Tbsp. olive oil
1 garlic clove, minced
1 small eggplant, peeled and cut into ¼-in. slices
1 Tbsp. minced fresh basil or 1 tsp. dried basil
1 Tbsp. grated Parmesan cheese
1 medium tomato, thinly sliced
½ cup shredded mozzarella cheese
   Additional basil, optional

1. Combine oil and garlic; brush over both sides of eggplant slices. Place on a greased baking sheet. Bake at 425° for 15 minutes; turn. Bake until golden brown, about 5 minutes longer. Cool on a wire rack. Reduce oven setting to 350°.

2. Place half the eggplant in a greased 1-qt. baking dish. Sprinkle with half the basil and half the Parmesan cheese. Arrange tomato slices over top; sprinkle with remaining basil and Parmesan. Layer with half the mozzarella cheese and remaining eggplant; top with remaining mozzarella. Cover and bake for 20 minutes. Uncover; bake until cheese is melted, 5-7 minutes longer. Garnish with additional basil if desired.

1 SERVING 275 cal., 21g fat (6g sat. fat), 24mg chol., 164mg sod., 16g carb. (9g sugars, 5g fiber), 9g pro.

"Exceptionally good recipe. It's just perfect, especially if you indulge in fresh mozzarella. I made this for a friend who loves eggplant Parmesan and fatty foods, and he dubbed this the best ever. The fresher the ingredients, the better."
—SUMMY, TASTEOFHOME.COM

PORTOBELLO RISOTTO WITH MASCARPONE

Portobello mushrooms add a beefy flavor to this creamy classic. Each serving is topped with soft, buttery mascarpone cheese, which makes it extra special.

—Carmella Ryan, Rockville Centre, NY

PREP: 20 min. • **COOK:** 25 min. • **MAKES:** 6 servings

1½ cups water
1 can (14 oz.) reduced-sodium beef broth
½ cup chopped shallots
2 garlic cloves, minced
1 Tbsp. canola oil
1 cup uncooked arborio rice
1 Tbsp. minced fresh thyme or 1 tsp. dried thyme
½ tsp. salt
½ tsp. pepper
½ cup white wine or additional reduced-sodium beef broth
1 cup sliced baby portobello mushrooms, chopped
¼ cup grated Parmesan cheese
½ cup mascarpone cheese

1. In a saucepan, heat water and beef broth and keep warm. In another large saucepan, saute shallots and garlic in oil for 2-3 minutes or until shallots are tender. Add rice, thyme, salt and pepper; cook and stir for 2-3 minutes. Reduce heat; stir in wine. Cook and stir until all the liquid is absorbed.

2. Add heated broth, ½ cup at a time, stirring constantly. Allow liquid to absorb between additions. Cook just until risotto is creamy and rice is almost tender, about 20 minutes.

3. Add mushrooms and Parmesan cheese; stir gently until cheese is melted. Garnish each serving with 1 heaping Tbsp. of mascarpone. Serve immediately.

FREEZE OPTION Before adding mascarpone cheese, freeze cooled risotto mixture in freezer containers. To use, partially thaw in refrigerator overnight. Heat through in a saucepan, stirring occasionally; add broth or water if necessary. Garnish as directed.

¾ CUP RISOTTO MIXTURE WITH 1 HEAPING TBSP. MARSCARPONE CHEESE 350 cal., 21g fat (10g sat. fat), 51mg chol., 393mg sod., 31g carb. (1g sugars, 1g fiber), 7g pro.

TUSCAN-STYLE ROASTED ASPARAGUS

This is especially wonderful when locally grown asparagus is in season.
It's so easy for celebrations because you can serve it hot or cold.

—*Jannine Fisk, Malden, MA*

PREP: 20 min. • **BAKE:** 15 min. • **MAKES:** 8 servings

1½ lbs. fresh asparagus, trimmed
1½ cups grape tomatoes, halved
3 Tbsp. pine nuts
3 Tbsp. olive oil, divided
2 garlic cloves, minced
1 tsp. kosher salt
½ tsp. pepper
1 Tbsp. lemon juice
⅓ cup grated Parmesan cheese
1 tsp. grated lemon zest

1. Preheat oven to 400°. Place asparagus, tomatoes and pine nuts on a foil-lined 15x10x1-in. baking pan. Mix 2 Tbsp. oil, garlic, salt and pepper; add to asparagus and toss to coat.

2. Bake 15-20 minutes or just until asparagus is tender. Drizzle with remaining 1 Tbsp. oil and lemon juice; sprinkle with cheese and lemon zest. Toss to combine.

1 SERVING 95 cal., 8g fat (2g sat. fat), 3mg chol., 294mg sod., 4g carb. (2g sugars, 1g fiber), 3g pro. **DIABETIC EXCHANGES** 1½ fat, 1 vegetable.

WHICH OLIVE OIL?

Common olive oil works better for cooking at high heat than virgin or extra-virgin oil. The higher grades have ideal flavor for cold foods, but they smoke at lower temperatures, so when it comes to roasting, stick with regular olive oil

PARMESAN RISOTTO

Risotto is a creamy Italian rice dish. In this version, the rice is briefly sauteed, then slowly cooked in wine and seasonings. Watch for that magic moment when the risotto transforms from just rice in liquid to creamy, tender deliciousness.
—Taste of Home *Test Kitchen*

PREP: 15 min. • **COOK:** 30 min. • **MAKES:** 12 servings

8 cups chicken broth
½ cup finely chopped onion
¼ cup olive oil
3 cups arborio rice
2 garlic cloves, minced
1 cup dry white wine or water
½ cup shredded Parmesan cheese
¼ tsp. salt
¼ tsp. pepper
3 Tbsp. minced fresh parsley

1. In a saucepan, heat broth and keep warm. In a Dutch oven, saute onion in oil until tender. Add rice and garlic; cook and stir for 2-3 minutes. Reduce heat; stir in wine. Cook and stir until all liquid is absorbed.

2. Add heated broth, ½ cup at a time, stirring constantly and allowing liquid to absorb between additions. Cook just until risotto is creamy and rice is almost tender, about 20 minutes. Add remaining ingredients; cook and stir until heated through. Serve immediately.

¾ CUP 260 cal., 6g fat (1g sat. fat), 2mg chol., 728mg sod., 41g carb. (1g sugars, 1g fiber), 6g pro.

SAUSAGE MUSHROOM RISOTTO Reduce olive oil to 2 Tbsp. In a large skillet, cook 1 lb. bulk Italian sausage over medium heat until meat is no longer pink; drain. Set aside and keep warm. Add onion, oil and ½ lb. quartered fresh mushrooms to skillet and cook until tender. Proceed as directed.

ASPARAGUS RISOTTO Trim 1 lb. asparagus and cut into 2-in. pieces. Place asparagus in a large saucepan; add ½ in. water. Bring to a boil. Reduce heat; cover and simmer for 3 minutes or until crisp-tender. Drain and set aside. Stir into risotto just before serving.

ORZO WITH CARAMELIZED BUTTERNUT SQUASH & BACON

The year my garden produced a bumper crop of butternut squash, I made so many new dishes trying to use up my bounty! This is a tasty, easy side with pretty colors, and it makes plenty to fill your hungry family. To make it into a main dish, add shrimp or shredded chicken.

—*Kallee Krong-McCreery, Escondido, CA*

PREP: 20 min. • **COOK:** 20 min. • **MAKES:** 6 servings

1½ cups uncooked orzo pasta
4 bacon strips, chopped
2 cups cubed peeled butternut squash (½-in. cubes)
½ cup chopped onion
1 cup cut fresh or frozen green beans, thawed
1 garlic clove, minced
1 Tbsp. butter
1 tsp. garlic salt
¼ tsp. pepper
¼ cup grated Parmesan cheese
Minced fresh parsley

1. In a large saucepan, cook orzo according to package directions.

2. Meanwhile, in a large skillet, cook bacon over medium heat until crisp, stirring occasionally. Remove with a slotted spoon; drain on paper towels. Cook and stir squash and onion in bacon drippings for 8-10 minutes or until tender. Add beans and garlic; cook 1 minute longer.

3. Drain orzo; stir into squash mixture. Add butter, garlic salt, pepper and bacon; heat through. Sprinkle with Parmesan cheese and parsley.

¾ CUP 329 cal., 11g fat (4g sat. fat), 20mg chol., 533mg sod., 47g carb. (4g sugars, 3g fiber), 11g pro.

⏲ CREAMY PUMPKIN TORTELLINI

My kids love the creamy, rich sauce on these tortellinis so much that they don't even realize there's pumpkin inside. Use freshly grated Parmesan cheese for the best nutty and delicious flavor.
—*Trisha Kruse, Eagle, ID*

TAKES: 30 min. • **MAKES:** 6 servings

2 pkg. (9 oz. each) refrigerated cheese tortellini
1 Tbsp. butter
3 Tbsp. finely chopped onion
1 cup canned pumpkin
   Pinch ground nutmeg
1 cup half-and-half cream
¼ cup grated Parmesan cheese
½ tsp. salt
¼ tsp. pepper
1 Tbsp. minced fresh parsley
   Additional grated or shredded Parmesan, optional

1. Cook tortellini according to package directions; drain, reserving ½ cup cooking liquid.

2. Meanwhile, in a large nonstick skillet, heat butter over medium heat. Add onion; cook and stir 1-2 minutes or until tender. Add pumpkin and nutmeg; cook and stir 1 minute longer. Stir in cream; bring to a boil. Reduce heat to medium-low; simmer, uncovered, 4-5 minutes or until thickened, stirring occasionally. Remove from heat; stir in cheese, salt and pepper.

3. Add tortellini; toss with sauce, adding enough reserved pasta water to coat pasta. Sprinkle with parsley and, if desired, additional cheese.

1 CUP 363 cal., 14g fat (8g sat. fat), 65mg chol., 610mg sod., 45g carb. (5g sugars, 3g fiber), 14g pro.

GLUTEN-FREE
PIZZA CRUST
(PAGE 266)

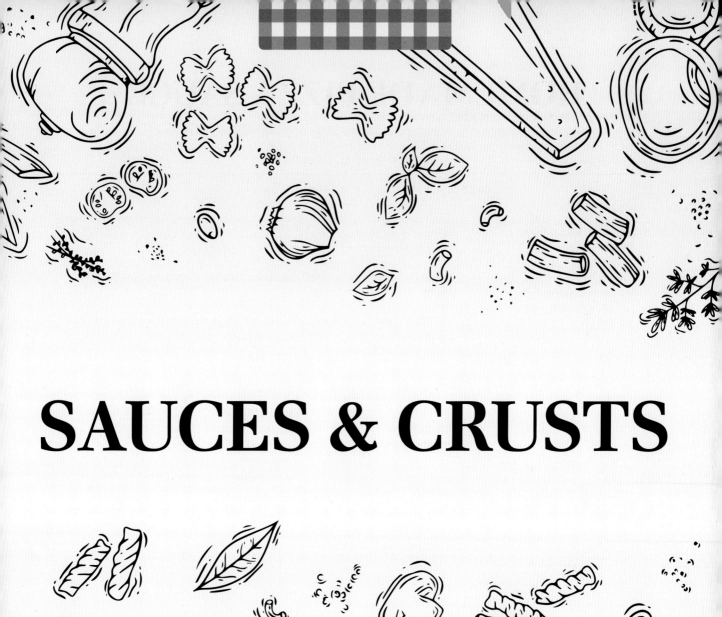

SAUCES & CRUSTS

HOMEMADE PIZZA SAUCE

For years, I had trouble finding a pizza sauce my family liked, so I started making my own. The evening I served it to company and they asked for my recipe, I knew I'd finally gotten it right! When I prepare my sauce, I usually fix enough for three to four pizzas and freeze it. Feel free to spice up the sauce to suit your own taste.

—*Cheryl Kravik, Spanaway, WA*

PREP: 10 min. • **COOK:** 70 min. • **MAKES:** about 4 cups

2 cans (15 oz. each) tomato sauce
1 can (12 oz.) tomato paste
1 Tbsp. Italian seasoning
1 Tbsp. dried oregano
1 to 2 tsp. fennel seed, crushed
1 tsp. onion powder
1 tsp. garlic powder
½ tsp. salt

1. In a large saucepan over medium heat, combine tomato sauce and paste. Add remaining ingredients; mix well. Bring to a boil, stirring constantly. Reduce heat; cover and simmer for 1 hour, stirring occasionally. Cool.

¼ CUP 26 cal., 0 fat (0 sat. fat), 0 chol., 189mg sod., 6g carb. (3g sugars, 2g fiber), 1g pro.

FREEZE OPTION Pour cooled sauce into jars or freezer containers, leaving ½ in. headspace. Freeze up to 12 months. Thaw frozen sauce in refrigerator overnight before serving.

"I have tried at least six homemade pizza sauce recipes— this one is the best! It was delicious when I first made it, and today I used the sauce I had frozen, and it was perfect!"
—KELLY FLAHERTY, TASTEOFHOME.COM

CAULIFLOWER PIZZA CRUST

Make your next pizza night a little healthier with this recipe.
The herbs and cheese add a ton of flavor to the pizza crust!
—Taste of Home *Test Kitchen*

PREP: 30 min. • **BAKE:** 30 min+ cooling • **MAKES:** 6 servings

1½ heads cauliflower (about 1½ lbs.), chopped (about 6 cups)
½ cup shredded part-skim mozzarella cheese
½ cup grated Parmesan cheese
1 large egg, lightly beaten
1 tsp. dried oregano
1 tsp. garlic powder
½ tsp. salt

1. Preheat oven to 425°. Working in batches, place cauliflower in food processor; process until finely ground. Transfer to a large microwave-safe bowl; repeat with remaining cauliflower. Microwave, covered, until cauliflower is tender, about 8 minutes. When cool enough to handle, squeeze dry; return to bowl.

2. Stir in remaining ingredients until combined. Line a baking sheet with parchment. Press and shape cauliflower mixture into an 10-in. circle or 13x6-in. oval.

3. Bake for 20-25 minutes or until edge is browned. Add toppings of your choice. Bake until toppings are heated through, 10-12 minutes longer.

1 PIECE 71 cal., 4g fat (2g sat. fat), 32mg chol., 316mg sod., 5g carb. (2g sugars, 2g fiber), 5g pro. **DIABETIC EXCHANGES1** medium-fat meat, 1 vegetable.

MARINARA SAUCE

My mother, who was Italian American, called marinara sauce "gravy." She made
this sauce in big batches several times a month, so it was a staple on our dinner table.
A mouthwatering aroma filled the house each time she cooked it.

—James Grimes, Frenchtown, NJ

PREP: 20 min. • **COOK:** 1 hour • **MAKES:** 5 cups

3   Tbsp. extra virgin olive oil
1   large onion, finely chopped
4   garlic cloves, minced
2   cans (28 oz. each) whole tomatoes
¼   cup chopped fresh basil
1½ tsp. dried oregano
¾   tsp. salt
¼   tsp. pepper

In a large saucepan, heat oil over
medium-high heat. Add onions; cook
and stir until tender, 3-5 minutes.
Add garlic; cook and stir 1 minute
longer. Stir in remaining ingredients.
Bring to a boil. Reduce heat; cover
and simmer until thickened and
flavors are blended, 30-45 minutes,
stirring occasionally and breaking up
tomatoes with a wooden spoon.

½ CUP 44 cal., 4g fat (1g sat. fat), 0 chol.,
178mg sod., 2g carb. (1g sugars, 0 fiber),
0 pro.

WHY MAKE YOUR OWN?

There are quite a few benefits to making your own marinara sauce.
First off, homemade marinara is free of sugars and preservatives,
and you know everything that is inside it. Plus, you can customize the
flavors to your liking. Try adding roasted garlic, sun-dried tomatoes
in oil, roasted red peppers and fresh oregano (instead of dried). You
could also add tomato paste to thicken your sauce and add a deeper
tomato flavor.

⏱ RAMP PESTO

Flavorful ramp pesto is a great way to extend the short season that ramps are available. Use it in all the delicious ways you'd use traditional pesto—toss it with pasta, spread it on sandwiches or pizza, or serve it with grilled fish or chicken. If you don't have enough ramps for this recipe, you can add basil, parsley or cilantro to make up the difference.
—Taste of Home *Test Kitchen*

TAKES: 10 min. • **MAKES:** 2 cups

10 oz. ramps (bulbs and greens), about 30 medium
½ cup grated Parmesan cheese
2 garlic cloves, halved
1 tsp. salt
½ cup pine nuts
½ cup olive oil

1. In a small saucepan, bring 8 cups water to a boil. Add ramps; cook, uncovered, just until ramps turn bright green, about 30 seconds. Drain and immediately drop into ice water. Drain and pat dry.

2. Place ramps, cheese, garlic and salt in a food processor; cover and pulse until chopped. Add nuts; cover and process until blended. While processing, gradually add oil in a steady stream. Store in an airtight container in the refrigerator for up to 5 days or freeze for up to 1 year.

2 TBSP. 105 cal., 10g fat (2g sat. fat), 2mg chol., 196mg sod., 2g carb. (1g sugars, 1g fiber), 2g pro.

IS BLANCHING A MUST?

Blanching the ramps before making the pesto helps prevent the vibrant green color from turning brown due to oxidation. If you don't have time to blanch, you can skip this step. The pesto will be safe to eat, even though the color will change. Blanching the herbs for homemade basil or parsley pesto will also help maintain their bright green color.

⏱ VEGAN BECHAMEL SAUCE

As one of the original classic "mother sauces," bechamel is a vital part of a wide variety
of recipes, including casseroles, white lasagnas and mac and cheese.
(For the classic version of this sauce, see Lasagna with Bechamel Sauce, page 206.)
—Taste of Home *Test Kitchen*

TAKES: 20 min. • **MAKES:** 4 servings (2 cups)

3 Tbsp. vegan butter-style sticks,
   such as Earth Balance
2 Tbsp. all-purpose flour
1½ cups unsweetened refrigerated
   soy milk
2 Tbsp. nutritional yeast
½ tsp. salt
¼ tsp. pepper
   Dash ground nutmeg
   Hot cooked pasta

In a small saucepan, melt vegan butter over medium heat. Stir in flour until smooth; gradually whisk in soy milk. Bring to a boil, stirring constantly. Remove from heat; stir in nutritional yeast, salt, pepper and nutmeg until smooth. Let rest 3 minutes or until thickened. Serve with pasta.

½ CUP 135 cal., 10g fat (4g sat. fat), 0 chol., 433mg sod., 7g carb. (2g sugars, 1g fiber), 4g pro.

HOW TO PREVENT LUMPS

Add the flour gradually, while constantly stirring; adding the flour all at once will make it harder to incorporate. Use a whisk to stir in your ingredients, and keep stirring while the sauce comes to a boil. Stir the sauce once more after it has thickened to make sure it is smooth.

⏱ NUT-FREE PESTO

This pesto recipe was handed down from my grandmother. Nuts were considered a filler in my Italian family, so this recipe does without them and just uses the good stuff! Everyone I serve this to says it's the best.
—*Mary Jo Galick, Portland, OR*

TAKES: 10 min. • **MAKES:** 1 cup

2 cups loosely packed basil leaves
1 cup grated Parmesan cheese
1 cup packed fresh parsley sprigs
3 Tbsp. butter, softened
2 garlic cloves, halved
¼ tsp. salt
½ cup extra virgin olive oil

Place first 6 ingredients in a food processor; pulse until coarsely chopped. While processing, gradually add oil in a steady stream until mixture is smooth. Store in an airtight container in refrigerator for up to 1 week.

2 TBSP. 206 cal., 21g fat (6g sat. fat), 20mg chol., 293mg sod., 2g carb. (0 sugars, 0 fiber), 3g pro.

HOMEMADE ALFREDO SAUCE

When I found out I had celiac disease and could no longer have fettuccine Alfredo, I was determined
to figure out a way to re-create it. This has now become one of my most-requested dishes.
I use gluten-free multigrain pasta, but you can use any style of pasta.
—*Jackie Charlesworth Stiff, Frederick, CO*

PREP: 20 min. • **COOK:** 20 min. • **MAKES:** 6 servings

3 Tbsp. butter
½ cup finely chopped shallots
5 garlic cloves, minced
2 cups heavy whipping cream
1¼ cups shredded Asiago cheese
1 cup grated Parmesan cheese,
   divided
¾ cup grated Romano cheese
¼ tsp. salt
¼ tsp. pepper
1 pkg. (12 oz.) fettuccine

1. In a large saucepan, heat butter
over medium heat. Add shallots;
cook and stir until tender, 2-3 minutes.
Add garlic; cook 1 minute longer. Add
cream; cook and stir until heated
through. Stir in Asiago cheese, ½ cup
Parmesan cheese, Romano cheese,
salt and pepper; bring to a boil, stirring
constantly. Reduce heat; simmer,
uncovered, until thickened, about
10 minutes, whisking occasionally.

2. Meanwhile, cook pasta according to
package directions. Drain, reserving
1 cup pasta water. Place pasta in a
large bowl. Add sauce; toss to coat.
Thin as desired with reserved pasta
water. Serve with remaining ½ cup
Parmesan cheese.

1 CUP 732 cal., 50g fat (31g sat. fat), 153mg chol., 710mg sod., 47g carb.
(6g sugars, 3g fiber), 27g pro.

WHY PASTA WATER?

Pasta cooking water helps both smooth out and thicken sauces
due to the starch from the pasta. Without it, the sauce will be a little
grainy, so be sure to save some of the water before you drain your
pasta. Stir a little bit into the sauce at a time, just enough to get the
desired consistency.

HEARTY RAGU BOLOGNESE

My robust ragu combines ground beef, sausage and chicken. Serve it over any type of pasta,
or baked or fried polenta. It's even good on its own with a slice of hot buttered garlic bread.
—*Caroline Brody, Forest Hills, NY*

PREP: 20 min. • **COOK:** 3¾ hours • **MAKES:** 12 servings (2½ qt.)

2   medium onions, coarsely chopped
2   celery ribs, coarsely chopped
1   medium carrot, coarsely chopped
4   garlic cloves, peeled
2   Tbsp. olive oil
1   Tbsp. butter
¼   tsp. ground nutmeg
1   lb. ground beef
¾   tsp. salt
½   tsp. pepper
1½ lbs. bulk Italian sausage
1   cup dry white wine
1   can (14½ oz.) beef broth
½   lb. boneless skinless
    chicken breasts
2   cups heavy whipping cream
3   cans (6 oz. each) tomato paste
    Hot cooked pasta
    Grated Parmesan cheese, optional

1. Place onions, celery, carrot and garlic in a food processor; pulse until finely chopped. In a Dutch oven, heat oil and butter over medium heat. Add vegetable mixture and nutmeg; cook and stir 6-8 minutes or until vegetables are softened.

2. Add beef; cook 6-8 minutes longer or until beef is no longer pink, breaking up beef into crumbles. Stir in salt and pepper. Remove with a slotted spoon; discard drippings from pot.

3. In same pot, cook sausage over medium heat 6-8 minutes or until no longer pink, breaking into crumbles; drain. Return beef mixture to pan. Stir in wine. Bring to a boil; cook and stir until wine is evaporated. Add broth and chicken breasts; return to a boil. Reduce heat; simmer, covered, 12-15 minutes or until a thermometer inserted in chicken reads 165°. Remove chicken; cool slightly. Finely chop chicken.

4. Add cream and tomato paste to pot; bring to a boil, stirring occasionally. Return chicken to pot; reduce heat and simmer, covered, 3-4 hours or until flavors are blended, stirring occasionally. Serve with pasta. If desired, sprinkle with Parmesan cheese.

FREEZE OPTION Freeze cooled sauce in freezer containers for up to 3 months. To use, partially thaw in refrigerator overnight. Heat through in a saucepan, stirring occasionally and adding broth if necessary.

¾ CUP 461 cal., 35g fat (16g sat. fat), 112mg chol., 712mg sod., 13g carb. (6g sugars, 2g fiber), 21g pro.

GLUTEN-FREE PIZZA CRUST

This is an ideal dough for children and adults alike who are gluten intolerant
but also crave pizza. You don't need to visit a health food store to find the flours for
this recipe—I buy both at local grocery stores here in my small town in Wyoming.
—*Sylvia Girmus, Torrington, WY*

PREP: 20 min. + standing • **BAKE:** 20 min. • **MAKES:** 6 servings

1   Tbsp. active dry yeast
⅔   cup warm water (110° to 115°)
½   cup tapioca flour
2   Tbsp. nonfat dry milk powder
2   tsp. xanthan gum
1   tsp. unflavored gelatin
1   tsp. Italian seasoning
1   tsp. cider vinegar
1   tsp. olive oil
½   tsp. salt
½   tsp. sugar
1   to 1⅓ cups brown rice flour
    Pizza toppings of your choice

1. Preheat oven to 425°. In a small bowl, dissolve yeast in warm water. Add tapioca flour, milk powder, xanthan gum, gelatin, Italian seasoning, vinegar, olive oil, salt, sugar and ⅔ cup brown rice flour. Beat until smooth. Stir in enough remaining brown rice flour to form a soft dough (dough will be sticky).

2. On a floured surface, roll dough into a 13-in. circle. Transfer to a 12-in. pizza pan coated with cooking spray; build up edge slightly. Cover and let rest for 10 minutes.

3. Bake crust until golden brown, 10-12 minutes. Add toppings of your choice. Bake until crust is crisp and toppings are lightly browned and heated through, 10-15 minutes longer.

NOTE Read all ingredient labels for possible gluten content prior to use. Ingredient formulas can change, and production facilities vary among brands. If you're concerned that your brand may contain gluten, contact the company.

1 PIECE 123 cal., 1g fat (0 sat. fat), 0 chol., 217mg sod., 25g carb. (1g sugars, 2g fiber), 3g pro.

MAKE IT IN ADVANCE

You can make this pizza crust a day ahead of time. Bake the crust as directed and let cool completely before storing in an airtight container in the fridge. Or freeze your parbaked pizza crust by wrapping it in plastic wrap and then in foil securely. Thaw in the refrigerator overnight before adding toppings, then proceed with the second bake as directed.

INDIVIDUAL PIZZA CRUSTS

This dough is great for parties. Everyone can pick their own toppings and it's always fun to do some cooking together. You can also use this dough recipe to make two 12-inch pizzas.

—Beverly Anderson, Sinclairville, NY

PREP: 10 min. + resting • **BAKE:** 15 min. • **MAKES:** 10 servings

2 pkg. (¼ oz. each) active dry yeast
2 cups warm water (110° to 115°)
¼ cup canola oil
2 tsp. sugar
½ tsp. salt
5 to 5½ cups all-purpose flour
Cornmeal
Pizza toppings of your choice

1. In a large bowl, dissolve yeast in warm water. Add oil, sugar, salt and 3 cups flour. Beat until smooth. Stir in enough remaining flour to form a firm dough. Turn onto a floured surface; cover and let rest for 10 minutes.

2. Divide dough into 10 pieces. Roll each portion into an 8-in. circle; prick each circle of dough several times with tines of a fork. Transfer dough to greased baking sheets lightly sprinkled with cornmeal, building up edges slightly. Do not let rise. Bake at 425° until lightly browned, 6-8 minutes. Add toppings as desired; bake 8-12 minutes longer.

1 CRUST 285 cal., 6g fat (1g sat. fat), 0 chol., 120mg sod., 49g carb. (1g sugars, 2g fiber), 7g pro.

A NEW KIND OF PIZZA PARTY

For your next pizza party, forget ordering in a stack of pies—let your guests build their own! Supply individual pizza crusts (above) and a selection of sauces, then fill a table with fresh veggies, proteins, cheeses and more, including both kid-friendly items and more grown-up picks. Let everyone create their own pizza, then bake it for them!

SUGGESTED ITEMS:

- Red onion, sliced
- Deli ham, thinly sliced
- Pepperoncini
- Pineapple, chopped
- Tomatoes, sliced
- Bacon, cooked and diced

- Sliced black olives
- Green peppers, sliced
- Mushrooms, sliced
- Sliced pepperoni
- Shredded mozzarella
- Sausage, cooked and crumbled

- Parmesan wedge
- Crushed red pepper flakes
- Fresh basil

⏱ CREAMY PESTO SAUCE

I love pesto sauce but adding it to noodles is too heavy and greasy for me.
This recipe softens the pesto and makes for a great noodle topper.
—Justin Weber, Milwaukee, WI

TAKES: 25 min. • **MAKES:** 2¾ cups

⅓ cup pine nuts
4 cups loosely packed basil leaves
½ cup grated Parmesan cheese
2 Tbsp. lemon juice
4 garlic cloves, minced
1 tsp. grated lemon zest
½ tsp. salt
½ tsp. pepper
½ cup extra virgin olive oil
1 cup heavy whipping cream

1. Cook and stir pine nuts in a small skillet over low heat until lightly browned, 3-5 minutes, stirring occasionally. Remove from heat; cool.

2. Transfer pine nuts to a food processor. Add basil, Parmesan cheese, lemon juice, garlic, lemon zest, salt and pepper; cover and pulse until blended. While processing, gradually add oil in a steady stream, scraping down side if needed. Add cream and pulse to combine.

3. In a small saucepan, cook pesto sauce over medium-low heat. Cook and stir until slightly thickened, 5-10 minutes.

2 TBSP. 105 cal., 11g fat (4g sat. fat), 14mg chol., 90mg sod., 1g carb. (0 sugars, 0 fiber), 1g pro.

THE BEST PIZZA DOUGH

This easy dough is the key to making an extraordinary homemade pizza. All-purpose flour does just fine here, but if you're lucky enough to live near an Italian market or can purchase double zero flour online, it will take your crust to the next level. You can also customize your crust by adding dried basil or oregano, and by substituting garlic or onion salt for the sea salt.

—*Josh Rink, Milwaukee, WI*

PREP: 30 min. + chilling • **MAKES:** 2 crusts (8 servings each)

1¼ cups warm water (110° to 115°)
2 tsp. sugar, divided
1 pkg. (¼ oz.) active dry yeast
3½ to 4 cups all-purpose or 00 flour
1 tsp. sea salt
1 tsp. each dried basil, oregano and marjoram, optional
⅓ cup vegetable or olive oil

1. In a small bowl, mix warm water and 1 tsp. sugar; add yeast and whisk until dissolved. Let stand until bubbles form on surface. In a large bowl, whisk 3 cups flour, salt, remaining sugar and, if desired, dried herbs. Make a well in center; add yeast mixture and oil. Stir until smooth. Add enough remaining flour to form a soft dough.

2. Turn onto a floured surface; knead, adding more flour to surface as needed until no longer sticky and dough is smooth and elastic, 6-8 minutes. Place in a large greased bowl; turn once to grease top. Cover and let rise in a warm place for 30 minutes; transfer bowl to refrigerator and chill overnight. Allow dough to come to room temperature, about 30 minutes, before rolling.

1 PIECE 144 cal., 5g fat (1g sat. fat), 0 chol., 121mg sod., 22g carb. (1g sugars, 1g fiber), 3g pro.

TO MAKE PIZZA

Preheat oven to 400°. Divide dough in half. With greased fingers, pat each half onto an ungreased 12-in. pizza pan. Prick dough thoroughly with a fork. Bake until lightly browned, 10-12 minutes. Add toppings of your choice. Bake at 400° until golden brown and cheese is bubbling, 12-15 minutes.

⏱ WHITE PIZZA SAUCE

If you favor the rich flavor of white pizzas, this sauce will become your new favorite.
Add even more garlic or your favorite herbs to give it more flavor.
—Taste of Home *Test Kitchen*

TAKES: 15 min. • **MAKES:** 2 cups

2 Tbsp. butter
2 garlic cloves, minced
2 Tbsp. all-purpose flour
2 cups half-and-half cream
⅓ cup grated Parmesan cheese
½ tsp. Italian seasoning, optional

1. In a small saucepan, melt butter over medium heat. Add garlic; cook and stir 1 minute. Stir in flour until blended; gradually add cream. Bring to a boil; cook and stir 1-2 minutes or until thickened. Remove from heat.

2. Stir in Parmesan cheese and, if desired, Italian seasoning.

¼ CUP 128 cal., 10g fat (6g sat. fat), 41mg chol., 113mg sod., 4g carb. (2g sugars, 0 fiber), 3g pro.

GRAMMY'S
ZUPPA INGLESE
(PAGE 281)

ITALIAN-STYLE SWEETS

TUSCAN SUN ORANGE CRANBERRY CAKE

This recipe came to be through much trial and error. Growing up, my family used farina flour in desserts, and I thought it would lend a nice texture to this cake. It's an old-world Italian-style cake, delicious but not too sweet. The orange-cranberry combination is perfect!
—*Ninette Holbrook, Orlando, FL*

PREP: 25 min. • **BAKE:** 20 min. + cooling • **MAKES:** 8 servings

⅓ cup sugar
⅓ cup canola oil
2 large eggs, room temperature
1 Tbsp. grated orange zest
1 Tbsp. orange juice
⅓ cup all-purpose flour
⅓ cup cream of wheat or farina flour
½ tsp. salt
¼ tsp. baking powder
⅓ cup dried cranberries, chopped
¼ cup sliced almonds

ORANGE GLAZE
¾ cup confectioners' sugar
1 Tbsp. orange juice
2 tsp. 2% milk
 Grated orange zest, optional

1. Preheat oven to 350°. Grease an 8-in. round baking pan.

2. In a large bowl, beat sugar, oil, eggs, orange zest and juice until well blended. In another bowl, whisk flour, cream of wheat, salt and baking powder; gradually beat into oil mixture. Stir in cranberries.

3. Transfer to prepared pan; sprinkle with almonds. Bake until a toothpick inserted in center comes out clean, 20-25 minutes.

4. Combine glaze ingredients; pour over warm cake. Cool 10 minutes before serving. If desired, sprinkle with orange zest.

1 PIECE 263 cal., 12g fat (1g sat. fat), 47mg chol., 182mg sod., 36g carb. (25g sugars, 1g fiber), 4g pro.

SOFT ALMOND BISCOTTI BARS

These bars are a variation on the fabulous cinnamon almond biscotti that my mother and grandmother always made for the holidays. Instead of crisp, crumbly cookies that are difficult to shape, these bars are chewy and satisfying with cinnamon flavor and toasted almonds inside and out.

—*Jannine Fisk, Malden, MA*

PREP: 20 min. • **BAKE:** 20 min. • **MAKES:** 4 dozen

1   cup sugar
1   cup packed brown sugar
⅓   cup canola oil
2   large eggs
4   Tbsp. water, divided
2½ cups all-purpose flour
2   tsp. baking powder
1   tsp. ground cinnamon
2   cups coarsely chopped almonds, toasted
1   large egg yolk
1   cup sliced almonds

1. Preheat oven to 375°. Line a 15x10x1-in. baking pan with parchment, letting ends extend up sides; grease paper.

2. In a large bowl, beat sugars and oil until blended. Beat in eggs, then 3 Tbsp. water. In a second bowl, whisk flour, baking powder and cinnamon; gradually beat into sugar mixture. Stir in chopped almonds (dough will be sticky).

3. Press dough into prepared pan, lightly flouring top as needed. Mix egg yolk and remaining 1 Tbsp. water; brush over dough. Top with sliced almonds, gently pressing into dough. Bake 20-25 minutes or until golden brown.

4. Cool in pan on a wire rack. Lifting with parchment, remove from pan. Cut into 24 squares; cut each square into 2 triangles.

NOTE To toast nuts, bake in a shallow pan in a 350° oven for 5-10 minutes or cook in a skillet over low heat until lightly browned, stirring occasionally.

1 BAR 118 cal., 6g fat (1g sat. fat), 12mg chol., 25mg sod., 15g carb. (9g sugars, 1g fiber), 3g pro.

LEMONY LIMONCELLO TIRAMISU

This is a great citrus twist on a classic Italian dessert. It's always a favorite at holiday meals and summer family gatherings! The lemon curd can be a little difficult to spread; a neat trick is to use a piping bag to add it in an even layer, then use a spatula to smooth it.

—Deena Resnick, Oregon City, OR

PREP: 25 min. + chilling • **MAKES:** 12 servings

2 cartons (8 oz. each) mascarpone cheese
6 large egg yolks
¾ cup sugar
⅔ cup 2% milk
1¼ cups heavy whipping cream
½ tsp. vanilla extract
¼ cup lemon juice
½ cup limoncello
1 pkg. (7 oz.) crisp ladyfinger cookies
1 jar (10 oz.) lemon curd
Candied lemon slices, optional

1. Stir mascarpone cheese; let stand at room temperature 30 minutes. Whisk egg yolks, sugar and milk in top of a double boiler until mixture is thickened (ribbon stage) and a thermometer reads 160°. Remove from heat; cool completely. Whisk in mascarpone cheese until almost smooth.

2. Whip heavy cream and vanilla until soft peaks form. In a shallow dish, combine lemon juice and limoncello.

3. Briefly dip 24 ladyfingers into limoncello mixture; place in bottom of an 11x7-in. baking dish. Top with half the mascarpone mixture, half the lemon curd and half the whipped cream. Repeat layers. Refrigerate, covered, 6 hours or overnight. To serve, garnish with candied lemon slices as desired.

1 PIECE 509 cal., 31g fat (17g sat. fat), 204mg chol., 80mg sod., 47g carb. (40g sugars, 0 fiber), 7g pro.

ITALIAN TOTO COOKIES

For many years, I tried to find a good recipe for this Italian cookie. With tips from fellow bakers and some experimenting, I came up with this version. I think it's the perfect combination of chocolate, orange and coffee flavors with a satisfying moist, dense texture.

—*Lilly Rudiy, Medina, OH*

PREP: 1½ hours. + chilling • **BAKE:** 10 min./batch + cooling • **MAKES:** about 10½ dozen

- 2 Tbsp. instant espresso powder
- ¼ cup hot water
- 1 cup butter, softened
- ¾ cup sugar
- ½ cup packed light brown sugar
- 3 large eggs, room temperature
- 3 Tbsp. chocolate syrup
- 4 tsp. grated orange zest
- 1 tsp. orange extract
- 1 Tbsp. coffee liqueur, optional
- 2 tsp. coffee extract, optional
- 1 tsp. vanilla extract
- 4½ cups all-purpose flour
- ½ cup dark baking cocoa
- 4 tsp. baking powder
- 1 tsp. ground cinnamon
- ½ tsp. baking soda
- ½ tsp. ground allspice
- ¼ tsp. salt
- 1 cup finely chopped walnuts, toasted
- 1 cup (6 oz.) miniature semisweet chocolate chips

GLAZE

- 1 pkg. (2 lbs.) confectioners' sugar
- 4 tsp. grated orange zest
- ¾ to 1 cup orange juice

1. Preheat oven to 350°. In a small bowl, dissolve espresso powder in hot water; cool slightly. In a large bowl, cream butter and sugars until light and fluffy, 5-7 minutes. Beat in eggs, cooled espresso mixture, chocolate syrup, orange zest and extract, coffee liqueur and extract if desired, and vanilla (mixture will look curdled). In another bowl, whisk flour, baking cocoa, baking powder, cinnamon, baking soda, allspice and salt; gradually beat into creamed mixture. Stir in walnuts and chocolate chips. Refrigerate 30 minutes or until firm enough to roll.

2. Shape dough into 1-in. balls; place 2 in. apart on parchment-lined baking sheets. Bake until firm, 10-12 minutes.

3. Meanwhile, for glaze, in a large bowl, mix confectioners' sugar, orange zest and enough orange juice to reach dipping consistency. Remove cookies from oven. Immediately dip cookies into glaze; allow excess to drip off. Place on wire racks; let stand until set. Drizzle cookies with remaining glaze; let stand until set. Store between pieces of waxed paper in airtight containers.

NOTE To toast nuts, bake in a shallow pan in a 350° oven for 5-10 minutes or cook in a skillet over low heat until lightly browned, stirring occasionally.

1 COOKIE 80 cal., 3g fat (1g sat. fat), 8mg chol., 38mg sod., 14g carb. (10g sugars, 0 fiber), 1g pro.

ITALIAN CHOCOLATE-HAZELNUT CHEESECAKE PIE

I first prepared an Italian-style cheese pie years ago. When I changed it up by adding a chocolate-hazelnut topping, it proved so popular that I had to give out copies of the recipe.
—Steve Meredith, Streamwood, IL

PREP: 25 min. • **BAKE:** 30 min. + chilling • **MAKES:** 8 servings

2 pkg. (8 oz. each) cream cheese, softened
½ cup sugar
½ cup mascarpone cheese
¼ cup sour cream
1 tsp. lime juice
1 tsp. vanilla extract
2 large eggs, room temperature, lightly beaten
1 chocolate crumb crust (9 in.)

TOPPING
½ cup semisweet chocolate chips
⅓ cup heavy whipping cream
½ tsp. vanilla extract
Whole or chopped hazelnuts, toasted

1. Preheat oven to 350°. In a large bowl, beat cream cheese and sugar until smooth. Beat in mascarpone cheese, sour cream, lime juice and vanilla. Add eggs; beat on low speed just until blended. Pour into crust. Place on a baking sheet.

2. Bake 30-35 minutes or until center is almost set. Cool 1 hour on a wire rack.

3. Meanwhile, for topping, place chocolate chips in a small bowl. In a small saucepan, bring cream just to a boil. Pour over chips; stir with a whisk until smooth. Stir in vanilla. Cool to room temperature or until mixture thickens to a spreading consistency, stirring occasionally.

4. Spread chocolate topping over pie; refrigerate overnight. Just before serving, top with hazelnuts.

NOTE To toast nuts, bake in a shallow pan in a 350° oven for 5-10 minutes or cook in a skillet over low heat until lightly browned, stirring occasionally.

1 PIECE 590 cal., 47g fat (25g sat. fat), 152mg chol., 319mg sod., 38g carb. (28g sugars, 1g fiber), 9g pro.

GRAMMY'S ZUPPA INGLESE

This was a dessert for special occasions that my Italian paternal grandmother used to make.
As a young girl I loved the creamy center, but I didn't really appreciate the liqueur-soaked ladyfingers
until I was older. It's been a family favorite ever since I can remember and we are teaching
the next generation in our family how to make this wonderful dessert.
—*Ann Marie Eberhart, Gig Harbor, WA*

PREP: 1 hour + chilling • **MAKES:** 16 servings

1 cup sugar
4 Tbsp. cornstarch
¼ tsp. salt
4 cups 2% milk
8 large egg yolks
1 tsp. vanilla extract
¾ cup Cognac
¾ cup anise liqueur
½ cup Rosolio liqueur
3 pkg. (3 oz. each) soft ladyfingers, split

1. In a large heavy saucepan, mix sugar, cornstarch and salt. Whisk in milk. Cook and stir over medium heat until thickened and bubbly. Reduce heat to low; cook and stir 2 minutes longer. Remove from heat.

2. In a small bowl, whisk a small amount of hot mixture into egg yolks; return all to pan, whisking constantly. Bring to a gentle boil; cook and stir for 2 minutes. Remove from heat. Stir in vanilla. Cool for 15 minutes, stirring occasionally.

3. In a small bowl, combine Cognac and liqueurs. Line sides of an ungreased 10-cup mold with ladyfinger halves, rounded sides out; brush with 1 cup Cognac mixture. Reserve remaining ladyfingers and Cognac mixture for layering. Pour ⅓ of pudding mixture into mold; layer with ladyfingers. Brush with ½ cup Cognac mixture. Repeat layers; top with remaining pudding. Refrigerate, covered, until set, at least 4 hours. Invert onto a serving plate; lift off mold.

1 PIECE 191 cal., 4g fat (2g sat. fat), 108mg chol., 108mg sod., 22g carb. (18g sugars, 0 fiber), 4g pro.

STRAWBERRY GELATO

You'll love this smooth and creamy gelato with bright strawberry flavor and just a hint of sea salt and honey.
Fresh raspberries or blackberries can be substituted for the strawberries if you prefer.
If your berries are tart, add a touch more sugar or honey.
—*Shelly Bevington, Hermiston, OR*

PREP: 10 min. + chilling • **PROCESS:** 25 min./batch + freezing • **MAKES:** 12 servings

2 cups whole milk
2 Tbsp. light corn syrup
1 Tbsp. honey
¾ cup sugar
½ tsp. sea salt
2½ cups fresh strawberries (about 12 oz.), halved
½ cup heavy whipping cream
1 tsp. lemon juice

1. Place first 6 ingredients in a blender; cover and blend. While blending, gradually add cream, blending just until combined. Remove to a bowl; stir in lemon juice. Refrigerate, covered, until cold, about 4 hours.

2. Fill cylinder of ice cream maker no more than two-thirds full; freeze according to manufacturer's directions. (Refrigerate any remaining mixture until ready to freeze.)

3. Transfer ice cream to freezer containers, allowing headspace for expansion. Freeze until firm, 3-4 hours.

½ CUP 160 cal., 6g fat (4g sat. fat), 18mg chol., 124mg sod., 26g carb. (25g sugars, 1g fiber), 2g pro.

WORK IN BATCHES

This recipe makes 4¾ cups strawberry mixture before freezing and yields about 6 cups after freezing. If you have a 1-qt. ice cream maker, you will probably need to make the gelato in two batches. Be sure to follow your manufacturer's instruction manual.

TORCETTI

Our Sicilian grandmother often had my sister and me roll out the dough for these tasty torcetti. They are melt-in-your-mouth good without being overly sweet.

—Joy Quici, Upland, CA

PREP: 30 min. + rising • **BAKE:** 15 min./batch + cooling • **MAKES:** 6 dozen

5 cups all-purpose flour
1 cup cold butter, cubed
1 cup shortening
1 pkg. (¼ oz.) active dry yeast
½ cup 2% warm milk (110° to 115°)
2 large eggs, room temperature
1 Tbsp. sugar
1½ tsp. vanilla extract
2 cups confectioners' sugar
  Additional confectioners' sugar

1. Place flour in a large bowl; cut in butter and shortening until mixture resembles coarse crumbs. Set aside. In another large bowl, dissolve yeast in warm milk. Add eggs, sugar, vanilla and 2 cups crumb mixture; beat until well blended. Gradually beat in the remaining crumb mixture.

2. Turn dough onto a floured surface; knead 3-4 minutes. Place in a greased bowl, turning once to grease top. Cover and let rise in a warm place until doubled, about 1 hour.

3. Punch dough down; divide into 6 portions. Shape each portion into twelve 6-in. ropes about ¼ in. thick; roll in confectioners' sugar. Shape each rope into a loop. Holding both ends of loop, twist together 3 times.

4. Place twists 2 in. apart on greased baking sheets. Bake at 375° until golden brown, 12-14 minutes. Roll warm cookies in additional confectioners' sugar. Cool on wire racks.

1 COOKIE 102 cal., 5g fat (2g sat. fat), 13mg chol., 21mg sod., 12g carb. (5g sugars, 0 fiber), 1g pro.

FROSTED LEMON-RICOTTA COOKIES

I work for a special education school and our students run their own catering business. Every time they make this recipe for a catering event, they get praise. The students chose these cookies to submit as their favorite cookie recipe. They say they are the yummiest and chewiest cookies ever!

—*Renee Phillips, Owosso, MI*

PREP: 20 min. • **BAKE:** 10 min./batch + cooling • **MAKES:** 3 dozen

½ cup butter, softened
2   cups sugar
2   large eggs, room temperature, lightly beaten
1   carton (15 oz.) ricotta cheese
3   Tbsp. lemon juice
1   Tbsp. grated lemon zest
2½ cups all-purpose flour
1   tsp. baking powder
¾ tsp. salt

FROSTING
1½ cups confectioners' sugar
3   Tbsp. lemon juice
2   tsp. grated lemon zest

1. Preheat oven to 375°. In a large bowl, beat butter and sugar until well blended, about 5 minutes. Beat in eggs, ricotta, and lemon juice and zest. In a second bowl, combine flour, baking powder and salt; gradually add to butter mixture and mix well.

2. Drop by heaping tablespoonfuls 3 in. apart onto greased baking sheets. Bake until lightly browned, 10-12 minutes. Cool for 2 minutes before removing to wire racks to cool completely.

3. In a small bowl, combine frosting ingredients. Spread over cookies.

1 COOKIE 139 cal., 4g fat (2g sat. fat), 22mg chol., 101mg sod., 24g carb. (17g sugars, 0 fiber), 3g pro.

STORING & FREEZING

These cookies will stay fresh for 3-4 days when stored in an airtight container at room temperature. You can also freeze them before you add the frosting—place them between layers of waxed paper in an airtight container and they'll keep for up to 3 months. Add the frosting after thawing.

CUCCIDATI

The compliments from family and friends make these Sicilian cookies worth the effort. It's the best recipe I've found!
—Carolyn Fafinski, Dunkirk, NY

PREP: 30 min. + chilling • **BAKE:** 10 min./batch + cooling • **MAKES:** about 5 dozen

2 cups raisins
¾ lb. pitted dates
¾ cup sugar
2 small navel oranges, peeled and quartered
⅓ lb. dried figs
⅓ cup chopped walnuts
¼ cup water

DOUGH
1 cup shortening
1 cup sugar
2 large eggs, room temperature
¼ cup 2% milk
2 tsp. vanilla extract
3½ cups all-purpose flour
1 tsp. salt
1 tsp. baking powder
1 tsp. baking soda

GLAZE
2 cups confectioners' sugar
2 to 3 Tbsp. 2% milk

1. Place first 7 ingredients in a food processor; cover and process until finely chopped. Set aside.

2. In a large bowl, cream shortening and sugar until light and fluffy, 5-7 minutes. Beat in eggs, milk and vanilla. Combine flour, salt, baking powder and baking soda; gradually add to creamed mixture and mix well. Divide dough into 4 portions; cover and refrigerate for 1 hour.

3. Preheat oven to 400°. Roll out each portion between 2 sheets of waxed paper into a 16x6-in. rectangle. Spread 1 cup filling lengthwise down center of each rectangle. Starting at a long side, fold dough over filling; fold other side over top. Pinch seams and edges to seal. Cut each rectangle diagonally into 1-in. strips. Place seam side down on parchment-lined baking sheets.

4. Bake until edges are golden brown, 10-14 minutes. Cool 10 minutes before removing from pans to wire racks to cool completely. For glaze, combine confectioners' sugar and enough milk to achieve desired consistency; drizzle over cookies. Store in an airtight container.

1 COOKIE 132 cal., 4g fat (1g sat. fat), 7mg chol., 67mg sod., 24g carb. (17g sugars, 1g fiber), 1g pro.

SUGGESTED ADDITIONS

Traditional cuccidati are flavored with dried figs, toasted walnuts and raisins. You can put your own spin on this classic cookie by adding chopped semisweet chocolate, ground cinnamon or sweet marsala wine to the filling. Before the glaze sets, top with rainbow sprinkles for added color.

ITALIAN SESAME COOKIES

These nontraditional European cookies aren't overly sweet and have a wonderful crunch from sesame seeds. They're the ideal accompaniment to a freshly brewed cup of coffee or tea.

—*Sarah Knoblock, Hyde Park, IN*

PREP: 35 min. • **BAKE:** 10 min./batch • **MAKES:** 8 dozen

½ cup butter, softened
1 cup sugar
3 large eggs, room temperature
1 tsp. vanilla extract
3 cups all-purpose flour
3 tsp. baking powder
½ tsp. salt
1¾ cups sesame seeds
¾ cup 2% milk

1. Preheat oven to 350°. In a large bowl, cream butter and sugar until light and fluffy, 5-7 minutes. Add eggs, 1 at a time, beating well after each addition. Add vanilla. In a second bowl, combine flour, baking powder and salt; gradually add to creamed mixture and mix well.

2. Turn dough onto a lightly floured surface, knead 10-12 times or until smooth. Divide dough into 8 portions. Shape each portion into a 24-in. log. Cut logs into 2-in. pieces.

3. Place sesame seeds and milk in separate shallow bowls. Brush pieces with milk, then roll in sesame seeds. Place 2 in. apart on greased baking sheets. Bake until set and bottoms are lightly browned, 7-9 minutes. Cool for 2 minutes before removing from pans to wire racks.

1 COOKIE 45 cal., 2g fat (1g sat. fat), 9mg chol., 35mg sod., 6g carb. (2g sugars, 0 fiber), 1g pro.

TRIPLE CHOCOLATE RICOTTA ICE CREAM

You're going to fall in love with this thick, luxuriously rich ice cream made with ricotta cheese. It has a creamy texture that can't be beat.
—*Colleen Delawder, Herndon, VA*

PREP: 20 min. • **PROCESS:** 20 min. + freezing • **MAKES:** 1½ qt.

1   carton (15 oz.) whole-milk ricotta cheese
1¼ cups whole milk
1   cup sugar
4   oz. cream cheese, softened
½   cup baking cocoa
½   tsp. instant espresso powder
¼   tsp. salt
1   cup heavy whipping cream
3½ oz. milk chocolate, melted and cooled
3½ oz. dark chocolate candy bar, chopped

1. Place first 7 ingredients in a blender; cover and blend until combined, about 1 minute. Add cream and cooled melted chocolate; cover and blend until slightly thickened, about 30 seconds.

2. Fill cylinder of ice cream maker no more than two-thirds full; freeze according to manufacturer's directions, adding dark chocolate during the last 5 minutes of processing in proportion to amount of mixture in the cylinder. Refrigerate any remaining mixture until ready to freeze.

3. Transfer ice cream to freezer containers, allowing headspace for expansion. Freeze until firm, 2-4 hours.

½ CUP 321 cal., 20g fat (12g sat. fat), 53mg chol., 141mg sod., 33g carb. (30g sugars, 2g fiber), 8g pro.

NONNI'S FRITOLE

My Italian grandmother was famous for her *fritole* and made these treats for her family and friends. Years later we found her recipe card and tried making them without success for several years. We finally figured out the missing part— self-rising flour! Now we can have these as often as we like. It brings back so many wonderful memories.
—*Ann Marie Eberhart, Gig Harbor, WA*

PREP: 15 min. • **COOK:** 5 min./batch • **MAKES:** 4 dozen

4 cups self-rising flour
½ cup sugar
3 large eggs, room temperature
1 cup 2% milk
3 oz. whiskey, rum or orange juice
2 medium apples, peeled and grated
8 tsp. grated orange zest
  Oil for deep-fat frying
  Confectioners' sugar

1. In a large bowl, whisk flour and sugar. In another bowl, whisk eggs, milk and whiskey until blended. Add to dry ingredients, stirring just until moistened. Fold in apples and orange zest.

2. In an electric skillet or deep fryer, heat oil to 375°. Drop batter by tablespoonfuls, a few at a time, into hot oil. Fry until golden brown, about 2 minutes on each side. Drain on paper towels. Dust with confectioners' sugar.

NOTE As an alternative for each cup of self-rising flour, place 1½ tsp. baking powder and ½ tsp. salt in a measuring cup. Add all-purpose flour to measure 1 cup.

1 FRITOLE 69 cal., 2g fat (0 sat. fat), 12mg chol., 131mg sod., 11g carb. (3g sugars, 0 fiber), 2g pro.

MAKE AHEAD TIP

If you're not going to eat these right away, don't put the confectioners' sugar on. When you are ready to serve, heat the *fritoles* slightly in the microwave and then dust with sugar.

LAVENDER PEACH GELATO

This sophisticated herbal gelato can be served as an appetizer, a palate-pleaser
between courses or a sweet, elegant dessert that tastes like heaven on a spoon.
—*Christine Wendland, Browns Mills, NJ*

PREP: 40 min. + chilling • **PROCESS:** 20 min. + freezing • **MAKES:** 3 cups

2 cups 2% milk
2 Tbsp. cardamom pods, crushed
1 Tbsp. dried lavender flowers
1 vanilla bean
¾ cup sugar
5 large egg yolks, beaten
2 medium peaches, peeled
and finely chopped

1. In a large heavy saucepan, combine milk, cardamom pods and lavender. Split vanilla bean and scrape seeds; add bean and seeds to milk mixture. Heat until bubbles form around side of pan. Remove from heat; cover and let steep for 10 minutes. Strain, discarding flowers and spices.

2. Return milk to heat; stir in sugar. Cook until bubbles form around side of pan. Whisk a small amount of hot mixture into egg yolks. Return all to pan, whisking constantly.

3. Cook and stir over low heat until mixture is thickened and coats the back of a spoon. Quickly transfer to a bowl; place bowl in ice water and stir for 2 minutes. Press waxed paper onto surface of custard. Refrigerate for several hours or overnight.

4. Fill cylinder of ice cream maker two-thirds full; freeze according to manufacturer's directions. When gelato is frozen, stir in peaches. Transfer to a freezer container; freeze 2-4 hours before serving.

NOTE Look for dried lavender flowers in spice shops. If using lavender from the garden, make sure it hasn't been treated with chemicals.

½ CUP 206 cal., 5g fat (2g sat. fat), 177mg chol., 47mg sod., 35g carb. (32g sugars, 1g fiber), 5g pro.

CARAMEL CHIP BISCOTTI

The combination of caramel and chocolate in these delicate Italian biscuits is simply fabulous.
These treats are divine dunked in coffee or a sweet wine, or even enjoyed on their own.
Feel free to use any flavor chocolate chips.
—*Tami Kuehl, Loup City, NE*

PREP: 30 min. • **BAKE:** 40 min. + cooling • **MAKES:** 2 dozen

½ cup butter, softened
1 cup sugar
2 large eggs, room temperature
1 tsp. vanilla extract
2½ cups all-purpose flour
1½ tsp. baking powder
¼ tsp. salt
1 cup Kraft caramel bits
1 cup semisweet chocolate chips
3 oz. white candy coating, melted

1. Preheat the oven to 325°. Cream butter and sugar until light and fluffy, 5-7 minutes; beat in eggs and vanilla. In another bowl, whisk together flour, baking powder and salt; gradually beat into creamed mixture (dough will be stiff). Stir in caramel bits and chocolate chips.

2. Divide dough into 3 portions. On parchment-lined baking sheets, shape each portion into a 7x3-in. rectangle. Bake until a toothpick inserted in center comes out clean, 20-25 minutes. Cool on pans on wire racks for 5 minutes.

3. On a cutting board, use a serrated knife to cut each rectangle crosswise into 8 slices. Place slices on baking sheets, cut side down. Bake until crisp, 10-12 minutes per side. Remove from pans to wire racks; cool completely.

4. Drizzle melted candy coating over tops; let stand until set. Store between sheets of waxed paper in airtight containers.

1 COOKIE 206 cal., 8g fat (5g sat. fat), 26mg chol., 115mg sod., 32g carb. (21g sugars, 1g fiber), 2g pro.

MASCARPONE CHEESECAKE

This rich dessert is sure to delight with its creamy filling, whipped topping and
sweet caramel drizzle. It makes a fitting ending to a special meal.

—Deanna Polito-Laughinghouse, Raleigh, NC

PREP: 30 min. • **BAKE:** 1 hour + chilling • **MAKES:** 16 servings

¾   cup graham cracker crumbs
3   Tbsp. sugar
3   Tbsp. butter, melted

FILLING
2   pkg. (8 oz. each) cream cheese,
    softened
2   cartons (8 oz. each) Mascarpone
    cheese
1   cup sugar
1   Tbsp. lemon juice
1   Tbsp. vanilla extract
4   eggs, room temperature,
    lightly beaten

TOPPING
1   carton frozen whipped topping,
    thawed
1   Tbsp. caramel ice cream topping

1. Preheat oven to 325°. Place a greased 9-in. springform pan on a double
thickness of heavy-duty foil (about 18-in. square). Securely wrap foil around pan.

2. In a small bowl, combine cracker crumbs and sugar; stir in butter. Press onto
bottom of prepared pan. Place pan on a baking sheet. Bake for 10 minutes. Cool
on a wire rack.

3. For filling, in a large bowl, beat the cheeses, sugar, lemon juice and vanilla until
smooth. Add eggs; beat on low speed just until combined. Pour over crust. Place
springform pan in a large baking pan; add 1 in. hot water to larger pan.

4. Bake until center is just set and top appears dull, 1-1¼ hours. Remove
springform pan from water bath. Cool on a wire rack for 10 minutes. Carefully
run a knife around edge of pan to loosen; cool 1 hour longer.

5. Refrigerate overnight. Remove side of pan. Garnish cheesecake with whipped
topping; drizzle with caramel. Refrigerate leftovers.

1 PIECE 339 cal., 26g fat (15g sat. fat), 121mg chol., 160mg sod., 21g carb. (18g sugars,
0 fiber), 6g pro.

ALMOND BISCOTTI

I've learned to bake a double batch whenever I make these crisp
dunking cookies, because one batch always goes too fast!
—*H. Michaelsen, St. Charles, IL*

PREP: 15 min. • **BAKE:** 35 min. + cooling • **MAKES:** 3 dozen

½ cup butter, softened
1¼ cups sugar, divided
3 large eggs, room temperature
1 tsp. anise extract
2 cups all-purpose flour
2 tsp. baking powder
   Dash salt
½ cup chopped almonds
2 tsp. 2% milk

1. Preheat oven to 375°. In a large bowl, cream butter and 1 cup sugar until light and fluffy, 5-7 minutes. Add eggs, 1 at a time, beating well after each addition. Beat in extract. Combine dry ingredients; gradually add to creamed mixture and mix well. Stir in almonds.

2. Line a baking sheet with foil and grease the foil. Divide dough in half; on the foil, shape each portion into a 12x3-in. rectangle. Brush with milk; sprinkle with remaining ¼ cup sugar.

3. Bake until golden brown and firm to the touch, 15-20 minutes. Lift foil with rectangles onto a wire rack; cool for 15 minutes. Reduce oven heat to 300°.

4. Transfer rectangles to a cutting board; cut diagonally with a serrated knife into ½-in. slices. Place cut side down on ungreased baking sheets.

5. Bake for 10 minutes. Turn and bake until firm, 10 minutes longer. Remove to wire racks to cool. Store in an airtight container.

1 COOKIE 207 cal., 9g fat (4g sat. fat), 50mg chol., 129mg sod., 29g carb. (16g sugars, 1g fiber), 4g pro.

COCONUT ITALIAN CREAM CAKE

I'd never tasted an Italian cream cake before moving to Colorado.
Now I bake for people in the area, and this beauty is one of the most requested.
—Ann Bush, Colorado City, CO

PREP: 50 min. • **BAKE:** 20 min. + cooling • **MAKES:** 16 servings

5   large eggs, separated
1   cup butter, softened
1⅔ cups sugar
1½ tsp. vanilla extract
2   cups all-purpose flour
¾   tsp. baking soda
½   tsp. salt
1   cup buttermilk
1⅓ cups sweetened shredded coconut
1   cup chopped pecans, toasted

FROSTING
12 oz. cream cheese, softened
6   Tbsp. butter, softened
2¼ tsp. vanilla extract
5⅔ cups confectioners' sugar
3   to 4 Tbsp. heavy whipping cream
½   cup chopped pecans, toasted
¼   cup toasted sweetened shredded coconut, optional

1. Place egg whites in a small bowl; let stand at room temperature for 30 minutes.

2. Preheat oven to 350°. Line bottoms of 3 greased 9-in. round baking pans with parchment; grease paper.

3. In a large bowl, cream butter and sugar until light and fluffy, 5-7 minutes. Add egg yolks, 1 at a time, beating well after each addition. Beat in vanilla. In another bowl, whisk flour, baking soda and salt; add to creamed mixture alternately with buttermilk, beating well after each addition. Fold in coconut and pecans.

4. With clean beaters, beat egg whites on medium speed until stiff peaks form. Gradually fold into batter. Transfer batter to prepared pans. Bake until a toothpick inserted in center comes out clean, 20-25 minutes. Cool in pans for 10 minutes before removing to wire racks; remove paper. Cool completely.

5. For frosting, beat cream cheese and butter until smooth. Beat in vanilla. Gradually beat in confectioners' sugar and enough cream to reach spreading consistency. Spread frosting between layers and over top and side of cake. Sprinkle with pecans and, if desired, coconut. Refrigerate leftovers.

NOTE To toast pecans and coconut, spread 1 ingredient at a time in a 15x10x1-in. baking pan. Bake each pan at 350° for 5-10 minutes or until lightly browned, stirring occasionally.

1 PIECE 667 cal., 36g fat (18g sat. fat), 128mg chol., 402mg sod., 82g carb. (68g sugars, 2g fiber), 7g pro.

BLACK TIE CHOCOLATE MOUSSE CAKE

This cake is the definition of indulgence! To slice this cake, run a sharp knife under hot water and dry it, then cut the first slice. Repeat, rinsing and drying the knife after every slice—it will keep the rich cake from sticking and ensure clean cuts.
—Taste of Home *Test Kitchen*

PREP: 1½ hours + chilling • **BAKE:** 25 min. + cooling • **MAKES:** 16 servings

½ cup baking cocoa
1 cup boiling water
½ cup butter, softened
1 cup sugar
2 large eggs, room temperature
¾ tsp. vanilla extract
1⅓ cups all-purpose flour
1 tsp. baking soda
¼ tsp. baking powder
¼ tsp. salt

CHOCOLATE CHEESECAKE
4 oz. cream cheese, softened
¼ cup confectioners' sugar
½ tsp. vanilla extract
½ cup dark chocolate chips, melted and slightly cooled
½ cup heavy whipping cream

WHITE CHOCOLATE MOUSSE
1 cup heavy whipping cream
2 Tbsp. sugar
3 oz. cream cheese, softened
3 oz. white baking chocolate, melted and cooled

GANACHE
3 cups semisweet chocolate chips
1½ cups heavy whipping cream

GARNISH
2 cups miniature semisweet chocolate chips
¼ cup white baking chips, melted

1. Preheat oven to 350°. In a small bowl, combine cocoa and water; set aside to cool completely. In a large bowl, cream butter and sugar until light and fluffy, 5-7 minutes. Add eggs, 1 at a time, beating well after each addition. Beat in vanilla. Whisk together flour, baking soda, baking powder and salt; add to creamed mixture alternately with cocoa mixture, beating well after each addition.

2. Pour batter into a greased parchment-lined 9-in. round baking pan. Bake until a toothpick inserted in center comes out clean, 25-30 minutes. Cool for 10 minutes before removing from pan to a wire rack to cool completely.

3. For chocolate cheesecake layer, in a small bowl, beat cream cheese, confectioners' sugar and vanilla until smooth. Beat in dark chocolate until combined. In another bowl, beat cream until soft peaks form. Fold into cream cheese mixture. Place cake layer in bottom of a 9-in. springform pan; spread cheesecake mixture over top. Refrigerate until chilled, about 1 hour.

4. For white chocolate mousse, beat cream until it begins to thicken. Gradually add sugar, beating until stiff peaks form; set aside. In another bowl, beat cream cheese until fluffy. Add white chocolate; beat until smooth. Fold in whipped cream. Spread over chocolate cheesecake layer. Refrigerate until set and chilled, about 1 hour.

5. For ganache, place chips in a large bowl. In a small saucepan, bring cream just to a boil. Pour over chocolate; stir with a whisk until smooth. Cool slightly, stirring occasionally. Reserve 1 cup for frosting; cover and refrigerate until cold.

6. Remove cake from pan; place on a wire rack. Pour remaining ganache over cake, allowing it to coat side. For garnish, press miniature chocolate chips into side of cake. Drizzle melted white chips over top. Refrigerate, covered, until chilled. Beat reserved ganache until piping consistency, about 15 seconds. Pipe around top edge. Refrigerate until serving.

1 PIECE 696 cal., 48g fat (29g sat. fat), 102mg chol., 241mg sod., 71g carb. (56g sugars, 4g fiber), 8g pro.

RICH & CREAMY TIRAMISU

Tiramisu is Italian for "pick-me-up," and this one is definitely true to its name! My version of the classic Tuscan trifle has both coffee and espresso for layers of java flavor.
—*Lauren McAnelly, Des Moines, IA*

PREP: 15 min. + standing • **COOK:** 10 min. + chilling • **MAKES:** 16 servings

2 cartons (8 oz. each) mascarpone cheese
5 large egg yolks
½ cup plus 2 Tbsp. sugar, divided
⅓ cup plus 2 Tbsp. Marsala wine, Kahlua (coffee liqueur) or rum, divided
½ tsp. salt
1 cup heavy whipping cream
¾ cup strong brewed coffee, room temperature
2 tsp. instant espresso powder
1 pkg. (7 oz.) crisp ladyfinger cookies
1 Tbsp. Dutch-processed cocoa

1. Stir mascarpone cheese; let stand at room temperature for 30 minutes.

2. Whisk egg yolks, ½ cup sugar, ⅓ cup Marsala and salt in top of a double boiler until mixture is thickened (ribbon stage) and a thermometer reads 160°. Remove from heat; whisk in mascarpone until almost smooth. Beat cream and remaining 2 Tbsp. sugar until soft peaks form; fold into mascarpone mixture.

3. Combine coffee, espresso powder and remaining 2 Tbsp. Marsala. Briefly dip 8 ladyfingers into coffee mixture and place in bottom of a 9-in. springform pan. Top with 1½ cups mascarpone mixture. Repeat 2 more times. Refrigerate, covered, 6 hours or overnight. To serve, loosen and remove rim; sprinkle with cocoa powder.

1 SERVING 280 cal., 21g fat (11g sat. fat), 123mg chol., 115mg sod., 19g carb. (14g sugars, 0 fiber), 5g pro.

HOW HARD TO MIX?

Feel free to vigorously whip the yolk mixture in the double boiler to add volume and get that ribbonlike texture. But work more gently when mixing in the mascarpone cheese. You can even leave it a little lumpy; the carryover warmth from the yolk mixture will soften those lumps while you whip the cream. When you fold in the whipped cream, they'll disappear entirely.

CANNOLI WAFER SANDWICHES

My family loves to visit a local Italian restaurant that has a wonderful dessert buffet.
The cannoli is among our favorite choices, so I just had to come up with my own simple version.
These sandwiches are best served the same day so the wafers remain nice and crisp.

—*Nichi Larson, Shawnee, KS*

PREP: 35 min. + standing • **MAKES:** 3½ dozen

1   cup whole-milk ricotta cheese
¼   cup confectioners' sugar
1   Tbsp. sugar
¼   tsp. vanilla extract
1   pkg. (11 oz.) vanilla wafers
12 oz. white candy coating, melted
½   cup miniature semisweet
      chocolate chips
      Additional confectioners' sugar

1. In a small bowl, mix ricotta cheese, confectioners' sugar, sugar and vanilla until blended. Spread 1 scant tsp. filling on bottoms of half the wafers; cover with remaining wafers.

2. Dip each sandwich cookie halfway into candy coating; allow excess to drip off. Place on waxed paper; sprinkle with chocolate chips. Let stand until set, about 10 minutes.

3. Serve within 2 hours or refrigerate until serving. Dust with additional confectioners' sugar just before serving.

1 SANDWICH COOKIE 93 cal., 5g fat (3g sat. fat), 4mg chol., 38mg sod., 13g carb. (10g sugars, 0 fiber), 1g pro.

"These cookies are my husband's absolute favorite. They are delicious and do taste like cannoli. My only recommendation is not to freeze them—they become mushy when thawed."
—MYSHAGREEN, TASTEOFHOME.COM

APRICOT ALMOND TORTE

This pretty cake takes a bit of time, so I like to make the layers in advance and assemble it the day of serving, which make it an easier option for entertaining.

—*Trisha Kruse, Eagle, ID*

PREP: 45 min. • **BAKE:** 25 min. + cooling • **MAKES:** 12 servings

3   large eggs
1½ cups sugar
1   tsp. vanilla extract
1¾ cups all-purpose flour
1   cup ground almonds, toasted
2   tsp. baking powder
½   tsp. salt
1½ cups heavy whipping cream, whipped

FROSTING
1   pkg. (8 oz.) cream cheese, softened
1   cup sugar
⅛   tsp. salt
1   tsp. almond extract
1½ cups heavy whipping cream, whipped
1   jar (10 to 12 oz.) apricot preserves
½   cup slivered almonds, toasted

1. Preheat oven to 350°. In a large bowl, beat eggs, sugar and vanilla on high speed until thick and lemon-colored. Combine flour, almonds, baking powder and salt; gradually fold into egg mixture alternately with whipped cream.

2. Transfer to 2 greased and floured 9-in. round baking pans. Bake until a toothpick inserted in the center comes out clean, 22-28 minutes. Cool for 10 minutes before removing from pans to wire racks to cool completely.

3. For frosting, in a large bowl, beat cream cheese, sugar and salt until smooth. Beat in extract. Fold in whipped cream.

4. Cut each cake horizontally into 2 layers. Place 1 layer on a serving plate; spread with 1 cup frosting. Top with another cake layer; spread with half the preserves. Repeat layers. Frost side of cake; decorate the top edge with remaining frosting. Sprinkle with almonds.

1 PIECE 546 cal., 25g fat (12g sat. fat), 115mg chol., 284mg sod., 75g carb. (51g sugars, 2g fiber), 8g pro.

CHOCOLATE CANNOLI

We made two Italian treats into one with beautiful pizzelle cookies wrapped around a rich, chocolaty cannoli filling. The chopped pistachios are a pretty added touch.

—Taste of Home *Test Kitchen*

PREP: 45 min. + cooling • **BAKE:** 5 min./batch • **MAKES:** 1 dozen

1 large egg, room temperature
¼ cup sugar
¼ cup butter, melted
½ tsp. vanilla extract
¼ tsp. grated lemon zest
⅛ tsp. almond extract
½ cup all-purpose flour
¼ tsp. baking powder

FILLING
¾ cup sugar
3 Tbsp. cornstarch
1 cup whole milk
1⅛ tsp. vanilla extract
1 drop cinnamon oil, optional
1¾ cups ricotta cheese
1 milk chocolate candy bar with almonds (4¼ oz.), chopped
½ cup chopped pistachios

1. In a large bowl, beat egg, sugar, butter, vanilla, lemon zest and almond extract until blended. Combine flour and baking powder; stir into egg mixture and mix well.

2. Bake in a preheated pizzelle maker according to manufacturer's directions until golden brown. Remove cookies and immediately shape into tubes. Place on wire racks to cool.

3. For filling, in a small saucepan, combine sugar and cornstarch. Stir in milk until smooth. Bring to a boil; cook and stir until thickened, about 2 minutes. Stir in vanilla and, if desired, cinnamon oil. Cool completely.

4. In a large bowl, beat ricotta cheese until smooth. Gradually beat in custard mixture. Fold in chopped chocolate. Spoon or pipe filling into shells. Dip each side in pistachios. Serve immediately. Refrigerate leftovers.

1 FILLED PIZZELLE 289 cal., 15g fat (8g sat. fat), 47mg chol., 124mg sod., 33g carb. (25g sugars, 1g fiber), 8g pro.

DARK CHOCOLATE PANNA COTTA

Everything about this dessert, from the pretty presentation to its silky smooth texture, says special. Rich chocolate is accented by the flavor of sweet, ripe berries perfectly.

—Susan Asanovic, Wilton, CT

PREP: 25 min. • **COOK:** 10 min. + chilling • **MAKES:** 8 servings

1 can (14 oz.) whole-berry cranberry sauce
5 Tbsp. raspberry liqueur, divided
1 envelope unflavored gelatin
1 cup cold 2% milk
4 oz. 53% cacao dark baking chocolate, chopped
1½ cups heavy whipping cream
½ cup sugar
⅛ tsp. salt
2 tsp. vanilla extract
Optional: Fresh raspberries and mint leaves

1. Place cranberry sauce in a food processor; cover and process until pureed. Strain and discard pulp. Stir in 3 Tbsp. liqueur; set aside.

2. In a small bowl, sprinkle gelatin over milk; let stand for 1 minute. Meanwhile, place chopped chocolate in another small bowl. In a small saucepan, bring cream, sugar and salt just to a boil. Pour over chocolate; whisk until smooth.

3. Stir a small amount of chocolate mixture into gelatin mixture until gelatin is completely dissolved. Stir in 1 cup cranberry puree and vanilla. Pour into eight 6-oz. custard cups. Cover and refrigerate for 8 hours or overnight.

4. In a small bowl, combine remaining cranberry puree and liqueur; cover and refrigerate until serving.

5. Unmold onto serving plates. Serve with sauce and garnish with raspberries and mint if desired.

1 SERVING 397 cal., 22g fat (14g sat. fat), 63mg chol., 81mg sod., 45g carb. (36g sugars, 2g fiber), 4g pro.

LEMON & BLUEBERY
PIZZA (PAGE 317)

DESSERT PIZZAS

CHOCOLATE PUDDING PIZZA

My sister Brenda and I made up this recipe while talking on the phone. My family loved
the classic pairing of chocolate and peanut butter presented in a whole new way.
—*LaDonna Reed, Ponca City, OK*

PREP: 35 min. + chilling • **MAKES:** 12 servings

1   pkg. (17½ oz.) peanut butter
    cookie mix
1   carton (12 oz.) spreadable
    cream cheese, softened
1¾ cups cold whole milk
1   pkg. (3.9 oz.) instant chocolate
    pudding mix
1   carton (8 oz.) frozen whipped
    topping, thawed
¼   cup miniature semisweet
    chocolate chips

1. Preheat oven to 375°. Prepare
cookie mix dough according to
package directions. Press into a
greased 12-in. pizza pan. Bake for
15 minutes or until set; cool.

2. Beat cream cheese until smooth.
Spread over crust. In another bowl,
beat milk and pudding mix on medium
speed for 2 minutes. Spread over
cream cheese layer. Refrigerate until
set, about 20 minutes. Spread with
whipped topping. Sprinkle with chips.
Chill 1-2 hours.

1 PIECE 449 cal., 26g fat (12g sat. fat),
37mg chol., 376mg sod., 46g carb.
(13g sugars, 1g fiber), 7g pro.

*"My family loved it; it's quick and so easy. I didn't have
chocolate chips so I used milk chocolate toffee chips and
added some chopped pecans. It's great for a light dessert
on a hot day."*
—ALETA FREEMAN, TASTEOFHOME.COM

APPLE CRISP PIZZA

While visiting the bakery at a Wisconsin apple orchard, I tried this tempting treat. At home, I put together this recipe.
As it bakes, the enticing aroma fills my kitchen, and friends and family linger waiting for a sample.

—Nancy Preussner, Delhi, IA

PREP: 15 min. • **BAKE:** 35 min. • **MAKES:** 12 servings

Dough for single-crust pie
⅔ cup sugar
3 Tbsp. all-purpose flour
1 tsp. ground cinnamon
4 medium baking apples, peeled and cut into ½-in. slices

TOPPING
½ cup all-purpose flour
⅓ cup packed brown sugar
⅓ cup rolled oats
1 tsp. ground cinnamon
¼ cup butter, softened
¼ to ½ cup caramel ice cream topping or caramel apple dip
Vanilla ice cream, optional

1. Preheat oven to 350°. On a lightly floured surface, roll dough to fit a 12-in. pizza pan; fold under or flute edge. In a large bowl, combine sugar, flour and cinnamon. Add apples and toss. Arrange apples in a single layer in a circular pattern to completely cover crust. Combine first 5 topping ingredients; sprinkle over apples.

2. Bake until apples are tender, 35-40 minutes. Remove from oven; immediately drizzle with caramel topping or dip. Serve warm with ice cream if desired.

DOUGH FOR SINGLE-CRUST PIE Combine 1¼ cups all-purpose flour and ¼ tsp. salt; cut in ½ cup cold butter until crumbly. Gradually add 3-5 Tbsp. ice water, tossing with a fork until dough holds together when pressed. Shape into a disk; wrap and refrigerate 1 hour.

1 PIECE 286 cal., 12g fat (7g sat. fat), 30mg chol., 159mg sod., 44g carb. (26g sugars, 2g fiber), 3g pro.

MAKE AHEAD OPTION

In our busy photo studio, we cut the apples the day before and brushed them with lemon-lime soda to keep them from browning.

FRUITY BROWNIE PIZZA

I start with a basic brownie mix to create this luscious treat that's sure to impress company. Sometimes I add mandarin oranges for even more color.

—*Nancy Johnson, Laverne, OK*

PREP: 20 min. + chilling • **BAKE:** 15 min. + cooling • **MAKES:** 12 servings

1 pkg. fudge brownie mix
   (8-in. square pan size)
1 pkg. (8 oz.) cream cheese, softened
⅓ cup sugar
¾ cup pineapple tidbits with juice
1 small firm banana, sliced
1 medium kiwifruit, peeled
   and sliced
1 cup sliced fresh strawberries
¼ cup chopped pecans
1 oz. semisweet chocolate
1 Tbsp. butter

1. Preheat oven to 375°. Prepare brownie batter according to package directions. Spread onto a greased 12-in. pizza pan. Bake until a toothpick inserted in center comes out clean, 15-20 minutes. Cool completely.

2. In a large bowl, beat cream cheese and sugar until smooth. Spread over brownie crust. Drain pineapple, reserving juice. Toss banana slices with pineapple juice; drain well. Arrange banana, kiwi, strawberries and pineapple over cream cheese layer; sprinkle with pecans.

3. In a microwave, melt chocolate and butter; stir until smooth. Drizzle over fruit. Cover and refrigerate for 1 hour.

1 PIECE 366 cal., 21g fat (7g sat. fat), 38mg chol., 220mg sod., 44g carb. (30g sugars, 2g fiber), 4g pro.

SUGGESTED ADDITIONS

Depending on your preferences, you can add blueberries, raspberries, sliced peaches, or cubed melon to your pizza. If you don't want cream cheese frosting, try a traditional vanilla or chocolate frosting instead.

CHOCOLATE PEANUT BUTTER PIZZA

Kids go crazy for this gooey dessert pizza, although adults snap it up too. Everyone loves the chewy crust and the amazingly delicious combination of chocolate and peanut butter.
—*Bernice Arnett, Marshfield, MO*

TAKES: 30 min. • **MAKES:** 16 slices

½ cup shortening
½ cup peanut butter
½ cup sugar
½ cup packed brown sugar
2 large eggs, room temperature
½ tsp. vanilla extract
1½ cups plus 5 Tbsp. all-purpose flour
2 cups miniature marshmallows
1 cup semisweet chocolate chips

1. Preheat oven to 375°. Cream shortening, peanut butter and sugars until light and fluffy, 5-7 minutes. Beat in eggs and vanilla. Add flour and mix well. Pat dough into a greased 12-in. pizza pan. Bake 16 minutes.

2. Sprinkle crust with marshmallows and chocolate chips; bake until lightly browned, 3-5 minutes longer.

1 PIECE 220 cal., 11g fat (4g sat. fat), 21mg chol., 42mg sod., 28g carb. (19g sugars, 1g fiber), 4g pro.

SUMMER DESSERT PIZZA

Especially refreshing during the summer months, this dessert lets fresh fruit shine.

—Ida Ruth Wenger, Harrisonburg, VA

PREP: 35 min. + chilling • **BAKE:** 15 min. + cooling • **MAKES:** 16 servings

¼ cup butter, softened
½ cup sugar
1 large egg
¼ tsp. vanilla extract
¼ tsp. lemon extract
1¼ cups all-purpose flour
¼ tsp. baking powder
¼ tsp. baking soda
¼ tsp. salt

GLAZE
¼ cup sugar
2 tsp. cornstarch
¼ cup water
¼ cup orange juice

TOPPING
4 oz. cream cheese, softened
¼ cup confectioners' sugar
1 cup whipped topping
1 firm banana, sliced
1 cup sliced fresh strawberries
1 can (8 oz.) mandarin oranges, drained
2 kiwifruit, peeled and thinly sliced
⅓ cup fresh blueberries

1. In a small bowl, cream butter and sugar until light and fluffy, 5-7 minutes. Beat in egg and extracts. Combine flour, baking powder, baking soda and salt; add to creamed mixture and beat well. Cover and refrigerate for 30 minutes.

2. Press dough into a greased 12- to 14-in. pizza pan. Bake at 350° until light golden brown, 12-14 minutes. Cool completely on a wire rack.

3. For glaze, combine sugar and cornstarch in a small saucepan. Stir in water and orange juice until smooth. Bring to a boil; cook and stir until thickened, 1-2 minutes. Cool to room temperature, about 30 minutes.

4. For topping, in a small bowl, beat cream cheese and confectioners' sugar until smooth. Add whipped topping; mix well. Spread over crust. Arrange fruit on top. Brush glaze over fruit. Store in refrigerator.

1 PIECE 176 cal., 7g fat (4g sat. fat), 29mg chol., 118mg sod., 27g carb. (17g sugars, 1g fiber), 2g pro.

TIME SAVERS

Use premade sugar cookie dough to save a bit of time. If you're in a pinch, orange marmalade works in place of the glaze.

⏱ WATERMELON FRUIT PIZZA

Fruit pizza is an easy and refreshing way to end a summer meal. Top it with any fruit you may have on hand and add other toppings like fresh mint, toasted shredded coconut or chopped nuts.

—Taste of Home *Test Kitchen*

TAKES: 10 min. • **MAKES:** 8 servings

4 oz. cream cheese, softened
4 oz. frozen whipped topping, thawed
½ tsp. vanilla extract
3 Tbsp. confectioners' sugar
1 round slice of whole seedless watermelon, about 1 in. thick
Assorted fresh fruit
Fresh mint leaves, optional

1. In a small bowl, beat cream cheese until smooth. Gently fold in whipped topping, then vanilla and confectioners' sugar until combined.

2. To serve, spread watermelon slice with cream cheese mixture. Cut into 8 wedges and top with your fruit of choice. If desired, garnish pizza with fresh mint.

1 PIECE 140 cal., 7g fat (5g sat. fat), 14mg chol., 45mg sod., 17g carb. (16g sugars, 0 fiber), 1g pro. **DIABETIC EXCHANGES** 1½ fat, 1 fruit.

PIZZA CAKE

Our kids had a great time putting this dessert together for a Cub Scout cake auction.
A boxed cake mix forms the crust, prepared vanilla frosting tinted red makes the sauce,
grated white chocolate is the cheese and fruit rolls cut into circles are the pepperoni. The recipe
makes two cakes, so we took one to the auction and enjoyed the other one at home.

—*Caroline Simzisko, Cordova, TN*

PREP: 15 min. • **BAKE:** 20 min. + cooling • **MAKES:** 2 cakes (8 servings each)

1 pkg. yellow cake mix (regular size)
1 cup vanilla frosting
   Red liquid or paste food coloring
3 oz. white baking chocolate, grated
2 strawberry Fruit Roll-Ups

1. Preheat oven to 350°. Prepare cake mix according to package directions. Pour batter into 2 greased and floured 9-in. round baking pans.

2. Bake until a toothpick inserted in center comes out clean, 18-20 minutes. Cool 10 minutes before removing from pans to wire racks to cool completely.

3. Place each cake on a 10-in. serving platter. Combine frosting and food coloring; spread over top of each cake to within ½ in. of edges. Sprinkle with grated white chocolate.

4. Unroll Fruit Roll-Ups; use a 1½-in. round cutter to cut into circles. Arrange on cakes.

1 PIECE 277 cal., 11g fat (4g sat. fat), 35mg chol., 285mg sod., 43g carb. (28g sugars, 0 fiber), 2g pro.

OTHER TOPPINGS

Make your pizza cake look even more realistic by recreating the look of your favorite pizza toppings. Try chopping green Sour Punch Straws into short pieces to look like green peppers. Shape brown fondant into mushroom shapes and cut black jelly beans in half to look like black olives. If you're a fan of pineapple on pizza, add some candied pineapple. If you like sausage on your pizza, mix chocolate cake crumbs with a bit of frosting—like you would for cake pops—and sprinkle the small crumbles on top of the pizza cake.

LEMON & BLUEBERRY PIZZA

Light and lemony, this blueberry dessert pizza is nice to serve after dinner, as an accompaniment to a cup of afternoon tea or as a special breakfast pastry. You can use a 13x9-inch pan instead of a pizza pan—just pat the crust over the bottom and ½ inch up the sides of the pan.

—Jeanne Holt, Mendota Heights, MN

PREP: 30 min. • **BAKE:** 25 min. + chilling • **MAKES:** 16 servings

1 pkg. lemon cake mix (regular size)
1¼ cups quick-cooking oats, divided
8 Tbsp. butter, softened, divided
1 large egg, room temperature, lightly beaten
¼ cup sugar
⅓ cup sliced almonds
1 pkg. (8 oz.) cream cheese, softened
½ cup lemon curd
1 can (21 oz.) blueberry pie filling

1. Preheat oven to 350°. In a large bowl, beat cake mix, 1 cup oats and 6 Tbsp. butter on low speed until coarse crumbs form. Reserve 1 cup mixture for topping. To remaining mixture, beat in egg. Press dough onto an ungreased 12-in. pizza pan; pinch edge to form a rim. Bake for 12 minutes.

2. Meanwhile, to reserved topping, add sugar and remaining ¼ cup oats and 2 Tbsp. butter. Stir in almonds. In another bowl, beat cream cheese and lemon curd until smooth. Spread par-baked crust with cream cheese mixture. Gently spoon pie filling over top. Sprinkle with almond mixture. Bake until topping is lightly browned, 20-25 minutes. Cool completely on a wire rack. Refrigerate at least 4 hours before serving. Refrigerate leftovers.

1 PIECE 363 cal., 14g fat (8g sat. fat), 49mg chol., 324mg sod., 57g carb. (37g sugars, 2g fiber), 3g pro.

INDEX